A POKE IN MY EYE

A POKE IN MY EYE

WHEN HOPE IS OUR ONLY EXCUSE TO LIVE AGAIN

ERIC OBENG EDMONDS

FOREWORD BY PRATT ROBINSON JR.

Copyright © 2011 Eric Obeng-Amoako Edmonds

All Rights Reserved.
No part of this publication may be reproduced, stored in a retrieval system, or transmitted, in any form or by any means, electronic, mechanical, photocopying, recording, or otherwise, without the written prior permission of the author.

A poke in my eye: When hope is the only excuse to live again by Eric Obeng-Amoako Edmonds.

Includes bibliographical references and index
1. Motivational   2. Personal Growth.   I. Title

ISBN: 978-0-9973519-3-4 (Hardcover)
ISBN: 978-0-9973519-4-1 (Paperback)
ISBN: 978-0-9973519-5-8 (e-book)

Editor: Brenda F. Welcome

Second Edition
Printed in the United States of America
Library of Congress Control Number: 2011918863

Rights for publishing this work outside the United States of America or in non-English languages are administered by the publisher.

For Mama

FOREWORD

I have been constantly encouraged and prodded by the author of *A Poke In My Eye*, and just this once, will have to permit myself to salute him for this inspirational story. Many people say "We all have a story to share," but not many will have the opportunity to make that a reality, and most may not have the discipline and passion to follow through. I am honored to lend my thoughts as an introduction to the book.

A Poke In My Eye is particularly encouraging for any reader because of the very fundamental and straightforward dialogue centered on a simple idea, hope. The chapters are a testament to a person's state of mind discovering hope throughout the challenges in life.

All of us, at critical times in our lives, will have to find the elements that trigger a deep-seated faith, especially when we are trapped in a quandary, to help us discover a reason to live. I am certain that the words in this book will strike a deep chord inside the reader who takes the time to reflect on the author's encounters and stories.

Put otherwise, each and every one of us has the ability to reason, but we often rely too heavily on reacting to situations. Our own indecisiveness may cause us to expend more energy to face our problems. It is inspiring that Eric's stories are written through the eyes of a man who struggles through challenges in life, but is grateful for God's grace and mercy that guides him through the storm to a brighter place in life.

Many of our experiences in life parallel one another, but when the odds are against you, you must choose to persevere. I am confident that the powerful statements will leave the reader renewed and encouraged to press through life's levels of challenging moments.

We all have had moments of despair and discover life isn't always fair. Why, then, does our subconscious record and retain the negative experiences in our lives more than the positive ones?

When our back is against the wall, many of us retreat to our internal sanctuary to ponder our next move, reflect on life's traveling grace, and re-energize our progress. Lessons are to be learned from our own footsteps and missteps, and we all must treat each landmark as an opportunity to remain steadfast and not lose focus of where we want to be.

Our life is a comparative puzzle of pieces; at a glance they may not always fit in the slots until we can visualize the image taking shape. As with most of you, it may be the stories of endurance from our past that we fall back on when our hopes and plans seems to be unraveling at the seams.

For this reason, I am certain that this book's real triumph will be the lasting effect it has in the lives of many people around the world who embrace daily challenges and deal with their unique, but hardly novel, life's adventures. Despite their failures, some people have an appetite for self-reinvention and they meticulously reconstruct their intensely personal journeys with optimism.

Remember God is always in control, tomorrow is not promised, but learn to celebrate each day as if it were your last. It is my hope that through this book, you will get your own *poke in the eye* moment.

– Pratt Robinson Jr.

CONTENTS

Foreword ix
Introduction xiii
Acknowledgments xix

CHAPTER 1
Gravity 1

CHAPTER 2
Ode to Sunshine 15

CHAPTER 3
Lilies and Butterflies 31

CHAPTER 4
Green Grass Vapors 43

CHAPTER 5
At the Water's Edge 53

CHAPTER 6
Two Black Polka Dots 67

CHAPTER 7
Eternity's Cabin 77

CHAPTER 8
Still a Trace in the Horizon 91

CHAPTER 9
Porcelain 105

CHAPTER 10
Finger Markings in Foggy Screens 113

CHAPTER 11
A Hummingbird's Ride 125

CHAPTER 12
Tears from the Grave 135

CHAPTER 13
Saving Rains 149

CHAPTER 14
Nightingale 161

CHAPTER 15
A Refuge for the Burning Candle 169

CHAPTER 16
Sidewalk 181

CHAPTER 17
The Color of Dreams 193

CHAPTER 18
Smiles and Cries 207

CHAPTER 19
The Loudest Wind There 219

CHAPTER 20
Back to Being Little 237

CHAPTER 21
Threads of Life's Tapestry 249

CHAPTER 22
When December Comes 265

CHAPTER 23
Halfway Home 287

Afterword 303
End Notes 307
Index 309

INTRODUCTION

A few years ago my life hit rock bottom. My disappointments had piled onto a heap of regret, flanked by uncertainty on both sides, as I watched my life being crushed by adversity. An emotional tailspin had begun. It is impossible for any of us to escape the ups and downs of life, but when the sadness overwhelms you and the unsettling feelings seem to push you closer and closer to a black hole, suddenly all you see are red lights and stop signs.

For me, the self-loathing, strong feelings of guilt and negative sense of adequacy kicked in. It was at this lowest point, and on the verge of giving up on life itself, that I experienced my life-changing moment.

I questioned God. I doubted hope. My greatest fear was *tomorrow*. Yes, tomorrow . . . the very thing that most people look forward to. I had enough of the solitude, the frustration and the anger. I decided this was where my journey ought to end. Coincidentally, this introspective dialogue was where the paradigm shift began.

The voices in my head multiplied, some with pleasant memories, others with gloomy images, and even more with doubtful reminders. Suddenly, the pieces added up, and in the middle of the mental chaos, the power of simple stories with extraordinary lessons is what gave birth to a symbolic *poke in my eye*. It was a sudden consciousness that made me aware that there was a lot more to live for, and many more reasons to hang on for one more day.

The prominent sportswear manufacturer Adidas once produced a television commercial that caught my attention. The commercial featured different prominent athletes walking together with the confidence and buoyancy that comes along with attaining the summit of a glamorous sports career.

The athletes were basketball, soccer, baseball, and hockey stars, all of whom had accomplished incredible feats in their sports. They all began their careers from very modest beginnings; all faced incredible odds, but now had become the best performers in their respective fields. They all wore white Adidas suits and together, signaled the ultimate picture of excellence. As they walked towards the camera, the narrator said;

"Greatness is not a birthright.
So why is it a surprise when someone from nowhere becomes great?
Maybe nowhere had something to do with it."

Afterwards the background music gradually fades out and the athletes turn to walk away from the camera brimming with coolness and self-assurance. On the backs of their white Adidas suits were the black Adidas symbol and the words *Impossible is Nothing*.

The visual insinuation is not hard to comprehend. Adidas made their successes and accomplishments possible. Not quite that simple. Instead I am convinced that the different athletes were all successful in their individual sports before the Adidas marketing employee thought about the clever advertising concept.

Wearing the Adidas clothing and playing sports in shoes may have had absolutely nothing to do with their individual ability to perform at such outstanding levels. The commercial's subtle message is inaccurate, but it's one striking truth is that an individual's coming from *nowhere* may have had *something to do with* their becoming who they are today.

A Poke In My Eye is the chronicle of my life journey and an inspirational account of the thoughts that I express in each one of my poems. The deliberate mix of prose, narration and candid facts, is intended to shed light on how the different personal, social or even historical events tie into the complex, interwoven and indispensable designs of the reality of life.

The *poke* is the sharp hand gesture to the eye and a metaphorical reference to the illumination of my life, free from any cognitive clout. That painful and sudden experience created a paradigm shift, gradual, but free from any ambiguity.

Amidst the daily struggle and tedium of living in this fast-paced society, it has taken me many years to appreciate the truth that there are certain things in life you can only learn through your own experiences. There are others that you may learn through other people's unique journeys. If there are any shortcuts, I missed them. Life is perhaps the only enlightening process for which you learn the lessons after the ordeal.

Some of these basic and extraordinary ideas have absolutely nothing to do with the supernatural, nor are they religious. Several schools of thought have spent enormous volumes of work on the Laws of Attraction, and the shades thereof. This book contains neither of such expeditionary concepts. This conscious reflection and interpretation of my life encouraged every word in the book.

I inspired myself to be full of hope and believe that life's lessons enable us to fight through it and emerge as champions. I share the interpretation of diverse themes from love, pain, hate, death, dreams, fear, joys, power, faith, and a host of everyday situations. I have to say, I am a product of an original thought, neither a lyricist nor a poet.

All the poems in this book reflect the authentic and bona fide reality of my life, the people I have known, and are mirror images of some of the deepest thoughts we all share. I traveled many roads with uncertain destinations in a wild world, places I called my Wild West. I learned about life through living and that has defined my character and my personality.

Maximizing one's life potential is no easy task, but it certainly is one worth fighting for. Irrespective of our colorful backgrounds or myriad of setbacks, where we go in life has absolutely nothing to do with where we have come from. If I am naïve in this assertion, naivety is occasionally a good thing.

Over the years, I have shared several of the stories in this book with many friends and strangers across the world. Most sought advice and life-changing philosophies, but I was always quick to express my inability to give any such counsel. All I know in life is what I have lived through and the personal experiences over three decades of incredible twists. So I told them stories about *A Poke In My Eye*.

Thus, in writing this book I make no apologies for individual opinions regarding faith or convictions, but my modest effort is to convey genuine thoughts in the most practical sequence. My belief is that by inspiring you to live through the challenges of life through a firsthand account of some simple truths that we all know, the invaluable thoughts will alter your life's course.

This book will not give anyone 10 steps to anything. The message is simple; free your mental framework from the excuse of not being good enough; and whichever of life's lenses that you choose to see yourself through, be sure to view it in the most constructive way.

Individual assessment of triumph and fulfillment varies; I am aware of this fact and that is why I am careful not to make any assumptions for anyone. The premise of this book seeks to suggest that everything in life should be a constant reminder that this is a journey of uncertainty and should challenge us to desire more.

No matter where you read this or what circumstance this book finds you in, I believe in my heart that you will see a genuine effort to encourage you to not only stay alive, but also fight to win. There will be days that waking up to a new morn will not be pleasant, if you are embalmed in the heaviness of nights before. Even in those days, learn to keep your inspiration alive and your chin up.

With every turn in my journey, I am reminded of the countless modest beginnings and the many years of unsure future I have known. Most importantly however, I am reminded of having to unshackle myself from my own preconceptions. My Adidas moments are the rewards of my tenacity, especially in the dismal days. It is the humbling reminder that I had come from a *nowhere,* and that *nowhere* has everything to do with the man I am today.

The narrative, anecdotes and simple analogies I share throughout this book are the same that I told myself over and again, and challenged myself to believe again. I lived through some difficult times and many desperate moments, but I am still here; and I am grateful for the opportunity to write about *A Poke In My Eye.*

ACKNOWLEDGMENTS

From its inception to this moment, it has taken many people and diverse insights for me to realize this project. To my parents, who will forever be my biggest fans, thank you for instilling faith and a courage guided by God. I have come to appreciate each day how much of my life has to do with the sacrifices you made.

This book is dedicated to my mama Rose, the mothers in my friends whose true partnership I have enjoyed and all the mothers around the world. Thanks to my father who imparted in me the love for reading and for forcing me to make coherent statements at five o'clock in the morning. The ordeal paid off and looking back, it all adds up.

I am indebted to my family whose invaluable support have carried me this far. Some helping hands give you the courage to keep on dreaming, and to them I owe so much of my accomplishments.

A heartfelt thank you to Nana Tetteh whose encouraging words kept me sane. Thank you for believing in big ideas and staying along for this topsy-turvy ride. We shared the wild disappointments, and the strength of mind to keep fighting; but most importantly, thank you for being my friend.

Writing is often a solitary adventure, but with every page I am thankful to Myesha House for her patience, friendship, and for challenging me to push harder. Your blend of untiring support and objective criticism through the years is the cornerstone of this project.

To my editor and insightful friend, Brenda J. Welcome, you are an angel that I will forever be thankful for. We worked overtime on this journey, and if I have been able to communicate my heart and deepest thoughts in print, I have you to thank for every moment of it.

My special thanks to many gentle individuals who graciously supported me, and through whose love I am able to make this incredible journey. To Lynn Guery and Delundra Williams for believing in this project even when it was only two ideas long. I owe sincere gratitude to Frank Adunyame who took the time to teach me about discovering potentials in life. Every page in this book reminds me of your seemingly radical ideology, and I am glad that our meeting in East London was not a coincidence.

To Melba Hamilton, thank you for the immeasurable support behind the scenes. You reminded me that *"some things don't matter much, and most things don't matter at all."* Debbie and Ben Boampong, you guys are an uncommonly generous duo, and have always been unfailingly inspirational to me.

Many thanks to Joe Union, Pratt Robinson, Timberly Williams, Rae Harris, Alisha Mallet, and Willie Small, all of whom I have had the chance to learn so much from. Ashley George, without your expertise and brilliant judgment this book would not have happened. You reviewed my thoughts so many times that I am sure you can almost recite it from memory. I sincerely thank you.

To Demetra Page and Caleb Fisher, your friendship, laughter and helping hands go much farther in my heart than a mention here; I am forever grateful. I have had the good fortune of knowing Adiba Pena and Erica Porter, for their hard work on early drafts, and entertaining a perfectionist.

Eddu Opare Addo, Eric Anim Ansah, Nii Ofori Lomastay and Eric Anim Nkansah, thank you guys for picking me up when I needed a lifeline. I owe a deep debt of gratitude to Kesha D. Miller for being a great person, and a great help, with a wonderful heart.

I am privileged to have met Deborah Goolsby, Deborah Triggs, Anthony and Tammy Cummings, Dr. Raul Cuero, and Julie Coan. My sincere gratitude to the House family in Memphis, the Page family in St. Louis, and the Brock family in Houston, all for their encouragement and invaluable support when I needed it most.

To Mrs. Charlotte Akyeampong for planting seeds of intellectual curiosity and love of literature in my heart many years ago. My superstar friend Patti Gras, thanks much for the Starbucks brainstorming sessions, and for pulling me along the ropes. Jill Pickett, thank you for opening a life door for me, and for always taking the time to let me know you're rooting for me. Julie Fix, thank you for reminding me of polite persistence—I owe you one. To Denise Castle and the team at Trafford, thank you for all your hard work.

For all of you who know how much you've meant to me at every turn—but I have skipped your name—please know that you have not gone unacknowledged in my heart. Pardon my oversight, I truly appreciate you also.

Finally, I am profoundly grateful to the hundreds of people I have met over the years and the millions more I reach with candid conversations about my life. I will not trade for anything the lessons I learned in my frustration, pain and despair. Each of them has served as a companion that make me grateful for my journey.

I am living every day the best I know how—and on the benchmarks I create for myself—and I am confident also that all of us can do all things with the help of God Almighty. *Impossible is nothing.*

GRAVITY

A sudden thought! It was less than a minute before I was about to run my car over the ledge on the empty road and plunge 30 feet to the ground, to end it all. The date was May 4. The most ridiculous and bizarre thought had crept into my mind, somehow.

"Wait a minute.
What if this is not all there is to my life?"

Where is the hope when a man is pushed through crushing adversity, heavy with disappointment and standing on the verge of his life's exit lane? How do I find the courage to live again when I am stretched thin and worn down by discontent and hurt? I pulled over to the shoulder lane and turned my car engine off. I paused for a moment, turned the radio off and leaned back in my seat to reminisce. How did I get here?

As a young boy, when I would sit quietly with a peaceful smile, my mother would say, "You seem to be at home in your head." It took more than 20 years for me to understand what she meant, and even though I never did have a fondness for riddles, I assumed that "being at home in one's head" was a good thing. She would always say, "Live life in real time and don't be perturbed by the fact that life is not always fair, has never been fair, and perhaps may never be."

There is nothing as scary as getting to the edge of a cliff and not having a very good recollection of how you got there. It feels as though the years gone by were nothing but a blur, one that left only scars of a dream you once had. Anyone in my shoes would be living their best years at the prime of their lives, and enjoying even the simplest things that came with each new day. My life had ceased to be ordinary a long time before now. Somehow, I had drifted away from everything I knew to be simple and routine. Like a pile of dust hides the beauty of a jewel left uncared for, my detachment had sent me out of touch with my life's ambition, and my hopes and destiny were left to chance. It is in those moments that it feels like the weight of the world rests on our too-feeble shoulders.

I never imagined writing a chapter of my life about "gravity," but a series of life events would force me to discover that the *unfair world* is what, over time, clogs our judgment. I am of the conviction that the person we are is the artifact of our surroundings, and even the most trivial event affects our makeup. We eventually become our own force, pulling our lives in one direction or another. Mine at this crucial stage of life was *gravity*.

There is an incredible sense of awakening when we find that our experiences, from our very first breath to this moment, have been both a good thing and sometimes an awful one. The knowledge through time allows us to learn from our own mistakes and missteps.

On the contrary, experience also has a potentially inhibiting ingredient. If not carefully channeled, it could become a deterring

Chapter 1: Gravity

agent to any further progress we make in life. Sitting on the edge of that highway, my stressful thoughts and feelings of inadequacy made me question everything, including my being.

The fast paced nature of life gives all of us ample opportunity to keep our sightline on the immediate steps we take. We are too busy living and it often feels like the hours lose their charm just as quickly as they come. If we have only a handful of images to ponder, the ones that make our heart's ache leap to the foreground. The shortcomings and our own disappointments have a way of magnifying their effect on our emotions to such an extent that if we are not careful, we will walk away from our destiny long before we have come to a proverbial end of the road.

"Gravity" happens to all of us. The weight pulls all of us from one side to another. It often pounds us the heaviest when we least expect it. What I have found is that we all learn to do a masterful job of covering our pain and disappointment until the implosion begins and we wonder how life turned out this way.

Our ingrained way of understanding life's circumstances presents an unending clash with every possibility of living our most fulfilling lives. This is where *gravity* kicks in. For most people that I have spoken to over the years, it is only when we look back in hindsight that we appreciate how easily we underestimated our own fighting power. It is not always a pleasant journey to appraise our own life judging from the tough moments in the day-to-day activities. It is important, however, that our daily battle does not redirect our focus away from what could be . . . the promise.

I told a story about two friends flipping coins. They tossed the coin five times and in each case, the coin landed on its head. They then began the guesswork process of what would happen in the sixth toss. One of them simply assumed that since the coin had landed on its head for the previous five tosses, there was a higher probability that it would land again in the same way. In fact he bet that the coin would also land on its head the sixth time.

I couldn't blame him; that was exactly the way most of us approach life's probabilities. The fact that we have applied ourselves to something and have not succeeded or do not reap the benefits of it does not necessarily mean that we will get the same results no matter what the odds are. Sometimes we have to push beyond the downside of probabilities and seek to achieve the other side, because that can be to our advantage.

The other school of thought in the coin-tossing game was that the coin has no memory. In fact, there is no way for the coin to know what has happened in the five times prior. In my calculation, that gives it a 50/50 chance of landing on either its head or tail. The only effect of gravity here is making sure the coins fall back down after a toss. It has absolutely nothing to do with which way is up.

There are many dealings in life that are dependent on decisions we have made in the past, but there are also many more opportunities for circumstances that are completely independent of one another. That equal probability of heads or tails on a coin is no different from the equal probability of winning or losing in life. Here I stood, *a man with ample opportunity at my wit's end,* but I had forgotten that I still had a 50/50 chance of winning, if not more. It is the same probabilities which drove me to that critical moment of asking, *"What if this is not all there is to my life?"*

I wrote the poem "Gravity" while I sat in the hospital lobby of Baylor College of Medicine in Texas. I had skimmed through every magazine in the waiting room and there was absolutely nothing else to do but wait for my turn to see a doctor. I decided to *peoplewatch*, a challenge to guess whose condition was worse just by observing their gestures.

It is remarkable how much a person's unconscious expressions tell about their deepest state of mind. The people in the hospital lobby were of all ages, all sizes and races, and with very stark differences in demeanor. Most of the people were yet to see a doctor but it didn't take much to see how some had already diagnosed themselves. Strange or not, some had given themselves a bad report even before the doctor could say hello. Suddenly a young lady with tears in her eyes walked out of a little door. Another woman who had been waiting in the lobby lifted her head and ran to hug the young lady.

"I knew it; I knew it!" she yelled, trying to cheer up the young lady. To this day, I do not know what the medical condition was, but I am sure the other woman did not help much. *Gravity's* pull on our individual lives is where we forget that probability is not a certainty. We forget that probabilities have more than just one outcome. All of us have at various points in life discounted the fact that our difficult circumstances today do not automatically change our next episode.

A fascinating thing about all of us is our inherent talent to look into a future even with many of the pieces yet to unfold. Maybe we do so because while we stand in middle of the long days and challenging situations, it takes almost no effort to imagine the same situation repeating itself over and again. We see ourselves almost stranded and jammed in the crushing waves of it. It is easy in hindsight to judge our actions, but embracing a contrary viewpoint to what we see could be the toughest proposition to accept. Coupled with this is the fact that life is not lived in hindsight.

No one staring at the doctor's report or living with a terminal illness would not wish to be well, and no one fighting an addiction or depression will not wish a little ray of sun would appear through the dark cloud. There is not a person with his dream fizzling away because he made a wrong turn that led to a dead end who will not wish to get back on track. Most of us would do anything to lift our heads up again. Most of us would probably give it another try if we knew what the future held in store for us. Yet we find that the present situation and the familiar territory pulls on our heels for so long that we forget how to walk again, and trust for a sun to shine again on our circumstance.

As I found out, the instant we doubt our resolve, we hand ourselves a bad report even before the evaluation begins. All of us, however, possess a powerful energy to transform our beliefs into action, whether in the affirmative or otherwise. Whenever you think the odds are stacked against you in a certain situation, how you approach it is surprisingly different from how you advance in another situation which places you on the winning side. *Doubt is the bandit in a winding road,* when our hopes are muddled with questions like, "What if this is all there is to life?"

Years ago, I was on a plane to San Diego, California. I sat next to a man who claimed to be a psychoanalytic thinker. I don't really know what that means, except that strangers on airplanes often mistake other passengers for their long-lost best friends and initiate conversations without regard for whether you care or not.

This *thinker* was one such person. He talked to me about his family, his dogs and also his career as a painter. Then he went on to explain why quitting his career as a lawyer was the best decision he had made in his adult life. My initial thought was to ask why he needed to tell me his life story, but I managed to be considerate.

Out of curiosity and some level of reluctant obligation, I continued to listen until he finally made his point. Whatever the reasoning that had led him to this moment, his advice was to "Find a bright spot even in the darkest days and magnify it." Sounds inspiring, but *"magnify what?"* The strange man on the plane had lived through some very thorny times and I am sure we would have become the best of friends if I had told him my version of life dragged down by gravity. The only thing that kept him alive is the thought that all it takes in life is just a *sudden turnaround.*

A sudden change, wherever it comes from, is all it takes to wipe tears and ease pain as if they never existed. Even more, we quickly look back to see that some of our tragedies have ironed out the wrinkles in our own lives, *creases clean through scorching blaze.* Maybe our attitudes and perceptions couldn't have been altered in any other way. This man managed to keep his eyes opened for that one bright spot; that was what he wanted to *magnify* in his life.

The cruel truth is that the *yoke of gravity* is like a veil to *ruined hearts* and a *splendor marred in ugly dust*. Just before we got off the plane, the man made an even more fascinating point of why he had chosen to become a professional painter. In his own mind, every time his paint brush would run over a spot, he was reminded that all it took was *one coat* to cover the *scuff* in our lives. Of course, life is not as simple as tweaking a tragedy and painting over our difficult circumstances, but perhaps that simple truth could be a remarkable start for most of us.

None of us stray too far from the emotional maps drawn by our own experiences. In our human nature, we cry when we hurt, when we are miserable or when we feel drowned in adversity. The opposite is also true; we rejoice when we are ecstatic and laugh when something is funny. These are often reactions that we have learned and practiced through the years and repeat without much effort.

One characteristic we all find endearing about firefighters and police officers is their instinctive reaction to run towards chaos when everyone else is fleeing for their own lives. In the company of other brave men and women, they answer the call and risk their own lives to save others. I am sure they are not completely oblivious to the fact that the crumbling buildings and burning fires could mean the end of their lives, but that is perhaps the last thing most of them think of when they hear the blast or see the flames. They have conditioned themselves through years of training and preparation, and hitched their confidence to the fact that if they do their job the best they know how, they will be standing tall when the chaos gives way to calm.

I never ceased to wonder if those same brave men and women would embrace the turmoil and chaos if it happened in their own lives, emotionally and psychologically. Unlike their reaction on the job, they probably have not run simulations of the rejection, have not practiced living through abuse, and spent hours planning on how best to confront the failures that happen in everyday life. We do not have the benefit of other brave men and women running behind and beside us in our personal journeys to give us the confidence that the raging fires will soon be gone. When the turmoil erupts in the different areas of our lives, we seldom know we are in the midst of a storm until we feel our feet trembling with doubt.

As a consequence, it becomes a natural recourse for us to continue in this routine. Occasionally, however, we all face decisions that will require us to run in opposite directions. I would be the first to admit that running against the wind and moving toward life's opposing currents is an enduring and taxing assignment.

The brunt of gravity is straightforward, and its consequence is even less complicated, but it will sometimes take the difficult moment before *the dirge* to recognize that. All of us on the contrary can manage the affirmation *"God can,"* instead of an inherent doubt of what could be possible, and reversing the words to read *"can God?"* Sitting at the edge of the empty road, I chose to hang on to the little hope rather than take a plunge into the ground below.

We have all heard of the story of a man who was convinced that life was not worth living, so he went to a bridge to jump off and die. To heighten the shock of his death, he took his clothes off and walked to the edge of the bridge. Much to his surprise, he turned around only to see another man picking up his old and tattered clothes with much gratitude. The first man paused for a second. His life wasn't so bleak and hopeless, he reasoned to himself. It didn't take much longer for him to grasp the idea that if another person was counting on his old clothes for their joy, surely his own could not be the worst of all. What if this is not *it*, he thought.

Gravity is what sends a fragile soul to the point where the ridiculous self-loathing thoughts become an alternative. If at any moment, we cannot easily find visible bright spots in our personal circumstances, I have come to find out that it does not automatically mean that none exist. Our own *weighty smiles* become our *attraction force* which weakens our willingness to forge ahead in what it takes to chart our own bright spots.

I have not always *been at home in my head*, but the one thing I learned in the course of my own life is how much momentum we get when we associate incentives with our attitude. As I wrote "Gravity," I cherished the 60 seconds I had to reminisce, and to remember the coin in the air, much like our own uncertain lives, which always has a 50/50 chance of landing on its head. We do not have to be physicists to predict our individual lives beyond temporary space and time.

There are countless examples in our individual lives to attest to the truth that if we can force ourselves to see past the empty vacuums, we will give ourselves a reason to believe again. If a certain frame of mind is what it takes to develop the psychological toughness to keep our insistent attitude, then it may be the most crucial factor in deciding whether we give up or keep on fighting. Who decides if *this* is *it*?

In "Gravity," all of us can rewrite our own story of despondency and pessimism with a personal decision to pull ourselves out of the slumps. *I am a man, sure as day and rising sun,* for I welcome the misfortunes as a part of the cycle of life, and the slumps could be just as instructive, if not more, than the high points. I am not suggesting that we ignore reality or pretend that life is some fancy puzzle, if only we can figure out the elusive trick.

In less than the minute when I wondered to myself if a desolate and bleak heart can ever find a place to start living again, something clicked. It was a reminder not to distort my own fate and definition of hopelessness, or blame *gravity* for my trip down into a black hole. When we feel pushed on all sides and cornered into a tight spot, I hate to be the bearer of bad news, but there is no cavalry coming to rescue us. You and I become our own rescue missions.

Most of us will come to a point in our lives where we imagine being at the end of our life's road. What must have once been full of joy is now laden with dismay. My encouragement is that if any force would direct our ambitions for the remainder of our lives, it shouldn't be *gravity* dragging us to the fences and the crossroads.

In my early 20's, I found a new fascination with Australia. One day, I imagined to myself that if only I can go so far away, maybe I could shake off my despair and start my life all over. I reasoned that I could then leave all the troubles of the fast lanes behind me, and evade the weight of the years gone by. I missed a vital point, in that there are miserable people everywhere, even in Australia.

Going far away on a radical relocation program is nothing but a change of address. The geography could change but the person remains essentially the same. It is true that unless we are ready to confront the basis of those dissatisfactions, no country in the world or hiding place under a rock can reorient our fate.

The mystery of "Gravity" is about a simple premise, that no matter how heavy the burden, we are never stretched so thin that we can't keep hanging on. Indeed all it takes is that one sudden turnaround, *one coat of paint to cover the scuff in our lives.*

One sudden turnaround. A tough sell yet a powerful truth. Of course if we had the power to look into tomorrow, and see what our lives could become, it would not be that difficult to comprehend the likelihood of "a sudden turnaround" in our lives. The challenge is finding the faith to remember that our footsteps have not been an accident all the way to where we stand now, and revel in the truth that having life to breathe again is a starting point in itself.

It may not look like very much because our minds have been programmed to expect a morning after each night. We have completely lost the miracle in the waking sounds, and forget that not everyone from the night before had the chance to hear them. What a difference the mundane side of life would make to us if it served as a reminder that as we continue to walk and continue to hope and continue to work, our outcome could change in our favor—maybe when we least expect it. Whatever we devote our time and effort to may end up being the catalyst that sparks the transformative moment we so desperately hope for.

Sitting at the crossroads, I had to create fresh options and find practical alternatives if I was not happy with the sequence that life was dishing out. I have always had a special message for people who are so stressed out and who have decided to give up on themselves. With all due respect, it takes a lot of guts to do the unthinkable even in our desperation.

If you have enough guts to pull a trigger, or plunge your car over a bridge, sure you have all the guts it takes to hang on and live life. Of course, for some of us perhaps a new home, a distant rock, or even far away Australia can help our psychological makeover; but ultimately how we fix our fears is our own business.

In many ways, my life was a microcosm of the millions of people whose journeys have brought them to the ledge of a highway and who are consumed by an ambiguous future. They are the people who ask themselves, "What if the present is all there is to life?" They happen to be those same people who will turn around and assure their hearts that, *"If this is all there is to it, every minute must count."* Somehow, we have to find a way within ourselves to defy *gravity*, mental or material, and give life our best shot.

Gravity takes its toll and leaves hearts in search of a glimmer of hope in the dark. Living our lives intentionally even when the odds stack up against us takes work, and so does shaking of the weight of "gravity." Someday we will honestly admit that the weight of the world was never on our shoulders, even when it felt that way. Nothing should bring us to the edge of our hopes, because one thing we all soon discover is that even when we are saddled with a barrage of missed opportunities and failures, the beautiful truth about life's many chapters is that another is soon to begin. Like the coin in the air waiting to land on either its head or tail, let's give ourselves a fighting chance to land with our right side up.

In the end, I am confident that the glimpses of hope, however little, are what gradually turn disorientation into reorientation, and into a time when our life finds its meaning and sets us on course again.

GRAVITY

1 A dot in a lane is a pounding heart at the crossroad
　A man and ample fortune at wits' end
　The yoke of gravity, a drag to the fences
　Cloudy is my faith, ground lost and time gone.
5 My mind is stuck in double lanes, and in the noise
　Providence is vague in ticking time
　I was a man, a time sooner than now
　Before a dirge loud with regret and signs.
　The weary vulture in a trance, my life pulls me down.
10 I'm somber here in a weighty smile
　The best is born to ruined hearts
　A man I am again, obsessed with vessels of wishes
　Avenging time to redeem faith
　Seasons change, so I'll live again.
15 Doubt is the bandit in a winding road
　The creases clean through scorching blaze
　Gravity, here I stand before the night falls
　To change a thing, or two, even four
　A splendor marred in ugly dust.
20 I feel the sand below my aching feet
　I am a man, sure as day and rising sun
　With more than a whiff of a grin
　My pompous heart led me here
　Loudmouth of hope held my hand
25 In time, I will be my rising tide here in faith
　To start where I stand,
　On dots of unsure lanes
　Gravity, ending here at the crossing road.

ODE TO SUNSHINE

So I stood in line, waiting for my turn to take a picture. I was mostly in shock but brimming with relief, that I could finally also walk the streets without having to explain who I am, and how everything I had owned had vanished many years before. I was standing in the same office that had rejected my petition three times and suggested that my only chance for approval would be a miracle.

I had lost everything; I had no reason to keep trying and nothing had changed over the years to make me assume that if I kept trying long enough maybe something would change in my favor. Then there was a flash, a smile, and my illogical tenacity and relentless gambling had paid off. In the years afterwards, I often recalled that the stakes were high for me. I saw my own life stuck in potential and its fulfillment depended on ridding myself of the roadblocks.

The word *irrational* is not entirely unreasonable. Consider choosing the distinction between black and white for instance. How much of the gray within the color spectrum is manufactured in our own minds, distorted by social impositions, and clouded by subjective definitions? Most of our normal predispositions are ones that operate with a *safety valve* in place.

For most of my life, I subscribed to a belief system that followed secure routes, those paths that others have carved and assured the rest of us that they did in fact exist. I still maintain that there is nothing wrong with living within socially accepted standards. A problem, however, arises when the standards define the frontiers of what we shoot for, and any action contrary to that becomes *irrational*. Gradually, like the meat from a processing plant, we come out on the other side looking, thinking and even feeling like every person next in line.

The years before now had had their fair share of unexpected bumps and intimidating turns for a young life. Yet everywhere I turned, I saw people dragging along in spite of their handicaps, some more obvious than others. The more I paid attention, the more I heard of the many wonderful—and some not so wonderful—stories of people taking chances when they had tried everything else they knew to do. When our own fears have become our faithful companions and we have found a way to settle in the present state, we easily gravitate towards the path in which we find the most comfort, even when we know deep in our hearts that we can climb a step higher. The air around us becomes too familiar to us to try anything different, and often even in the simplest things we do, we find ourselves doing our very best not to step on the wrong side of a line we drew a long time ago.

I met Ms. Fix in her office during my senior year in college. There I showed her my cover letter, cautiously crafted for my first job interview upon graduation. Her eyes rolled immediately to the last paragraph and she crossed it out with a big red marker. Without any hesitation, I asked her why she did that. "There is nothing wrong with humility and civility, Eric," she said without looking up.

She continued, "Most of us are so fixed on doing what everyone else does because someone said it is the right way of doing things." The notion was admirable, but it still did not answer my question. What was the problem with my cover letter, telling my prospective employer that, "I look forward to speaking with you at your earliest convenience?" Everything!

Until that afternoon, without fail, I always gave the option of a probable follow-up to the person on the other end. Without fail, I would give that person the opportunity to return my telephone calls and respond to my questions whenever they deemed convenient. What would easily be an emergency to me, and when I considered being "earliest convenience" may mean absolutely nothing to the next person.

Little did I know that in the simple cover letter, and the many other occurrences, I had failed to keep the advantage in my own half of the court. "There is something called *polite persistence*," she continued, "You do not play safe in anything in life because that is how everyone else does it."

My conversation with Ms. Fix gave me an intriguing insight into many other mental flaws that we often mistaken for humility. There is nothing radical about this concept; actually, there is probably nothing revolutionary about life itself. We do an excellent job at making it more complicated than it actually is.

Ode to Sunshine was born out of my realization that regardless of what internalized life principles we muster, unless we are prepared to rewire our thinking, nothing will change. In my pursuit of sunny days, I had to be cognizant of the fact that no one was keeping score on my roadblocks, no matter what they were.

The narratives in my *weary diary* would be my own, regardless of how *irrational* the hunt may seem. It is this same principle I would adopt later in life. Even when I had no rational explanation of how a decision could work in my favor, I still would keep my enthusiasm alive and gamble on keeping the advantage on my half of the court.

I know this also, that when a person is trapped between disappointment and uncertainty, the safety valves in our lives are not always as helpful as we would like to think.

Once I thought to myself, "This is all my father's fault." Or perhaps my mother's. Whatever different decisions and missteps have brought me to this juncture in my life, it can't possibly be my fault. I can at least blame my parents, my friends and even God for the things that didn't turn out well. Unfortunately, I never gave anyone credit when things worked out. How convenient!

In our search for just about anything to clasp on to and pass the buck of blame, we turn to other people, our own past, and our setbacks. Some of us have never learned to take ownership of events in life, especially when they are not so pleasant.

Sure, maybe there is a host of people at whose feet we could lay blame for why our lives turned out the way they did. What if this happened or that had not happened? If we invest time enough, we can find everyone who had done something wrong to us, or people who did not give us everything we think we deserve. I reasoned that even in the best case scenario, those people would apologize and own every bad thing they did to us. But then what?

Misfortunes and the parts of our lives that aren't like we wished create detours we could have gladly avoided, but they certainly don't have the power to alter our destiny. We do. When we assume for a moment that no one from our past or even our present owes us anything, we put ourselves in a rather unique position to view every waking moment through a renewed set of lenses in which we have a major role to play. That is the powerful truth which gives us the audacity to dust ourselves off and get back in line for what we are willing to work for. It is that freeing awareness that gives a person the energy to look for sunshine in places where he could have used every excuse to cave in.

Not long ago, I had a colleague who would usually stop by a drinking bar on his way home from work. He would swear that he was not an alcoholic, but that he had adopted the drinking routine because it helped him to forget his problems, at least for a short time. I never passed judgment as to whether or not his drinking alcohol really made his problems disappear. Rather, I acknowledged that his reaction to whatever the problem was in his life was that of a bifocal view. Is the problem absent at his feet slowly reappearing as he lifts his eyes?

On and on he went talking about the two horrible people in the world, both of whom happened to be his parents. Just as I was about to believe his story, he added that both had passed away before he was 11 years old. I never did understand how he managed to pass blame onto two people who had nothing to do with his life 20 years later. My colleague couldn't explain that either, but had made a very interesting observation. He would argue that some of us do not drink our problems away; we instead do the next best thing, which is to find someone else to blame.

Blame is a convenient scapegoat and it's often easier to think someone else made us feel the way we do, as though we did not have a conscious choice in the matter. Do we have an innate tendency to redirect the source of a problem, even when we know that the foundation rests with us? I do not purport to know the correct answers, but most of us have at several points in our lives had the privilege of creating that self-image of a victim.

For us, it is an unfortunate event or circumstance occurring without our having anything directly to do with it. Albeit true in some cases, it is often more than just *someone* doing something to *us*, but how differently we would approach our own lives if we were the *someone* performing the action, and not just a victim. How convenient is it to have someone to point fingers at for our shortcomings?

Sometimes we all have to get irrational, intentionally. The notion of polite persistence is developing a come-what-may persevering mindset, unheeding to off-putting reports, cautiously calculating recklessness and understanding that a repeat of the same action does not yield any results different from the present.

I met an unusual friend named David in high school many years ago. David was a strange boy in a curiously odd way. He imagined that since we are all bound to make mistakes at some point, he wanted to have control in what kind of mistakes he made and become the architect of his own disaster. Certainly, I thought to myself, this idiot cannot be serious; but he was.

It took a while for me to discover that the *idiots* who refuse to be chained to conventions and denials are the same *idiots* who end up basking in the sunny rays, enjoying the picture-perfect *Sunshine*. Many years later, I learned the lesson he attempted to teach me, except that I was too contented in my safe zone to think about anything that could leave me vulnerable. At that early age, I was sticking to the way things were done, and perhaps rehearsing that attitude for my adult life.

"Don't rock the boat, if you are not sure you can swim," I thought to myself. More than anything, I was afraid of losing the little things that I had accumulated with my shielding and myopic approach. What I did not understand about David's way of thinking was that, anyone seeking to engineer his own failure was not going to actively plan his own doom. Rather it involves having the mindset of constantly developing an active response to life's events.

A few years ago, I learned something peculiar about an old friend, Nicole. She did recall that sometimes our sensitivity is the breeding ground for many of the emotional train wrecks in which we find ourselves. She was not the first person to talk about love being the energy of life, which more than we often care to admit, gives life its meaning. Bad relationships, disappointments and vain associations are just a few of the many things that drain all of us, but ultimately are not the responsible party in our misery.

For as long as I had known Nicole, she had never made a mistake. A chunk of her problems, as she put it, resulted from her father leaving their home when she was young. Also when Nicole was young, her mother died. As Nicole claims, losing her parents left her with no meaningful relationships as she grew up. Nicole is in her mid-40's, and has yet to discover that she is the sole proprietor in this investment called life.

Later on in life, one of her bosses did not like her too much, which made her miserable at work. Outside of work, she was not a popular girl and was often depressed because no one made her feel good about herself. Nicole shared with me her strong feelings of wanting to be loved by someone or by most of the people around her. Also like most of us, she had made a series of emotion-centered decisions that rewarded her with disappointment and heartbreak. The flashbacks kept coming to her mind and she remembered every last detail.

On and on she described all the people she had met and devoted her time and energy to, but these relationships only led to one disappointment after another. She resorted to a resolve of blaming all the participants in her life for her shortcomings, as well as her subsequent loss of self-worth. I couldn't have said it any better than a comedian once explained, "There is a good reason why it is called *self-esteem*; you do it for yourself." The trick is that we may never acknowledge the *self* part if we are so busy looking for a willing culprit to shoulder our responsibility.

Soon after she had finished, I told her my story. I had similar disappointments and justifiable anger, legitimate reasons to resent most of the people I had known, and ultimately walk through life with a sour poor-me attitude. I have honestly had a great family all my life; but whenever possible, I pushed some of the blame to something someone else could have done for me. Sooner or later, I was forced to pause and wonder exactly what the role of others had been in my life, and surprisingly, there was often none.

In my case, it occurred to me one morning that perhaps I was standing in the revolving door of disillusionment and frustration. It is one of those moments when you suddenly realize that only you are responsible for your own happiness, and other people are too busy living their lives to worry about you.

The *aha moment* makes us wonder why we didn't think about this all along, and instead walk through life with a reversed outlook on why everything happens to *us*. Sometimes even the most generous of hearts, greatest talents and good intentions, suffer setbacks and that is not automatically someone else's fault.

I learned many years ago that the general rule of thumb for us is to address the *constants* in our lives and not expend all our valuable energy on the *variables*. The constants are the relatively unchanging elements, like who we are, where we are and the people around us. All others are those we can alter, whose effect on our lives may vary depending on our reactions to them. I know also, that there are still some aspects of our lives in the supposedly fixed arena that we can still change if we want to.

Sooner or later, we are entirely responsible for every element in our lives and the task is entirely ours. Instead of dealing with the one person that repeatedly endured the heartaches and the pain, Nicole, like most of us, turned to the other people whose presence in her life was only temporary. The flashbacks are endless when you have lived long enough to endure friends', families', or even strangers' letdowns. Our instinctive reaction isn't so much to reflect on where we missed the warning signals, but why a person would do an awful thing against us. Then we find someone to blame, even if all we have to blame is our own shadow.

I learned about people like that, who lose everything, may even have nothing, but still find the bravery to maintain their advantage.

Idiots like my friend, David, jump back in the line and are ready with a smile. In that same vein, almost anyone can think of many people who did not accomplish their objectives by accident, but were willing to risk shame and dare to fail. Those are the people who have come to understand the secret and live without safety valves locking their mental structures into a predetermined position.

Later in life, I was on assignment for a national television program and I met Mr. Holt. My job was to ask a string of questions about his philanthropic life and his work with high school youth in American cities. I was then to give him an idea of the type of questions that would be asked on the television interview.

Halfway through our conversation, he said to me, "The problem with most of us is that we are not prepared to fail." His comment was especially out of the ordinary for me, because his accomplished life didn't strike me as the failure kind. What could he possibly know about a child born into a ghetto and raised in poverty? Nothing maybe. However, he knew his own life story and that fulfilling lives are not reserved for a few people in a privileged class.

My eyes lit up as I tried to make the connection with his point. "Most of us are not trained to fail; so when we do, which we will, the only recourse is giving up," he continued. Mr. Holt is a prominent international executive, and my plan was to learn some remarkable pieces of business savvy from him, not the idea of *failing faster*. Nothing could come closer to the truth; every aspect of our lives revolves around an imagined sense of safety and security.

I remember us talking about a story of a scientist named Roy Plunkett. While experimenting with a chlorofluorocarbon, Plunkett inadvertently left a can of the compound on his laboratory radiator at night. By morning, the compound had polymerized and created a hard resistant surface on the bottom of the can. What any scientist would have easily written off as a mistake inadvertently became a significant product called Teflon. More often than not, we count ourselves out of the competition before the final whistle blows.

I recall a sentence many years ago in the *London Evening Standard*. I saw it in a crowded underground subway at King's Cross Station in Central London, when an old man across from my seat was reading the back page of the newspaper, with the front page glaring at me. The sentence ran: "Blame sits on the opposite side of the continuum from responsibility."

As I read that quote, I smiled and eventually spent the remainder of the journey reflecting on what the continuum was, and why blame and responsibility would sit on opposite ends. I thought to myself that, of all the people who would read the same newspaper, perhaps only a fraction of them will acknowledge, let alone understand, the relevance of those words to our daily actions.

The point of the sentence perhaps was that unless we assume responsibility for our actions and even the unforeseen events that happen to us, we will inhibit our own ability to find clarity and an appropriate resolve. At any point, I believe that we will either own the responsibility or find a scapegoat to carry the guilt, to ease our own. As I did in the case with my friend Nicole, I used a familiar analogy that coincidentally struck a chord. It often happens when two people in some form of relationship decide to go separate ways. There is that tense scene when one partner walks up to the other with the all-important smirk and says, "Honey it's not you; it's me."

In other words, the person is saying "Blame it all on me." That is usually an overused exit strategy that skirts the real problem, but it assumes that the next person will be content in knowing that whatever the issue was, it wasn't their fault. I call it *selective ownership*. The interesting truth is that it is playing the blame game in reverse to eliminate the prospect of a confrontation, and surprisingly it works quite well. Unfortunately, that is where most of us draw the line

Chapter 2: Ode to Sunshine

in the sand. In every other aspect of life, we blame everything and everyone else, but ourselves.

On the contrary, we do not fail at any endeavor and immediately *blame it on us*. I am convinced that some of our own lives may be a lot more fulfilling if we learn to apply this selective ownership trick in more productive ways and carefully avoid blaming others or accept blame rather than passing guilt in a life where each of us is responsible for our own undertakings. All of us have been disappointed, disheartened and seen our share of heartbreaking moments; but we also are the architects of our own happiness.

In our effort to apply our tunnel vision syndrome, we cheat ourselves out of seeing from another side. In our life's vocabulary, the word failure is an atrocity, yet it is the one steady variable that resurfaces in different magnitudes throughout life. It doesn't take much to reckon how this must be a tough idea to chew on for parents, and our society at large, so we do the next best thing, avoid it altogether.

The answer is much simpler. We are rational beings; and in our own wisdom, we imagine *sunshine* to be the dazzling and sunny days in a distant place. We could very well create our own sunshine just by getting back in line and trying again. That is why we deliberately get irrational, to allow us to rethink how our minds are wired in the first place.

There is a reason why most of us are rational, and hedge our bets on the safer side of things. However, my line of reasoning is that, if being rational and safe leaves us wondering why we are not getting much out of life, then maybe we need to start looking for the mental barricades. For that to happen, our preconditioned safety valve must come off.

All of us will have to learn to write new chapters of our lives and keep the advantage on our side. I assume that we will hurt some feelings, surprise others, disappoint a few friends, and endure some sleepless nights along the way but all those uncomfortable thoughts are crucial for a paradigm shift. Of course, in the hopes of being carefully irrational, I hope we would avoid somersaulting around town like lunatics eager to prove our newfound mental freedom.

The important thing here is to follow our hearts' ambitions, not to accept the first denial notice as divine mandate, but step outside the ordinary and tap into the infinite capacity of our mind at work. Our biggest gift to ourselves is the honest introspective conversations alone and without the rebuff and the denials.

When I first lived in Houston, rush-hour traffic jams and inconsiderate drivers were the standard practice that people had come to accept as part of the nuances of a booming city. After my first week, I knew I had to either rewire my coping mechanisms in order to get with the program, or leave. I had other options if I wanted to change the situation, but that would mean relocation to a small town in the countryside where there perhaps would be no crowded highways, no stop signs at every turn and no traffic to worry about.

On my way to my first day at work, it was as if everyone else in the city decided to drive on the same street at the same time. I ended up an hour late to work, and the manager had left a note on her office door with my name on it. It was weird, as if she knew what my excuse would be.

"How you get to work on time is your own problem," she wrote. It didn't take much for me to learn that blaming your lateness on traffic was no excuse here. That certainly was not the pleasant welcome I had hoped for but it was clear that I had to take charge of the problem if I planned on working at that job.

It was not my supervisor's job to wake me up early, encourage me to leave home early and plan for my commute. Any drop of empathy may have short-circuited my sense of owning the problem. In response, I changed my personal schedule and routine so I could leave home an hour early for a 15-minute journey.

I learned quickly that it was one of the simple situations in life with lessons sprinkled all over it. It is much easier to see every other person's effect on us, than it is to see ourselves at the helm. This simple experience had a profound affect many years later on how I would adjust to even the most precarious events in life. In making that practical adjustment, first I had to assume the personal responsibility.

I read of *self-serving biases* years ago. Even simpler is the *self-enhancing bias* which allows us to take credit for successes, and also the *self-protecting bias* that helps us to reject liability for our shortcomings. In either of these circumstances, I am of a firm belief that nothing triumphs over an honest assessment of our plights, whatever they might be.

Instead of misplacing the blame, looking within ourselves and genuinely assessing our part in any process requires pausing for a moment, and not ignoring our roles in our circumstances. In fact I suggest that we do not just pause, but rather learn to stop altogether. It is only helpful and wise to slow down and reevaluate our priorities.

I have forced myself to do this time and again; and the good part of the story is that once we have identified our role, we can rearrange the odds and eliminate the *someone* and *something* doing an action to *us*. I mentioned earlier the importance of always reevaluating the *constant* factors in our life's equation, rather than losing sleep over *variables* that can and will often change. By doing so, we can quit the blame game and learn to take ownership of the joystick instead of bending sideways to justify our misadventures and disasters as another's making.

The two people I had met from very different circumstances, Mr. Holt and Ms. Fix, encouraged me to draw images in my own heart, and endeavor and follow my heart in achieving them. They challenged me to not assume that all that there is to life are just the options life had given to me. They also warned me to not be so fixated on the gray lines, whether real or imagined, so much that I would lose the value and the exciting colors of life itself.

No matter how far I go in search of *sunshine*, I am the only one who can decide to get off life's fringes and radically reorganize how I think and act. Only then can I find the *sunshine* in life sitting outside the barricades I had been stuck inside all of my life.

ODE TO SUNSHINE

1   All I can, I write in blue lines in a weary diary
    The vibrant days I love
    And sacred nights I loathe
    Whose hope scrawled in ink, but faint with time
5   In search of a promise filled with subtle tricks.
    All I found, sour quests with nothing to savor.
    Far from sandy beaches, but the sands have sound
    And their words pile on a noisy mime.
    It's not another snivel either true or blue
10 For life is only a trail of deja-vu.
    All I write is in bold
    In marble frames on sale for pennies
    I'll give to myself after the summer's heat
    At picnic lunches in bright sunshine days.
15 The finest canvas of a heart's virtue
    Is all I know and filled my years.
    When my faith is swept under a rug,
    Both white and striped
    How thin is the string to the calm streets?
20 So I won't surf through empty words
    And a thousand mortals gone with the wind
    And doubts planted in my fragile soil.
    It's sunny still above, oh yes I see
    But torn between me and my faith
25 My arms open to my past and to never again
    I remember the discord lullabies
    Remember the black-eyes
    I remember life's lies in the blink of an eye.
    I remember hope too

30　And that makes me smile
　　　The color of my words, not vanity in moment perfect
　　　Is painted my world of gentle stillness
　　　Asleep on fine Belgian linens made through time
　　　And feet rested well on sunbrella pillows.
35　Peace lives next door, I saw it once before
　　　In elusive models of winding shores
　　　The beauty of the breeze blowing across my skin
　　　Soaking suns and dreaming for more
　　　Finding my way back to Manhattan
40　The same moments where songs live in the skies
　　　Where I'll find the same sunny rays and blue beaches
　　　And find the memories in a diary's line
　　　The perfect sunshine I passed long ago.

LILIES AND BUTTERFLIES

Bear in mind, if you are going to amount to anything, that your success does not depend upon the brilliancy and the impetuosity with which you take hold, but upon the everlasting and sanctified bulldoggedness with which you hang on after you take hold.

—Dr. A. B. Meldrum

An amazing natural phenomenon is the migration of birds across the globe following their instinctive wisdom. Regardless of where a bird breeds, or the air temperature it has become accustomed to, it resorts to an internal presence of mind to travel thousands of miles across oceans to compatible climate and conditions.

Unlike any of us, birds are not equipped with either technology or the ability to make logical deductions. They follow their instinct. They ride wind currents and circle the globe as many times as they can, all based on a natural gut direction. We as humans own something much more sophisticated than just instinct. We have conscience and an added ability to reason, but so often these birdlike instinctive signals add a unique dynamic to this thinking capacity.

Many happy people I have had the pleasure of listening to, and observing their extraordinary sense of purpose, have all mastered the art of listening to the voice in their head. For every pursuit, there are roadblocks, whether real or perceived, to throw us off our intended route.

Some individuals took the time to recognize the nature of these obstacles and, most importantly, to listen to the voice deep down from within themselves. For most of us, it is a gut feeling or that still small voice. Perhaps not quite as guiding as the birds traveling thousands of miles to spend their winter in the Antarctic, but it exists.

There are people who refer to the sixth sense phenomenon, extrasensory perception (ESP), or that almost eerie ability to sense things and events. Since it first appeared in scholarly work around 1837, our society still wrestles with whether a human soul or a subconscious mind is responsible for this intuitive sense. I don't know the answer either.

Call it what you will, but I will argue that unless we get to know ourselves and undoubtedly recognize the echo of this instinctive voice in our own heads or hearts, every decision we make will miss that crucial element from deep within us.

How many times have we done something or even completed a task only to learn that the correct answer was housed in our first thought? We had some strange feeling we were correct, but we ignored our own intuition. The imagery of my poem *Lilies and Butterflies* urges us all to stay connected to that freedom at heart to let our basic intuitions matter. It encourages us to stay in touch with our senses of those ambitions that are indeed still possible.

The internal dialogue we have with ourselves can be our harshest critic, but just as easily our most truthful motivator. In the quiet of our hearts, we can sift through whatever our minds encounter. It doesn't take long for any of us to come to terms with the fact that we cannot do anything to stop the constant barrage of thoughts and voices that whisper into our minds. The voices paint pictures in our mind's eye, stroke after stroke on a blank canvas. The nature of the voice we tune in to will in turn give us the image we will hang on to and the actions that will direct our daily walk. It is worth listening to the quiet voice that prompts us to dig our heels in, and let faith be our anchor as we find our way through the raging seas. Better yet, it makes a difference which of the voices we trust.

My friend Devale Simmons is an expert in *barriers*. After his advanced degree in psychology, he ventured into an arena in social life left largely to religious professionals. One evening we talked at length about his book, *Let Them Come*, in which he writes of pragmatic and insightful ideas on reshaping the minds of a new generation of youth.

There is an inescapable connection between what we all do, how much of it is defined by the world around us and how often that world conflicts with our individual intuitions. Devale Simmons spent many years as a minister and counselor to thousands of teenagers and young adults across America. His objective was to find the inherent connections between what most of us do, as it relates to the mental and emotional barriers in our individual lives.

From my own experiences and associations with many others, I came to learn how a fraction of us operate on impulse and natural feelings. We often acknowledge that only when our decisions are mistaken. Otherwise we are quick to ignore the process that led us to the point of decision in the first place. Thanks to our intrinsic, instinctive abilities, we know the answers to some of the questions long before we even ask.

My sister sent a long letter to me one summer about a heartbreaking moment, and how much of it she should have seen coming. She was consumed with regret, and gradually turning to the poor-me-why-me mindset. It must have taken her at least five grueling hours to craft such an extensive tale of why people do not keep their word. She was understandably devastated, but my sister's plight had everything to do with her choice to live against her better judgment, and a failure to make the tough choice even when she felt deep within her heart that it was the best option.

My sister had missed a chance for a *butterfly moment*. She later talked about failing to follow her intuition and doing what she felt in her heart was right. In retrospect, however, she chose not to beat on the same drum as before, but instead gave herself one more reason to dust off the pain and the disappointment of a broken heart; and for whatever it was worth, learn from it.

At a low point in my own life, I wondered if there ever was any difference between *beaten and broken*. I thought to myself. A crashed, trampled and trodden upon object still has one advantage: it is still unbroken. Even the wrecked and ruined object on the other hand may have a long way to go to get back in its prior shape, but this is definitely not impossible in any case.

While they may have lost their grandeur, with skill, time and patient reconstruction, even the seemingly hopeless objects can be put back together. They regain their prior value eventually, but it takes a significant effort for that to happen. Whether crushed, beaten or broken, every *butterfly* that is changed from its original nature will have the opportunity to relive its utmost potential.

We may be beaten but we are not broken. We may have cracks on either side of our hearts but we are still made to stand tall and persevere. We may be crushed by the series of missteps and life's sharp turns, but nothing we go through in life can unravel the very core of who we are unless we give it permission to do so. Many days may feel like a raging storm dragging us through ruthless waves all around us, but the truth remains that on the other side of the ocean, not too far from where we are, are the calm waters. On the other side of that surging wave is the chance to begin again.

As I wrote the poem "Lilies and Butterflies," the difference in our reactions, I assume, is a personal conviction and individual decision not to cave in under pressure. It comes with being conscious of that which is possible and going beyond just wishing yourself into being. It takes work on our part, even on the most beautiful wings of a traveling butterfly to perch in the fields of lilies, in whatever area of life we find ourselves.

I have had to constantly remind myself of *butterfly moments*. Most of the time, what appears broken to us, is beaten instead. It is not shattered or ruined; our splendor is still intact and even when we have been the architect of our own failures, there is still no good excuse to live the remainder of our lives as a *frantic soul*.

My life as a figurative weary *butterfly* speaks of days and years spent crying about destitution, heartache and pain. Just like the caterpillar dragging through the dirt and mud, most of us are familiar with the moments where we think life has dragged us to our lowest point. Inside the caterpillar is that gentle butterfly, waiting for time to complete its transformation.

That process is what strengthens the wings of the butterfly; a change in both the internal characteristics and outward appearance is metamorphosis. Our circumstances may be different, but simply wishing ourselves out of the difficulties does not offer the best chance for success.

For the caterpillar, its metamorphosis from a tree-clinging 12-legged pest through a probably gruesome and dark world soon turns it into the majestic flying butterfly that soars. High in the sky, I wonder if it looks back at its caterpillar days and smiles at what made it what it has become. Will it remember the darkness when the once slimy world made it feel trapped and helpless? Will the butterfly remember how its many cells grew into body parts through a tough transformation— that defining moment—and gave it the wings it needed to fly?

Did the pupa one day outlive its inchoate state and was everything that happened to it provide just the muscles it needed to prepare for a new chapter?

Our sixth senses and gut instincts, if we learn to listen to them, help us to dig deeper and find the strength to go one step at a time. It may sound very simple or even unsophisticated but it is a powerful self-reforming approach that works. I like to think that the phrase "one step at a time" is only useful if we acknowledge and understand that the more we accomplish in step one, the more opportunities we have given to ourselves to accomplish more in step two, just like a single flap of the butterfly wings.

Gut instinct has a remarkable effect on changing the simplest actions into excellent pursuits. It is not a coincidence that the New York Giants won the 2008 Super Bowl against a tough New England Patriots team. I was particularly stunned as a Patriots supporter, as were many others; but winning the game involved something more than just drills and strategies for the Giants. During the most memorable parts of the game, in the precious final seconds, the players were not executing their coach's instructions.

As in our own pressure-filled situations, they had no time to think about offensive tactics. They had to resort to that one ability that I believe is in all of us, gut instinct. The obstacles were clear as day. The Patriots had finished their season unbeaten. Quarterback Tom Brady and wide receiver Randy Moss had record-setting seasons in epic fashion.

Leading up to Super Bowl Sunday, the New York Giants looked more like lambs awaiting slaughter, but they prepared against a formidable opposition and executed their plan to perfection. As it would turn out that evening, the Giants won against incredible odds and it would be forever known as one of the National Football League's biggest upsets.

After the game, team captain Eli Manning was asked how they managed to pull off that stunning upset; and his response was "We just took it one play at a time." A television commentator, however, noted something rather unconventional. In the deciding and game-changing performance that Sunday night, Eli Manning did something that he had never done before. He couldn't have possibly practiced that instinct from any training session; but when he felt that abrupt urge to throw the ball while the Patriots were swarming onto him and pulling him down, he did. *Something* told him to throw the ball at a time when any other quarterback would have played safe and fallen to the ground.

It was a daring-chance moment, even risky, but the Giants knew that both teams would have the same 48 minutes and 11 players on the field. Irrespective of their opponent's size, what was most important was how they approached every second. When the game was on the line, all the rules and strategies didn't seem to click! That butterfly instinct kicked in. It didn't matter how many losses they had suffered along the way. It didn't even make any difference that all the statistics were stacked heavily against them. The distant *lily* would be the joy of the championship story those men would tell their children someday.

In much the same way, as I responded to my sister's frustration, I reminded myself that nothing takes the place of being prepared to stay the course and to keep our focus on our goals. Something happens to our inner psyche when we seek to persevere, but the important part is that we have to allow our progression of one step and one flap of a wing at a time. We all have different sets of obstacles to overcome. Mine may have been difficult for me just as yours could have been demoralizing for you. I do not suggest any universal formula, but rather a humble suggestion to follow the New York Giants' Eli Manning's game plan.

Maybe no one told the Giants they would win. My guess is that the Giants did not tell themselves they would lose. They knew they couldn't just sprinkle stardust on their wishes and wipe their turbulent season away. They were willing to believe that the gutsiest and most risky decision might very well be the simplest of all the steps ahead of them. Getting onto the field and giving our best efforts will often demand that we rid ourselves of anything that only gives us a myopic view of the journey ahead, and dare to take a risk. Winning at life is not an entitlement. It is this orientation that gives us the steady heart to forge ahead, and leverage every small triumph along the way, even when we feel we have reached our wits' end.

My inspiration for writing "Lilies and Butterflies" may have been that we all listen to the voices in our head when they call. There is an old axiom that we can only appreciate the heartache of a man in a hole if we ourselves crawled out of the same hole before.

Until I have walked a mile in your shoes, I can only imagine what your fears and hopes are. I have no way to gauge your willpower but I humbly suggest that at any point in our own lives, we still have the opportunity for *butterfly moments*. We still have all that it takes to dust off the pain from past failures and keep our eye on the ball.

Throughout the poem "Lilies and Butterflies," it is important to know that as I encourage you to follow your sixth senses, even seventh or eighth if you have them, the vital part is giving yourself compelling reasons to believe that you can do it, too. I am living proof that we can all pursue our dreams with our self-made gusto and stubborn enthusiasm.

For the better part of our life journey, we may walk in similar scenarios, but the responsibility to reconstruct your thought processes is entirely yours. My modest suggestion is that even at that point in our lives where we feel like giving up is the best option, we remember the "startling calm in life's musical chairs," and that we still have life, and that in itself is hope for a better tomorrow.

Somewhere beyond our ability is an innate compass and a small voice only to be heard by you and me. The same intuition that guides birds thousands of feet high and many more thousands of miles across the globe, hints to us that we can all fly as high or travel as far as we set our minds to. The fact is that we build our own faith to believe a successful outcome is either possible or impossible. Soaring like butterflies beyond possibilities is the liberating adventure that sets us up for greater opportunities.

Out of the Korean War in American history came a powerful life lesson. Thousands of Chinese Communist troops, who had been hiding in North Korea's desolate valleys, attacked with overwhelming swiftness. They forced the battered Americans to retreat south across the Chongchon River, and many more attacks gave birth to what some have called the "longest retreat in American history."

It appeared the American forces had begun backpedaling in retreat. In the midst of the chaos and the uncertainty, his men asked General Oliver Smith what was his plan. "Gentlemen, we're not retreating," said Smith. "We are advancing in a different direction." This is by far one of my favorite declarations. The same is true about the everyday battle we fight.

Butterfly moments are more than knee-jerk reactions to something that instinctively feels right to do. How many times have we had to step back, presumably retreating, to move forward in whatever we are engaged in? Sometimes taking one step at a time will mean taking some backwards, but that should not be discouraging if it is part of a bigger plan forward.

Even in their instinctive journeys, as it is with their migration across the globe, birds' unrestrictive intuition causes them to stay in the moment. What can we learn from their level of freewheeling intuition? They surely can be a reminder that we will eventually smell the beauty in distant fields; and we can do so in our own unique way. We ought to approach each day in the conviction that our own experiences have given us enough wherewithal and reserve to draw from.

It is from this well of confidence that we draw our actions, especially when nothing in sight seems to be working. Like the football team in the face of insurmountable odds, we play the game of life one sequence at a time. Like the caterpillar transmogrified into a butterfly, our instinct and inclination will help us soar. As we forge ahead in our own lives, we ought to remember that life itself did not just happen within a blink of an eye; everything works with one step and one moment at a time.

"Once the abstract painting of my happy man," where even the most resolute and unwavering warrior has reached rock bottom and the picture of life is faded with every adversity. I am always reminded that we are what we choose to be; instincts and butterfly moments exist for those who take advantage of them.

The power of our subconscious is what reinforces our desire to keep holding on, marching on and fighting on. I adopted an affirmation that guided my every endeavor and all I choose to accomplish. Like the unusual life cycle of a butterfly and through its spectacular metamorphosis, I had to decide to live my life, follow my heart's instinctive wisdom, and not focus on the imperfections and turbulent rides of my life.

In the remarkable stories of butterflies, the caterpillar forms a chrysalis and eventually transforms the worn out, dragged around insect into a beautiful creature with a new lease on life. This is my inspiration for the poem "Lilies and Butterflies."

Logic says the road ahead is dismal, but something deep down inside us seems to say that our dreams are not bigger than our abilities. Brace yourself, listen to the small voice in your heart, for that is the "stunning lily gazing into the happy sky."

LILIES AND BUTTERFLIES

1   The wingtip of a checkered fly
      Leave the scars behind in the sand
      White paintings between my cheeks and eyes
      Were the pain and chills down my spine
5   And now left cravings within a frantic soul.
      The twilight's cool will save a mile
      A fad, whim or empty craze,
      Here to quietly perch
      I am no pest.
10 No, I am butterfly.
      The stargazer lily was beautiful from a distance
      Young and pure and heavenly scent
      So my scars, I can pretend are a hollow blotch.
      When life weighed heavy on a bruised neck
15 And the dazzle in my bloom lost its glamour.
      No captions in the midnight quivers
      But a thing within screams serenity still.
      My bleached smile fools everyone but me
      With sour memory trapped in smirks
20 Beauty of powdered murky mornings
      Enough to save a tear down my flabby cheeks.
      Once the abstract painting of my happy man
      I wish for a sun and a wing to fly
      Not some pretty homage to my wagging tail
25 But the smell of flower's field.
      The startling calm in life's musical chairs
      And a cheery, merry memoir left behind
      Clings to a stunning lily gazing into happy sky
      Nothing better than these pinky fields

30 Where checkered flies will die to bloom
     In tomorrow's sun
     And in peace after the twilight too.

GREEN GRASS VAPORS

I grudgingly walked into my doctor's office prepared for a health checkup. I always had good reasons why I did not fancy such trips; just the smell of the reception area and the graphic images on the walls gave me chills. Never mind the dentist. This particular morning was no different. The doctor gave me a prescription and said, "let's try this one first; i think it will work for you." "You think?" Is what i wanted to verbally express but i held my composure.

Ten minutes later, I was driving back home when his words clicked in my mind. For a while I ignored the fact that medicine is a *practice* in every sense of the word, and doctors are not God. I had amassed a plethora of unrelated reasons that justified my anxiety. I imagine doctors do not definitively know the correct answers simply by listening to our symptoms, and in some cases their *accurate* diagnosis ends up erroneous.

Most of what medical professionals do is intelligent trial and error, and the most knowledgeable doctors are the ones that have done the same thing over and over again. In fact they are kind enough to tell us that truth all the time, except that we often show up at a doctor's office in desperate mode, too busy to listen to probability disclaimers.

As I sought to make sense of the conversation, I recall the doctor patting my shoulder in an attempt to quell my fears. "You stress about things you have no control over," he said with a smile. To an extent, I did; but I believed that I had a justifiable explanation for it. The only problem is that my anxiety, regardless of the reasons for it, does not change the facts in what happens or does not happen in life.

It is interesting how so many of the things we agonize over never happen. Consequently, our worry about the elements around us shapes our own self-limiting beliefs. According to author Les Brown's outlook, "Far too many people sit back and coast just when they should be moving to the edge of their seats and hitting the accelerator."

The figurative drive through life is in a fast lane, with many sharp turns and unmarked exit roads. Our instinctive concern prompts us to hit the brakes and pull over on the side of the street. We give up on ourselves when we cannot visualize any immediate and practical answers within our reach. We panic, and start looking for the EXIT sign when we ought to be searching for another way forward.

I will be the first to tell you that there are endless opportunities for us to *freak out,* especially when it feels as if someone had *pulled the rug* from beneath us. When setbacks and life obstacles slow us down and oncoming traffic appear to be heading for a direct collision, that is when we ought to be hitting the accelerator and forging ahead. We should hang on when we are pressed on either side, push past the edge of our fears, and confront those same mental signposts that could have sent us crashing. For me, such a signpost was "Green Grass Vapors."

Chapter 4: Green Grass Vapors

In 1915, Walter Cannon defined an acute stress reaction, commonly known as the fight-or-flight response. His theory stated that animals react to threats with a general discharge of the sympathetic nervous system, which in turn primes the animal for fighting or fleeing. Other researchers have found that the perception of danger triggers catecholamine hormones which facilitate immediate physical reactions.

In our simple everyday language, this implied that as the action of our heart and lungs accelerates, blood vessels in many parts of the body constrict, and blood vessels for muscles dilate. In fact there are many more physiological responses that occur but which may very well require scientific clarification for us to even know what is happening to us.

The Cannon research is still true today; and I hate to admit, but there is often more *flight*, than there is *fight*. For most of us unfortunately, *flight* from the circumstances we encounter in our work, our marriages, lifestyles, or our numerous associations becomes our default response.

The last time I spoke with my friend Stuart, he was 62 years old. Eighteen years earlier he had been diagnosed with cancer and on the verge of a nervous breakdown. His doctor's attempt to accurately identify the origin of the malignancy or type of cells involved had taken a toll on Stuart and he was gradually falling off the edge of a depressive cliff.

Every one of his weekly visits to the hospital reminded him of how meaningless his life had become, with death probably imminent. His doctors told him to be of good cheer as they worked hard for some positive results, but Stuart had given himself the worst news already.

Stuart tells a story of leaning in a chair in the hospital lobby one afternoon when a weird thought crossed his mind. If he was indeed going to die from the cancer, he would anyway, and no amount of remorse and sadness would save him. What if he had sat there in self-pity and prepared for his own funeral but never died? It would probably be a wise idea to live the life he had with a positive outlook, instead of spending every waking moment lamenting over the illness.

An interesting area of medical study in health psychology is the biopsychosocial model. The premise is that health and illness are to some extent influenced by a combination of factors that are not necessarily biological or genetic in nature. It is very possible that behavioral factors like individual habits, lifestyle, health beliefs and social conditions like cultural influences and family relationships, play significant roles in a person's health.

However accurate this research may be, I contend that perceptions of a disease can become stressors by affecting an individual's psychological well-being. In some cases, these stressors can lead to depression and send a person into an emotional tailspin. It is for this same reason that the placebo effect is indeed possible; a hope of recovery has a positive relationship with our chances of recovery.

Stuart later told of how that afternoon in the hospital chair marked the most important moment in his life, because two years later, the doctors assured him that he would live a healthy life free of any cancer. He had already made up his mind to continue with the business of living, no matter what the odds were. If he had a choice of fight or flight, he imagined a fight was the better option, at least until he knew for a fact that he would die of the cancer. Eighteen years later, Stuart is too busy with life to fret over the events that he probably could do very little about.

The same evening Stuart shared his good news, I had just been fired from my job. My colleagues called it *downsizing* but it seemed more like *firing* to me. The night before, my bosses invited me to a baseball game and we spent the rest of the evening drinking and eating. When I showed up the next morning, these same bosses pulled me aside and told me that business was too slow, and that they had to let me go. In talking about my reaction, *confused* is a pretty nice way of putting it. Completely stunned, I had no idea what my next move would be, but I had no other choice but to walk out.

Our reactions in uncomfortable situations tell a lot about our character. Our resolve not only tells the person standing across from us the value we have placed on ourselves but often is a striking reminder of our own self-image. Often our instinctive actions are the true products of our hearts—the things we do or say when we haven't had the luxury of time to evaluate the thought options at our disposal. If I yelled or even screamed at the two men, even they would understand. If I told them that I felt betrayed and disappointed they would have probably understood my point of view and not take it personal.

Left with a host of choices in whatever I could have done, I knew also the principle that people who had developed a resolve to fight and push forward usually don't have too much time to wail at closed doors. In fact, they see closed doors as an inevitable part of life and make a deeply personal decision to be unfazed by them.

I did something interesting that morning, and in hindsight, I wonder what triggered the thought of it. Instead of waiting for the disappointment and stress to kick in, I walked across the street to the offices nearby to apply for another job. I didn't say a word about what had happened, but equally surprising, I was hired on the spot to start the next day. The first train of emotions didn't have the chance to sink in before it was replaced by another.

I believe wholeheartedly that you don't *fight* life with an escape through alcohol, drugs, or any compulsive behavior. In the times when we can only hope for a *fresh dew to fall on our fields of green,* that is when we need our clear minds the most. As clichéd as this may sound, the most potent recourse is to make up our minds to not be depressed. The company that fired me faced an insurance lawsuit a month later; and in another month, they closed their doors for good. I understood then that what, at one time, seemed so puzzling to me was actually a way of escape.

For some of us, there are ingrained enforcers of negative off-putting beliefs that we live by. Whether we accept it or not, what we believe makes the biggest difference in the ultimate progress we make in life. There is a price for every action and inaction; every turn in a day gives all of us another chance to start over or press ahead.

Imagine yourself with a Rubik's Cube, one of the most frustrating yet stimulating toys in the world. No matter how clever a person may be, it is easy to notice after a series of attempts that a particular sequence is not helping the solution. The simple toy makes the most analytical thinkers wonder if they are over-thinking a simple step.

Experts of the game talk about how most people try to solve the cube layer by layer. The central problem with the layer method is that when you have completed the first layer, you can do nothing without breaking it up. I honestly cannot recall the last time I attempted a Rubik's Cube, but I know that in a good situation, I would be doing something useful all the time; and every act would be a part of the solution, instead of an obstacle.

"Green Grass Vapors" is a proposition that if the journey thus far has not lived up to the promises we hoped it would, this is certainly not the time to flee. I am not in the business of prescribing tranquilizers or any shortcuts; but when the negative reports show up, let the sequence we follow be filled with reassuring and affirmative thoughts, instead of fear and watching the rest of the world spin right in front of our eyes.

> I soaked my feet in blissful beam.
> That the ringing bells will wake my soul.
> I am no pauper, I am a man.

The remarkable thought is that the value we place on our own potential, ignoring the disappointments of our past, is the only method to visualizing a brighter moment ahead. "Green Grass Vapors" is my humble proposition to encourage us all to *hold on* even when there is almost nothing but faith to hold onto, and expect the fresh dew to revive our nerve-racking days. Some psychology experts will suggest that the most important component to a happier life is to guard our minds against any information that negates our core ambitions.

In fact if we do not see ourselves making a difference in life, we will not. When my doctor calmly patted my shoulder and suggested that I refrain from unnecessary anxiety, there certainly was more to it than medical study. We compromise our own resolve more that we know. Most things in life may involve some trial and error, but the perception of impending doom in our own minds immediately freezes our ability to react proactively.

I have seen this principle work in the lives of people of faith, as much as it had worked excellently in people who believe nothing about faith or religion, and it led me to believe that it is not a principle of faith per se. An optimistic and constructive attitude about life and ourselves is a straightforward universal principle and the opposite is true as well.

How do you tell a young mother struggling to make ends meet or a father doing every menial job to provide for his family to have a constructive and optimistic attitude to life? To make it worse, these may be people who have done all they could and given life their very best but maybe one reason or another leaves them where they have to scramble to live. How do you tell a person lying on a sick bed, unable to move and wishing for the day when he can take a step on his own, that he should find a faith to hold on to, because that makes a difference in the path to recovery?

Truth is, the downcast days of our lives are when we need faith and courage the most. The alternative to digging our feet in and clinging to whatever drop of optimism we can muster will only be an endless drain on us. If indeed the dew falls on the fields to renew their strength and vivacity, then we can also afford to keep our eyes on the moment when we will be refreshed to begin again. Until then, we stand.

There is a story about a prominent American architect, Frank Lloyd Wright. Throughout his life, he produced innovative, original architectural masterpieces as well as many of the interior elements of buildings, such as furniture and stained glass. In his personal life, there were less masterful occurrences.

The failure of his first two marriages and the well publicized 1914 fire and murders at his Taliesin studio took a toll on him. Architectural historians have their differing recollections about Lloyd Wright, but not many will deny the fact that a little Wisconsin boy would leave an indelible mark on history. Did his failures carve a tunnel of gloom for the remainder of his life?

When I first read his story, I wondered what drove him and how he endured the turmoil and endeavor to create his amazing masterpieces. Lloyd Wright once wrote, "The thing always happens that you really believe in; and the belief in a thing makes it happen." Simple as that, it is the conviction and confidence in *the thing* that gives us energy for a positive expectation, a sense of purpose and an *eye-poking moment*. Only then can we see ourselves in a refreshing and renewed field of green, full of "Green Grass Vapors". Belief, though, is a complex system that I believe we develop over time.

In group discussions I had over the years, many individuals acknowledged a need to realign deep-seated beliefs in order to decode the never-ending cycles of worry and doubt. They direct our behaviors and define the kind of goal that we buy into. I have repeatedly reminded myself of Ms. Karen's story.

After she was diagnosed with breast cancer, a doctor told her that she had two months to live. Her children saw their mother's condition drastically deteriorate in the first few weeks. She then agreed to a full treatment of mastectomy and chemotherapy; but after the first session, Ms. Karen decided that she had enough. Doctors advised

Chapter 4: Green Grass Vapors

against her decision, but she had made up her mind to use homeopathy and any other alternative to the painful sessions.

I learned this from her son, who had a front-row seat to his mother's condition. Ten years later, medical tests indicated that her cancer had steadily been in remission. Today she is living a fulfilled life. An interesting remark she made was that she *never thought of herself* as a sick person. Sure, she had been sick, she had a medical condition, but she refused to label herself a cancer victim. In our mind's eye, each of us holds a mental picture of who we are or who we want to be. It is entirely possible that the manifestation of who we are today is a direct result of our yesterday's thoughts.

I have met many people who would say "my allergies," or "my migraine" when they talked about an illness. The possessive pronouns, I am sure, do more to our psyche than we care to acknowledge. I do not know how much of the woman's results had to do with a biopsychosocial thought process, but she was convinced she had played a crucial role in her own survival.

In Green Grass Vapors, because of the morning dew that showers on our lives after we decide to hang on, we *wait for changing day* in *golden fields of fluffy thorns*. When we manage to appreciate the journey of life and keep on pressing forward, we learn to not fret and stress at the first sign of trouble. Even more, we learn to *fight* and not take *flight*. We send different signals to our brains every day when we have an assenting idea or take any initiative.

I believe we do the same when we dwell needlessly on negative reports. Whatever data we send to our brain, it is correctly stored in a compartment and securely coded. Eventually, this becomes the filter with which we scrutinize every activity and consequently how we perceive ourselves. This is probably how our beliefs take root.

My humble suggestion is that these deep-rooted beliefs make or break us and cause us to lose sight of the imminent fresh dew, the "Green Grass Vapors."

Green Grass Vapors

1 One more snow cone is worth gold
   For a pauper in the dusty tent
   Like chaff,
   Blows away in open palms.
5 I am scared of the changing days
   When the price I paid for a sky and a star
   Is more than boxes of gold,
   And all I am
   And fading through a glare in lucid doors.
10 Will I stay,
   For hope in barter, or for a song?
   In the burrows in grass
   And the mounds they leave behind
   The pauper hides his empty hands
15 The smell treasure is stale in the unsure winds
   Yet, I wait for changing day.
   The grass, the green and the breeze of blue
   The spinning door, a tent has none.
   I soaked my feet in blissful beam
20 That the ringing bells will wake my soul
   That I'll sit in golden fields of fluffy thorns
   And there in a silent trance
   I am no pauper,
   I am a man.

AT THE WATER'S EDGE

It was in my first year at college that I bumped into Professor Janine Blitch. She had a no-nonsense aura around her, even in her smile. Nothing made her more intriguing than her insightful ideas about some of the simplest things we often overlook as everyday natural occurrences. I had enrolled in an English composition series and would later learn a fascinating lesson beyond the scope of any academic discipline. It was a simple but life-changing thought that took a moment to sink in.

A faint smile appeared on her face as she read my first essay. "Good work," she mumbled to herself grudgingly. The assignment was about choosing any current social issue and arguing a point of view. There were no right or wrong answers. It did not take much to notice that Professor Blitch was not overly impressed with something about my arguments, but she kept that to herself.

After the next lecture session, the professor pulled me aside and advised that I be careful about constructing sentences *in the first person*. I took it for a trivial critique, but those same words dawned on me over and over a few months later. She was referring to the excessive use of words like *I and me* to express how any situation relates to us.

I did not quite grasp her reasoning, especially since I had gone through most of my life writing about what *I do, have done, I want, will do,* and even those things which *I will not do*. As you would expect in normal human beings, our human nature is consumed with thoughts about how the smallest details influence our lives. Most of us live in the *first person* and consequently, it is no surprise that we also think in the *first person*. Unfortunately, our interpretation of any life action seemingly revolves around our well-being in one way or another.

Different from selfishness as a character trait, thinking of ourselves and our immediate concerns is a logical occurrence for all of us. In a strange way, Professor Blitch's advice sparked an internal dialogue in my mind. Quietly, I wondered how much of our lives would be different if we didn't see the next person as a total stranger, or an irrelevant living thing, but rather an extension of our own selves.

At the Water's Edge is the point where we learn how much of a stranger's happiness is woven into our own. Perhaps the only reason why we are not the only people on Earth is because all of our lives are connected somehow, in one way or another.

I learned later on that there was absolutely nothing wrong with first person narrations in English grammar. However, when Professor Blitch suggested paying attention to the *I phrases*, she was unknowingly suggesting that whatever I was writing about was possibly not just about me. From that moment, it wouldn't take much for me to notice how much of my own conversations and the most trivial of things were filled with *I did this* and *I want that*.

Chapter 5: At the Water's Edge

The intriguing thought came to my mind that life is not all about *I*. That unsuspecting classroom exercise many years ago would become my new frame of reference for deliberate actions with another person's happiness in mind. The magic of this selfless act is that we may never know how much of a difference we make for the next person, and in turn what impact a complete stranger could have on our own lives.

I am of the conviction that our daily lives could have much more meaning if we take the time to make a stranger's agenda and the struggles of others just as pertinent as our *first person narrations.*

At the Water's Edge is an imaginative and reflective story of my life as I sat on the serene and shallow banks of a gently flowing stream. There in the quiet, I looked back at my own life. I reflected on how much I have lived for anything or anyone but myself. As the gentle water washed across my feet, I looked back at the simple acts of compassion and concern that gave my existence true value. In our steady grind to fulfill our own ambitions, most of us never pause to imagine the magnitude of a simple smile, benevolence and of sowing *a seed of care* into another person's life.

So often all of us live in the *what's in it for me* mode. It would be hypocritical on my part to assert that I am not driven by some form of rewards in life's actions, but it is amazing how much a simple word and the smallest help without any obvious rewards for ourselves can brighten someone else's life, and even more surprising is how it changes our own life.

I was particularly taken aback as I recalled the different parts of the world in which I have lived, and the many people whose dismal days and hollow lives were in desperate need of a genuine smile. I had no idea how much of a difference there could be for a stranger who takes a second to show someone else that they care. I am aware that it is those simple and noble expressions that make the entire universe go round. It certainly was true in my world.

Professor Blitch was right about one thing: my life had always been about the *first person narration*, all about me and my insatiable desires, until I hit a roadblock. For the many years that followed, it was impossible to *catch a break*, or so it seemed. Even the simple tasks which had been so easy to do had become *mission impossible*. Every hope and ambition I had was falling apart and I struggled at every turn to keep my focus on "I." I was sitting at the banks of a dried up stream; I had self-centered hopes that inadvertently blocked the peaceful waters that should have flowed back to me.

Out of nowhere, a thought crossed my mind one Sunday afternoon. What if I stopped worrying about the things I cannot do, and concentrate on those things which I know I can certainly do? What if I changed the focus from what my limited resources cannot afford, and rather invest my energy in those things which my *sufficient* resources could accomplish?

What can I do for someone else and do it without a shadow of a doubt? It is important to understand also that in this simple paradigm shift, our own circumstances don't have to necessarily be affected. "Let me take myself out of the equation for a minute," I thought. The only difference therefore is our altered focus.

The remarkable, yet effortless idea was to change the object of my attention to helping someone else who probably had no idea who I was, and with no means of compensation for my time and my seemingly genuine consideration. This is especially significant even in those upside down moments when we have no idea how to fix our own problems. It may very well be a confidence booster if we can be an *answer* in some capacity. I have witnessed some of my most unique moments of calm when I get to be a solution, another person's way out of a problem, just by providing even the most trivial of answers to another person's worries.

In my own logic, I became convinced that if I could find a way to be exactly who another hurting person needed to soothe their pain, I would put myself in line for someone else to soothe my pain. I could be a hero to someone; which was, at that time, something I could not be to myself.

At the Water's Edge is where the same gentle waters and encouraging energy we give out flow back onto our own feet, and bring us the compassion and peace that we seek for ourselves. I am in no way suggesting that a calculated reciprocity scheme is the answer to our individual challenges. Instead, my intent was to shift the focus from the constant *"I"* thoughts and change the dynamic of my conversation from rehashing my problems to becoming someone else's solution.

In any case, I was unknowingly engineering my happiness through other strangers' lives, and I was no longer losing sleep about things I could not do. None of us may have a scholarly understanding of how *karma* works, and none of us know the full spectrum of seed and harvest time, but our agenda is not to reap a benefit because we gave time and energy to the next person who needed it.

This exercise led me to be cognizant of the fact that in some distant future, what will matter will not only be how much I have done for myself, but for the next person in whose life I have had abundant opportunities to lend a helping hand. I have found that the more I give, the more I am living.

> *In the strangest hopes in a stranger's eye, and his story shudders my feebly spine. Washed to my feet in a gentle stream.*

A colleague shared his story while we sat in a lunch room many years ago. I listened closely with my hand on his shoulder, even as the tears filled his eyes and his heart was heavy with pain. His 13-year old daughter may never live the healthy life that most of us so easily take for granted.

At six years old, the little girl was diagnosed with systemic lupus erythemathosus and her immune system has always been in a constant scuffle with body cells, kidneys and nervous system. He talked about how the antidepressants soothed his daughter's pain, but also of how she may never get to play with her friends like most of us did as children. My heart was heavy as I listened to his account, but I managed to hide my tears as I listened to how a little girl's days started with eight pills and ended with six more.

I would later learn something quite stirring, that in spite of how much our present adversities may seem overwhelming for us, I can bet that there is always someone else waiting in line to trade their frustrations with ours. The 13-year-old little girl is forced to find a miracle where the odds are piled against her at such an early age. My colleague held my hands firmly and said, "Thank you for listening."

All that the distressed father needed was a stranger who cared enough to listen to his story. He did not need my money or advice; my smile was enough. He was living with a condition that no amount of money or expert advice could change. I had no idea of what to say in response, so I lightly patted his shoulder. "Are you alright?" I asked. "Yes; yes I am," he replied as he wiped the tears off his face. *"You didn't have to do this, so thank you,"* he continued.

What my colleague did not know was that I was struggling with my own health problems, strapped in discomfort and ache. He had no idea that I also woke up every morning with a heavy heart, in search of a shoulder to cry on. I knew what it felt like. In the middle of my own chaos I had to pause for a moment, remembering that our lives were not all about *us*, even when we have our own set of issues to worry about. I believe that so often, a humble compassion that is not rooted in compulsion, guilt, duty, or some crafty expectation is a powerful resource which all of us have, and can give.

In some of my lowest points of misery, when the hard times became overpowering and I sought to find the pieces which could make my life just a bit more meaningful, I found them in the faces of strangers. In our own little way, we can search for openings in strangers' faces, a redirection of our inabilities to solve someone else's problem, no matter how small. The truth *at the water's edge* is that we will never know when the desperate person we touch with our compassion is our own selves.

A long time ago, I was driving on a busy street with a friend when the usual traffic jam forced us to a virtual standstill. The street hawkers approached cars with a variety of items to sell, while a few others held signs in hopes that strangers would be kind to them. A man in a wheelchair tapped on my car and without uttering a word, pulled out a sign that read, "I am your investment." I mumbled to myself "Investment in what." It seemed to me a very ingenious style of pleading for help, and I gave the beggar some money in admiration of his odd creativity.

My friend was not particularly impressed by my generosity, and he went on to explain his rationale for not paying any attention to beggars on street corners. He had a valid point, but I also believe that it is more important to follow our individual and inner guideposts, than try to rationalize our actions, especially when we have no way of knowing what brought someone else to the middle of the street with a sign. Sure I had no idea how the man got in the wheelchair. I certainly didn't know how he made it to the busy street, or even why he chose to tap on my window. All I know was that a stranger needed help, and he didn't ask for much.

I genuinely respect different opinions on altruistic intentions but I have learned to always be kind to the next person, regardless of the circumstances and despite the cardboard signs their hopes are written on. In all honesty, I was not expecting that someone else would be kind to me in return, but I considered it another exercise in learning to live beyond the *first person*.

It meant a lot more to me than just a simple act of random kindness. The empathy we pass on to the next person may very well be the empathy we need for ourselves in our often unrelated circumstances. Perhaps the beggar was right about one thing, *my investment* would be to shift the spotlight from the many things that I was incapable of and to focus on things of which I knew I was capable. If that was my seed of care to someone else, a few dollars would be worth my investment.

I learned about the hard work of social activist Jane Tewson's non-profit organization Timebank and the Pay It Forward Foundation. It became an idea for a Hollywood movie production. In 1990, the film *Pay It Forward* was based on the premise that it was indeed possible for one idea to change the world. A schoolboy in Las Vegas, Nevada named Trevor McKinney was given a project to complete by his social studies teacher Eugene Simonet, who had terrible burn scars on his face and neck.

The task was to come up with a plan that would change the world through direct action. Trevor was a 12-year-old boy who believed in the goodness of human nature and would plan to change the world for the better, using the imperfect people around him.

The moral of the film set forth the precedent that when someone does you a big favor, *don't pay it back; pay it forward*. As with Trevor's belief, a simple act of kindness and consideration can change the life of the next person, and that is always something any one of us can do. All of our lives are filled with elements like time and energy which are finite resources. A helping hand and a healing heart, however, are abundant in our every moment, if only we can take the time to hear the heavy heart next door.

Thanks to Professor Blitch, I learned to take out the *I* not only from my writing assignments in college, but in everyday life and find fulfillment in the peace of the strangers around me. Fortunately, I saw my reward in unexpected places, and this exercise became an incentive in itself for me. The more I thought I was helping another person, the more I learned I had been helping myself the whole time. This is the peace in my heart, the calming breeze and gentle stream as I sat *At the Water's Edge.*

At another point in my life, I attended a meeting to discuss my poem, "At the Water's Edge," and I met an old friend. He listened carefully to every story, the diction and meaning in every sentence. Unable to hold his silence much longer, he politely whispered, "Have you ever thought of becoming Buddhist?" *"Never,"* I replied, all the while thinking to myself, *"Where did that come from?"*

"I see you are happy being of service to a higher self," he said.

Apparently selflessness is a Buddhist teaching, and in my friend's opinion I was half way living that doctrine so it shouldn't be difficult for me to sign up altogether. "I think you would be a good teacher," he continued. *"Higher self"* I pondered.

Sounded nice, but no thank you. I honestly did not ponder that for too long. I am sure Buddhism, like most religions and doctrines, has fine and considerate ideas. Instead, I remembered vividly that when Professor Blitch taught me to not always think in *first person*, she wasn't talking about a higher self. I never thought of reasonable compassion towards another person as fulfilling a religious obligation, but rather extending a generous hand to a stranger or a neighbor.

It reminded me, however, of stories I first heard not too long ago. A Buddhist monk met a beggar. Starving and cold, he asked the monk for anything he could offer him. The monk handed the beggar the loaf of bread without much thought. As the man reached out to get the loaf, the monk felt his shivering hand and fingers. The monk took off his robe and handed it to the beggar to keep him warm. "Thank you," he muttered in a weak voice as he walked away.

A few minutes later the monk saw the beggar running towards him, with the loaf of bread and robe in his hands. "Are you okay?" the monk asked.

"Yes I am," the beggar replied as he handed over the bread and the robe. "But I don't want it!"

The monk asked, "What sir, do you want?"

"I want what you have that allowed you to give away the bread and the robe."

Oftentimes, our immediate sense of generosity points to the virtue of giving good things to others freely, and without reward. It is also entirely possible that this is a learned character trait, not a spiritual belief, but rather a mind-set.

I was familiar with the Buddhist's understanding of generosity stemming from two words—dana and caga. *Dana* means *distribution of gifts*, while *caga* translates to mean *a heart bent on giving*. *Dana*, or giving, is intimately tied to karma, or what is commonly understood to represent a cause and effect. *Caga* describes the state of mind of the generous giver, or the desire to give.

Coincidentally, most people we meet and many of the situations we find ourselves in, as dire as some may be, often ask for much less than giving up our lives for another person. It is the simple smiles, the considerate and compassionate gestures that make some of the biggest differences in the lives of many people.

The meaning of the chapter *At the Water's Edge* is that the more we are able to redirect the center of our attention to the person next to us, the more we are able to lend a helping hand to the ailing heart and stranger, especially when our seemingly insignificant efforts are all that they need. The powerful effect that I saw in my own encounters is that irrespective of how long it takes or how unaware we may be, that same act of kindness spirals back into our own lives, when we least expect it. Generosity and common kindness heals not only the people we have met, but our own selves also.

I had discovered my concern for other people not only as a way to change what concerned me, but as a strategy to remove myself from whatever my own shortcomings were. In this way, I didn't give myself

Chapter 5: At the Water's Edge

the time and the opportunity to dwell on life's many roadblocks and my laundry list of adversities. It had nothing to do with a religious doctrine, and I have similarly invited many individuals to genuinely incorporate this noble and self-sacrificing agenda into their daily lives.

There is a story of a woman who sat next to a man on a bench near a playground. "That's my son over there," she said, pointing to a little boy in a red shirt who was gliding down the slide. "He's a fine looking boy," the man said. "That's my son Todd on the swing in the blue shirt," he added.

Then, looking at his watch, he called to his son, "I'm ready to go, son." The little boy pleaded, "Just five more minutes, please!"

The man nodded and the little boy continued to swing. Minutes passed and the father stood and called to his son again. "Time to go now?"

Again the little boy pleaded, "Five more minutes. Just five more minutes." The man smiled and said, "O.K."

"My, you certainly are a patient father," the woman politely observed. The man smiled, as he leaned back in the chair thinking to himself. His older son Tommy was killed crossing a street while he was riding his bike home. Tommy was rushing home so he wouldn't break his father's rules. In fact everything revolved around what this father wanted, his time, his plans, and his rules. Now the man would give anything to spend just five more minutes with his son, Tommy.

The lesson is that he vowed not to make the same mistake with his younger son, Todd. The little boy thinks he has five more minutes to swing. But the truth is that the father has found out that he gets five more minutes to watch him play. Just as he finished telling the woman the story of his sons, he added *"happiness is not all about mine."*

At the Water's Edge follows the interwoven nature of each of our desires in life. Rather surreptitiously, each of our simple joys is connected to someone else's, whether we acknowledge it or not. We all use the cliché "Life is a game," which insinuates that some logical sequence of attitudes could increase the probabilities if all that mattered was winning and losing.

The often obscure logic, unique to this *game*, is that the rules on my side of the fence may very well be the same for you, and that maybe we can all find a way to a priceless investment in lives other than our own. There is no *one-size-fits-all* prescription to a self-sacrificing idea, but I am forever inspired by Albert Einstein's quote, "A person truly lives when he can live outside of himself."

We all have important things that we could be doing at any moment, but occasionally we could also pause and let another person's happiness become our load. Life certainly is not all about the *I*.

At the Water's Edge

1 It's in the eye of the stream
   Where the laden heart finds calm
   In the strangest hopes in a stranger's eye
   And his story shudders my feebly spine.
5 Broken life of a soul reaching out
   Washed to my feet in a gentle stream.
   His tears fill my eyes
   With the shock that never wears off
   My scratching scalp, my own to bear
10 And my veins filled with twinge and stings.
   Not a blemish on a cheek,
   No dimples and pretty freckles
   Or sparkle in the bulging brows
   When man is all shred, sore and turning blue.
15 The streaming splash is calm in my eyes
   My feet still wet with a stranger's tears
   Of a weeping man, a million pains to his name
   And left with a bamboo splinter faith
   Washing down the at the water's edge.
20 My sun-drenched days of baking heat
   Was his too
   In different colors and bigger bubbles
   The stranger's hope is clearer now
   In the ripples of a gentle stream
25 All my silent deeds are but a carnival at ending turn.
   Oh look!
   My life is slowly washing to land
   I was my stranger, closer now I can see
   The longest prayers at a water's trail
30 Gently washed my saving heart to land.

TWO BLACK POLKA DOTS

For almost five years, I lived in utmost paranoia as I saw my life unravel, with missed opportunities, bad decisions and my hopes falling apart bit by bit. Often when I talked of such moments, I met people who genuinely seemed compassionate or were able to personally connect to my story. Others stared in amazement at how a young person's life could possibly be so nerve-racking, to the point of near despondency.

You may have had such experiences for a longer or shorter period, or maybe not at all. My assertion is that, very often the crisis in our personal lives has the potential to snowball, and wreck everything we have worked and hoped for.

Most of us learned very early as we grew up how to live our lives behind a mask. After many years of hiding behind our emotions and deflecting the emotional surges, we succeeded in doing so. No one will know our quiet tears. The disappointments we go through will not show up on our faces, so we can go through life without letting the world see how broken we are on the inside. When a stain is left to reside on a piece of cloth, it soon finds company with another and then another. They exist together as part of a plan, just as we learn to live with the masks and the pain. Soon enough, what could have been an eyesore at one point in our lives the turmoil we learn to live with, and we find a way to go along with it instead of confronting it and moving on with our lives.

Life is not always straightforward, clear-cut and with roadmaps; it's not always easy to dust off the negative reports and keep moving on. My sad days were nothing new, and there was surely nothing magical about the simple choice of standing tall even when I was without reasons to try.

Why *Two Black Polka Dots?* Ambition is the energy for endurance but when this optimistic impetus is challenged, there comes a point in a person's life when it feels as though basic survival is completely shattered. I remember having to assure and reassure myself that there were brighter days ahead, although the pressure and the weight piled on year after year. In lieu of any uplifting experience, most of us eventually retreat from our immediate network or any support establishment. From that moment, all that matters to us is *self.*

Since I was young, I hoped to explore the world, except that I had no idea of how lonely adventures could be. My comfort in the familiar territory and company of family of friends changed two days after ending up in a small town in Arkansas. I had formed some of my most splendid memories living on Avon Avenue in Newark, New Jersey. The excitement and fun became commonplace and routine.

Life in Arkansas was on the extreme end of that happy spectrum. It was a small town with hardly anything to do and few job opportunities. There was no "Now Hiring" sign in any window across town.

Chapter 6: Two Black Polka Dots

Here I was, always wanting to travel somewhere far and different; but now I thought to myself that the bottom couldn't be any farther from where I stood. Luckily, I found temporary jobs through employment agencies enough to support my livelihood and I was determined not to leave town out of frustration.

On one such assignment, I met Duane. He was a supervisor at a polystyrene insulation processing plant and had an astonishingly charming persona and intellectual ability. He could memorize numbers and calculate even the most complicated combination of arithmetic without any effort, and without a calculator.

I learned this about him one afternoon, as we sat on the warehouse steps trying to calculate what our paychecks would be for that week. I was immediately intrigued and genuinely curious to find out why he had never cared to pursue any other opportunity that would employ his remarkable gift for mathematics.

Certainly, I wondered to myself, why was Duane arranging styrofoam blocks and sheets that required no mathematical ability? Why would anyone with such aptitude as his just waste their time here? Much to my surprise, he had earned an advanced degree in Applied Mathematics at a prestigious university. He had worked on several research projects that sought to retain his expertise for international projects. I assumed then that there ought to be a life-changing reason why he had given up on the career and the life he could have enjoyed.

Almost grudgingly, he reflected on his former life for a moment. "Something happened in December 1997," he admitted while staring at the concrete floor. Duane never told me what happened but I could imagine how much of an impact, whatever it was, had on his life. We were about to begin our shift when he began to talk some more about the events in his life that led up to this point.

His family and all his friends lived in Hackensack, New Jersey. He speaks to his family on the telephone every month but never agreed to anyone visiting him in the small town he now lives in. He claimed to be happy where he was now but it was evident Duane still hurt about something. I knew this, because I also had suffered what appeared to be grim psychological hopelessness.

Unfortunately, not many people around me took the time to notice. I had often said that I could not blame my immediate circle of friends and family, because whatever was the source of the misery, it eluded me also. What is there to know if you do not know what you're looking for? In retrospect, that was probably my encounter with paranoid personality disorder, especially with the pervasive and insidious feelings of emptiness.

My new friend had been living with a heavy heart. Once upon a time, he was a high achiever with the same optimism most of us have, and he had high expectations of himself. Duane was relearning the art of survival and giving himself a reason to continue living to the fullest.

His world crashed once because of a horrible car accident and he has been trying to move on ever since. He is learning to redirect his focus and not allow his past hurts and resentment to spill over into his present life. Someday, Duane will choose which memories to hold on to, and which to let blow away like chaff. I lived through mine and while I listened to him, I was thankful to get a second chance to tell a story of triumph today. This is why I wrote *Two Black Polka Dots*.

The two dots are the stains and spots which taint our otherwise pure and uninterrupted path in life. They are the many unexpected circumstances which derail our mandate for a fulfilling life and send us on a downhill spiral. They are also the indelible marks that are almost impossible to erase, those marks that glare at us at every turn. The stains are not a result of any subpar performance or any fault of our own; it is life and it happens. They are the unanticipated events out of the blue, after whose encounter we are never the same again.

Chapter 6: Two Black Polka Dots

Following the years of what I believed to be my recuperation, I learned something fascinating about myself and my experience. I noted that my fragile identity through this tumultuous emotional stage of my life was perhaps a direct result of chronic rejection and inability to pursue simple tasks. I had continually lived with the feeling of being locked outside my real world of infinite potential.

This is where some of us hit a depressive note and give up. As with my friend Duane, the negative setbacks had defined the person I was and what I could be the rest of the way. Although my life, figuratively, as a train was still moving, the only mental picture I saw was that of a train wreck. It is no secret anyone can be happy and enthusiastic in the good times.

We often miss the truth that it takes the same amount of energy to stay afloat, if not more, than it takes when you are riding through the slump. I remember how my world eventually became a bunch of absolutes: good or bad, friends or foes, with no middle ground and no shades of gray.

Having the right outlook begins with an honest appraisal of where we stand in life, not with a glamorous picture of who we want to be. By that same measure, a gloomy portrait of how we perceive ourselves will not help us in any way. It's like a huge board inside a shopping mall that does its job of listing all the stores in a diagram that makes sense of the chaos of a marketplace. Then it adds something even more powerful, a big red arrow to say "You are here" on the map. Finding where we are or what we are looking for, even where we desire to go, will not make a difference, unless we find the big red arrow.

Stripping away the fragments of sadness that linger around all of our lives will demand an honest acceptance of where we are. Like the map in the mall with the big red arrow, we have to know where we stand in a world where we can find a million trinkets to remind us of where we fell short and why our lives could be better than they are now. Only then will we know how to get to the destination ahead of us, because even when the paths get twisted and crooked and narrow and dim, the big red arrow will have guided us from where we once were to the place we ought to be heading.

The *Two Black Polka Dots* had formed images of the silent killer in my own interpretations of mistrustful people and a conniving world out to hurt me. I had lost sight of the fact that my life was my own, that life happens, and that the world is filled with a lot more than a handful of bitter images. My persona was mostly plain, with only *Two Black Polka Dots*, but adversity had magnified their impact beyond what it actually was.

When I left the little town in Arkansas, my life's hard days and difficult moments had shaped me into an ailing man who had nothing but self-therapy to change the course of my unfortunate trajectory. Even worse was that I could never once identify anything wrong in my life, until now, many years later. I had become fragile, on edge, suspicious of everyone and gradually sinking into a depressive condition. Unless I was able to ride through the overwhelming obstacles, it would be almost impossible for me to fix this miserable person.

Former Microsoft CEO Bill Gates once wrote this: "Whether you succeed or fail depends on how you greet bad news." Not whether or not you get bad news. In fact bad news is just as much a part of life as water and air, but even the lowest points of our lives possess windows of hope. Our unique challenges work like a bouncing ball, with likelihood to bounce upwards after a drop. Therein exists a critical lesson. I had to learn that the minor setbacks could unconsciously permeate into other areas of life and affect things I couldn't have imagined.

I suggest that a little winning step is an added momentum to keep on moving higher in spite of the odds. I have also come to learn that we should be very careful of the magnitude of events we casually classify as *trials by fire*. All of us are not equally wired to respond to

Chapter 6: Two Black Polka Dots

challenges in the same fashion and to endure the hardships of life. Maybe prolonged stress, lingering anxiety, and tremendous uncertainty about one's fate are enough to drive a person to his grave.

If we allow our minds to dwell on the downside of anything, and live with a defeatist posture, it may not be long before we allow the constraints on our days to morph into seemingly insurmountable hurdles. That will kill the little spark that ought to give us a sense of confidence to hang on for another moment. Maybe pushing ourselves to alter our perspective is more than just creating an alternate reality. Instead, those seemingly inconsequential steps give us a platform to hone in on any bright spot we can find and let that become the lighting rod that leads our way. The right perspective changes our vantage point and offers the energy we need to propel us into achieving our life's goals. Even more important, we will give ourselves permission to enjoy the journey along the way.

A young girl wrote a letter to her parents. It read, "Dear Mom and Dad, I'm sorry it has taken me so long to write but my stationery was destroyed the day the demonstrators burned down the dormitory. I am out of the hospital now and the doctors said my eyesight should be back to normal, eventually."

"The wonderful boy, Bill, who saved me from the fire kindly offered to share his cozy little apartment with me until the dorm is rebuilt. He comes from a good family and you should not be too surprised to learn that we are going to get married next week. In fact Mom and Dad, you always wanted me to give you grandchildren, so you should be real happy to learn that you're going to be grandparents—next month!"

The young girl signed her letter with a kiss and an arrow that instructed her parents to turn the page over. It read, "Mom and Dad, please disregard the above practice in English composition. There was no fire, I have not been in the hospital, I am not pregnant, and I do not even have a boyfriend. However, I did get a 'D' in Chemistry and an 'F' in Math, but I wanted to make sure you received this news in the proper perspective."

We easily imagine the parents' sigh of relief in realizing that their worst fear did not indeed happen. As with the recipients of this letter, that is how our circumstantial priorities are quickly altered and a problem that appeared insurmountable in one instance is almost irrelevant the next moment. Over and over again, I have shared personal experiences that had a potentially de-motivating element unless I made a choice to use that moment as a bridge builder to another level in life.

One advantage we all possess is that we know ourselves better than anyone else ever will. I am confident, also, in the fact that only you and I stand the best chance of shifting our focus at any point in our lives. People who live fulfilling lives learn to see past the apparent and the present, the here and now. If all it takes to ruin our joy is two stains, inconsequential setbacks, troubles we can sidestep, *Two Black Polka Dots*, then we may not have had much joy to begin with.

We cannot wait for everything around us to fall in line before we decide to live the best we know we can. In fact there is plenty of interruption along the way to ensure that we never have a stress-free, perfectly scripted life. Nothing may change immediately, but what we perceive of ourselves can force us to interpret where our God-given strength can take us, in a completely different way. This may indeed be the reason why our resolve should be to live in spite of the inescapable strain that can pile on us like the weight of many tiny rocks that soon become a boulder too heavy to carry. When the hurdles seem daunting and we find ourselves knee-deep in a pit we cannot easily dig our way out of, we will still have to summon a courage to do whatever we had our hearts set on, even when that means taking one feeble step after another.

At the end of the day, life goes on no matter how unfair and how many problems we think are unmerited. I told my friend Duane what my father once told me, that the world owed us nothing. There are some things that we have absolutely no control over. All we can do is to reevaluate what happens inside of us and around us, and not allow the two little dots to ruin the rest of the promises and rewards of our lives.

Two Black Polka Dots

1 On the verge of ripping in two
Roses dried in summer's breeze
Blots and spots have muddled purity
And dreamy eyes are afraid to sleep.
5 The sun burned happiness in freezing nights
The splotch killed the simple dreams
Burned the hope I had to give to self
A heart once pure and true
Now flee for a life and from a polka dot.
10 Virtue was born with strings to win
Until now, and the shock of sudden stain.
It's one or two and here and there
Scars in memories of yesteryear
Lost in the misery of moments gone
15 From what is pure and still so clear.
A blot that changed my very soul
See the burdens fade
Not just scatter,
Not just wider and wider.
20 Signs of life, a tinge and beauty lost
But how much more are the dots so poor?
When is a heart bare and fresh again?
To start anew living through purple stains.
Let one or two be a memory's mark
25 For in dirty mirrors the dots will blur.
Let my life restore to clean like before,
To my perfect life
Sparkling fresh, and happy smells
I am pure and whole and a hundred yards
30 Two black polka dots, but forever well
In my gleaming heart and stainless life.

ETERNITY'S CABIN

A man told a story of how an elephant adapts to illusory obstacles, to such an extent that over time, those false borders become their awareness of reality. An untamed baby elephant is captured and a long chain is tied around its foot. The other end of the chain is tied to a tree. The elephant pulls over and again but to no avail and it is unable to break free.

After repeating the process for several weeks, the elephant finally surrenders to the chain and stop trying to pull away. Later, the chain is taken off from the tree but the other end is still tied around the elephant's foot, and the elephant never attempts to break away because it remembers its foot was chained to a tree.

A remarkable aspect of our human existence is in our ability to transform and adjust ourselves to different circumstances. Whether we recognize it or not, there is a constant evolutionary force at work in and around all of us. For instance, none of us are exactly who we were as little babies many years ago. Somehow we have managed to change with the years and to a larger extent adjusted our world view along the way. Times change and certainly, people also do change, but perhaps within the progression of time itself are our changing roles and our opportunity to perfect our own routines.

The comforting news is that the oblivious elephant is not running a race with anyone. The only hope is that it recognizes at some point that it had been set free; beyond that, it has every chance in the world, like all of us, to live a fulfilling life.

Whatever we have been unable to do at one turn, there is no rule anywhere that suggests that we cannot do it now. None of us are stuck in *Eternity's Cabin*, forever chained to our past setbacks. Certainly there is nothing requiring us to stay at one spot, transfixed on a handicap.

I recall one afternoon when I bumped into an old friend. I had not seen my elementary school pal Linda for 15 years. Linda was married and had two children; and from what I could tell, she looked very happy. She wasn't. Halfway through the conversation, she mentioned also how many things she would do over if she could start again. In her mind, so much time had elapsed, and so many wasted years had killed the passion she once had.

"*Why can't you,*" I thought to myself quietly. She had previously seen my picture in a news magazine and went on to talk about how much of our lives seemed to her like an arty stage work. That I agreed with. The best part of the stage work then was that there was always a *scene two* if we ever faltered and froze in our opening act. The years have flown by so quickly that as Linda put it, she never got the chance to find her role, or play the leading character in her own play. The longer I listened to her, the more I recalled the many people who shared their regrets in much the same way.

Chapter 7: Eternity's Cabin

Occasionally I will take a moment to reflect on some of the invaluable life lessons my grandfather passed on over the years, especially those that he taught unintentionally, through his actions. He was one person who adamantly believed that the rules of any successful lifestyle are universal; and always reminded anyone to live this life not only for their own accomplishment, but also for many more people whose ideas, values and faith may be affected by their story someday.

When he died on June 4, 1994, my grandfather had lived a complete life, filled with deep-seated and self-regulating attitudes which made him the person he was. After the war in Burma, he had come home with a renewed set of ideas, including a fresh perspective on the value of life and death. "Life is worth a lot and nothing at all," he often said. In one instant you are here, but in a blink of an eye, you are gone. This is nonetheless one of the many crucial truths with a potential to recreate a sense of urgency in all of us.

It is one thing to fear the uncertainty that belies a future, but it is a completely different situation to allow those fears to obstruct our decision-making and any progress we would otherwise have made. Imagine yourself standing in the middle of a road. There you are, in the median and cars are speeding past you in both directions.

How you got there is irrelevant; how you make it across the street is what makes all the difference in the world. My father would suggest that any direction is better than standing on the yellow lines; because sooner or later, a car would veer into the median and whack you into either direction. Choose a side, take a chance, and cross the road.

Our fears inevitably lead to excuses of inability and helplessness. A very popular thought is the question of what each of us would do if we knew for a fact that we were not going to fail irrespective of the challenge? Many people we all know tried many things, failed at some of them, and still inspired themselves to do more than twiddle our thumbs. Sure enough, they had many more victories than others who played safe, stood in the middle of the road in fear and did nothing.

If failure was impossible, I can only imagine how many of us would try new careers and new adventures and revive our buried dreams. How many of us would ignore our past failures and start over in the confidence of an inevitable victory? I often talked about how some people are extremely clever at pointing a finger at everyone else except himself or herself. I know of people who blame society, their friends, government and even their own family for their personal misfortunes. I have been there.

The foremost motivation from *Eternity's Cabin* is that only you and I can redeem the time on our own behalf. We can take center stage and play the leading role in the one performance we are perfectly equipped for. Years ago, when we sat next to each other in elementary school, Linda and I joked about wanting to build a hospital together when we got older. Linda was passionate about helping others, and I talked about how much money we would make because everyone will get sick at some point.

Every child has a lavish dream filled with ambitions and hope, but it is possible that somewhere in the midst of our taxing performances we lose track of the beautiful desires that once filled our hearts. For some of us, it would take forever, almost *eternity* to acknowledge that the boundaries we imagined had been illusory obstacles all the while. By that same token, none of us can afford to shrink into our *cabins* and give up on whatever it is we want to accomplish.

Fifteen years ago, no one told Linda and me that our lives would go through dramatic ups and downs, of death, emotional losses, threats and even attempted suicide. With time, our passion had waned; the chains had weighed so heavy on our feet that we had nothing but *stifled optimism* left in us. Some people learned those lessons long ago and embraced the revolving doors even as fast as

Chapter 7: Eternity's Cabin

they came. Like others, we still struggle with the thought of starting over and dreaming again.

As in the case of the elephant, it soon realizes that the chain at his feet is no longer tied to a tree trunk, but whether or not it takes advantage of the new-found freedom has a lot more to do with the elephant than it has to do with the chain. As the times change, the effort and pressure to alter our idiosyncrasy into the positive are the same that it takes to direct them in the opposite direction.

We took turns sharing our experiences over the years, and most importantly the lessons they brought. It is fascinating how much all of us remain the same over time, as an extension of our old self at any point in time. At the core, I was no different from the nine-year-old boy in elementary school, but how we evolve and grow over the years hinges on a series of choices we make at each turn.

Generally, we all are who we have always been; and by that same token, no matter how long a passion lies dormant, it never dies. In the *timeless drama through dawn and dusk, eternity's cabin* keep our hopes secure, our spirits alive, and hands over another chance to deliver a stunning performance. The happiest elephants then are not the ones who imagine yanking the tree from the ground and dragging it through the rest of life, but the ones who recognize the liberty to pursue their deepest ambitions. Seldom do providence and our fortunes tilt the scales, but all of us have the power to start over in spite of what our story has been.

I learned an interesting fact many years ago. You realize that anytime you point one finger, there are always three pointing back at you and the thumb alone pointing up, as if to God, Heaven or somewhere above. My father told of how that simple hand gesture was probably God's reminder that the bulk of life's culpability is of our own making.

I did mention in the earlier chapters that we could choose to blame everyone else, but that temporary relief is far from a solution.

Many psychologists would say that the only way to take the initiative to rectify the negatives in any situation is to accept our share of the responsibility for their happening.

My grandfather would say, it is important to understand this balance and make considerable efforts to shake off the culture of blame-shifting. The extent to which we are willing to accept our individual roles in our own life story remarkably affects how we approach and handle even the simplest of actions. *Life is worth a lot and nothing at all*, and this renewed sense of urgency is the bridge to altering any portion of our lives, in our work, our home, with our friends, and with anything else we can imagine.

My first week's experiences in London and New Jersey had strikingly similar feelings, although several years apart. I had left behind the home, family and the many familiar faces I had known all my life and entered into another world which had an inherent shock factor. Although they both had a promise for a brighter future and the potential to advance my personal ambitions, none of the fresh starts offered any guarantees.

I had somehow developed a clear sense of what my priorities ought to be, hence it was easier to change locations and still hold on to the same set of values. I called my father a thousand miles away, and all he did was to remind me that they were the same internal ethical and moral guidelines which my grandfather had shared and the same principles which had shaped my mindset. Our motivating factors may lie in the most insignificant encounters, and it is up to you and me to stay tuned to how these associations affect our lives.

A long time ago, my grandfather would say that no matter where life takes you, the same universal principles apply. We are who we are for a reason. Imagine for a moment life as a market or a business process. Each of us in this market is always selling something. We sell a thought, a character, some knowledge, or our very presence. Interestingly, the fact that we may not even know what it is we have to sell does not change this rule. By that same gesture, with all of our dealings, each of us is buying something.

With every day that we live and with every one of our actions, we make a sales pitch either to the next person or even to ourselves. Often times another person's concept of who we are is what we have sold to them, whether consciously or otherwise. The axiom "Don't sell yourself short" was perhaps born out of this premise. It is only prudent that we take a cautious and honest inventory of ourselves and of our abilities. The purpose of this exercise is to be assertive on what it is we are selling at any point in time.

One of the most amusing but priceless recollections of my childhood was my evening strolls with my father, although it wasn't too much fun then. We would walk around the neighborhood, saying hello to almost anyone we met, and almost wandering aimlessly in the suburb. The interesting part is that we would dress in our best suits and shoes, as if we had just come home from an important event, and just winding down with a leisurely walk.

Frankly, I never thought much about it until later in life. We were poorer than most of our neighbors, but my father didn't want that to translate into a defect in our sense of self-worth. The evening walks in our finest clothes made us look important, feel important, and think importantly. In my naïve mind, we were the most important people in the neighborhood.

Even to this day, I am convinced that the fact that some of us do not have much does not automatically oblige us to walk around with long faces, and as if the weight of the world were strapped onto our shoulders. Reputation is undeniably based on other people's perceptions about who we are to them, which is often the key element that constructs their reality of us. I do not suggest that we scramble in search of others' approval or sell misconceptions, but by all means, that we pay attention to the images that we convey with every word and every action.

Eternity's Cabin expresses nostalgia for my childhood, but more importantly, it is a reflection on the subtle guiding thoughts on who I have become. We cannot drift aimlessly and carelessly through life and assume that luck, by some coincidence, will turn the odds in our favor. We all have an internal monitor that serves as a mental thermostat and that gives us an awareness of our own life map. What controls our thermostat are the signals we feed it. Thus if we convince ourselves that we are cold, we will feel cold even in a blazing summer day.

The reverse is true also. Truth is, we are all different, and it could very well be that these differences also influence how we approach daily living. What is not different is that life owes us nothing, and we are responsible for how much value anyone places on us, largely because we say how much we are worth. The emphasis is on the *individual*, the *unique* and the *self*. That means, my blueprint can only inspire or encourage yours, but it is not designed to be a photocopy of your life's path.

For many years, I shared these thoughts with friends and hundreds of people I spoke to. Ultimately, it is about having a personal mission statement in life. I am not referring to laid-back wishful thinking or wild desires of your glamorous imaginations. A mission statement requires a deep conscious and honest meditative process. Our life's mission statement is what will define who we are to ourselves, what we want out of life and how we plan to get there. Our having that clear sense of direction and a map allows us to navigate our lives in a careful, consistent and meaningful way.

Life is worth a lot and nothing at all, but the journey itself is long or short, fertile or futile, depending on how much we are getting out of it. My father would say, if you have *skin in the game*, you act differently. Skin in the game is a term coined by renowned financial investor Warren Buffet. It meant nothing more than taking an active interest in a company or an undertaking by making a significant investment or financial commitment.

Chapter 7: Eternity's Cabin

The events that motivate our deepest passions may not be the same as those that drive the next person. However, keeping our thoughts aligned with our carefully crafted mission statement can only enhance our options and increase the odds in our favor.

I wrote *Eternity's Cabin* one morning as I imagined how someday we would have lived out our lives and had the chance to look back at our own performances. At every turn, an act will have its own consequence, and as the moments change, every one of the consequences will affect our overall outcome.

Truth is, we cannot lay aside our identity for a moment and assume a character we would perform on a stage. Unlike a theatrical display, an anxiety-filled day will not soon go away simply because a new day arrives. It will be up to each one of us to consciously raise the curtains in our lives. On the days when there is nothing to cheer us into giving our best and even though the blustery days makes us prone to wander, we need a determination to pummel ahead to make it through the scene as best as we can, and set us up for the next. Little by little we will benefit from the groundswell of courage we have gathered through the simple moments we endure.

The big difference in this presentation is that the characters are not fictional; they are you and me. The dialogue, the script and the direction are carefully authored by every one of our choices toward an end product. Regardless of how clumsy our past has been, a rewarding life happens through a relentless effort to move when we have to, and deliver when it's our turn to. The director just screamed *"Action!"*

All of us are witnesses to the fact that life is a package deal; some good times accompany the not-so-good ones. Even when we have given our best performances, sometimes a solution breeds new problems. Some things do not make sense and probably never will, but we still have an audience waiting for our brilliant performance.

A harsh insight for me was when I came face to face with what I thought to be the villain in my life's story. It was the voices of desperation and emptiness. Anxiety does well to remind all of us of what we have done wrong, and how meaningless our achievements are. It bears mentioning again that none of our ambitions and hopes need to be validated by anyone except ourselves.

Our stories are our own. None of us could afford to cancel the show because we got tired along the way or did not feel like taking the stage. I am here to report that the act of living our fulfilling lives will not offer any of us dress rehearsals or green rooms to fine-tune our craft. I am even happier to report also that with every day, with every choice and even with our countless mistakes, we get better, adapt and become excellent at living our best.

Dr. Pearson was my sociology professor at Houston Community College who taught us about everything except what was in the school's curriculum. As radical and often controversial as his ideas were, I sat in the back row and listened to him carefully every Monday morning for three months. One day he said, "There are two most important questions you have to ask yourself. Some people never have, and in fact, most people never will."

That got our attention, as the rest of my colleagues turned to each other wondering what life-changing secret Dr. Pearson was about to reveal. Then he continued, "The first question is, *where am I going?* Second, *who am I going with?*"

Take a minute to ponder these questions. Take a whole day if you have to. These could be two of the most important questions any of us will have to ask ourselves throughout life. The condition is that these are questions we do not ask in reverse order, neither do we answer them in haste. I sat in the back row, squiggling on a notepad until the meaning of the words sank in.

Leading up to asking *where we are going* involves an honest fact check of who we are in the first place. Unless we find out who we are, and then where we are going in life, everyone else in our life is along for a roller coaster ride. Many years after I heard Dr. Pearson make his statement, I met many people who had no clear idea *where they were going* but without fail, had managed to find *who they were going with*.

Almost like clockwork, these relationships will come to a crossroad, or even in several cases a screeching halt. The same is true of any of life's endeavors and any aspect of our lives. If I could have shared Dr. Pearson's words with my grandfather, he would have added that if we know *where we are going*, we will quickly find out how many people are not heading in the same direction.

Throughout my many life experiences, I found one thing to be certain, that we either ask ourselves the supposedly tough questions or miss the chance to use them as a compass to navigate our journey. Even worse, we may crash in the next turn for not having a clue where we are heading. This assertion is remarkably vital but so effortlessly ignored. Life is worth living for people who plan for it and prepare themselves for the ensuing steps. The fulfillment and rewards of life make it worth everything.

Every action is of meaningful consequence to people with skin in the game. Unfortunately, some of us are dragging along through life, with no idea of what we are *buying or selling*, and life is just another event. There are enduring lessons that we continually learn as we go through the simplest routines in our day, but we ought to know where we are at any point in time in order to see the potential in the moment.

The reality is that if we understand the nuances of life's intricate design, it is worth living and bursts with fulfillment. It is when we fail to make decisions consistent with our own mission statement, that we conclude that this life is worth nothing at all.

The *lost birds* and *fighting sons* will *soar where dreams go*, and the encouraging words of my grandfather can live with all of us every step along the way, forcing us to hang on even when life seems to have taken a nosedive.

I am sure you have once felt as if you are running as fast as you can, only to find yourself in the same place. Other times, the daily challenges feels like we are swimming in a pool filled with ping pong balls, and our only job is to keep all of them under water. Those are desperate and seemingly pointless moments when even the best within us wonders what we are made up of.

The good part of life's drama is that we are our own audiences, and every member in the crowd who matters is on our side. Our life has evolved through our challenges, and all we have is ourselves. It is also true that if that is all we have to work with, we have plenty, and enough reasons to stand and deliver. Determine to live as if you would need to look back on it someday in the future.

"Eternity's Cabin" only conveys a metaphor, a theatre script. The scenes change and the drama heightens, but a performance designed for a happy ending always finds a way to achieve its purpose. I am living in the constant reminder that today is the day which did not exist yesterday; this is the best time to take center stage and take charge of our own lives. The storylines could be long and the dramatic effects unsettling at some moments; however, our stories of courage cannot just begin and end with *Act One and Scene One*. We have to find courage and dare to enter the next scene . . . and the next.

The times may change someday but we will have lived life and given it our very best effort. We find solace in the fact that our lives are still unfolding by some invisible design, regardless of our imperfections and our shortcomings.

Eternity's Cabin

1 The doors lock from inside and the curtain rises
No villains, no subplots
Only heroes, only me
Welcome to life's story, and the ironies on a stage
5 And the sound of life, long before eternity
Of where and why and when
And how I live in shiny cabins
Cry sometimes and long for tomorrow.
The morning's pure
10 But we'll soon be bald with age
And nights, a peep of all we feared
From eternity's cabin
My tête-à-tête with Saint John
Earned a cross and a striking soul
15 A lung to breathe
And a soul playing his part.
A morning bird's flying far into the west
The rising sun showing the way
No scenes precede anti-climaxes
20 From the lowest points on stage
I learn the most about forever alone.
A cast of stars of me and my fears
With marks and scars of fighting days
The tale about who I have become
25 A story of valor and I'm watching all alone.
Lenses never set on the twists and turns
Or even what the critics will say
Discomfort is the grouchy prop
So are the teardrops

30 A peek of the grand stage with beaming lights
   Darkness shields the audience, now alone.
   A cabin made of glass, so I stand on all sides
   Timeless drama through dawn and dusk
   Filled with time to start again
35 Lost birds find solace in a home
   And fighting sons, succor in faith.
   I sweat in the coldest winter
   Lost a beat in December's wind
   Soaring where dreams go
40 Long past the fields of Carolina
   And past the long country roads
   Sure it's play; no need for style, no flair, or scream cut!
   My life is my own, my act my victory
   My now my eternity
45 Time and time our story to tell
   Long before the reels are gone
   And days on stage are nothing but settling dust
   For our dreams to unlock from eternity's cabin.

STILL A TRACE IN THE HORIZON

In her 1974 book "Dare to Dream," 93-year old Rose Resnick wrote, "Without dreams, there would be no discovery, and no trips to the moon. The challenge, the reaching out and the exploration lift us out of everyday well-trodden paths into fresh fields of endeavor and fulfillment."

Her counsel seems straightforward, that even amidst the dull and mundane sequences of our day, we may have to force ourselves to *imagine the beautiful colors in the sky, no matter how unachievable it may seem.* Much like envisioning the existence of rainbows in a clear blue sky, the thought of setting goals is somewhat like staring into an open space and hoping for an object to appear with time.

The difference, however, is that our real work ought to happen simultaneously with the *staring*. Through my own experiences, I have come to find how irrespective of how ambitious our imaginations may be, they have the energy to potentially make all the difference in how much we accomplish in our lives. Over and over again, we learn that once we fit our ambitions into life's *big picture,* its enthusiasm motivates us to see the beauty in the *challenging colors* yet to take shape.

In writing the poem "Still a Trace in the Horizon," I often thought of the American civil rights organization, the National Association for the Advancement of Colored People (NAACP). Its catchy slogan is too powerful and potent to be limited to just the uplift of any group of people or just one aspect of living. In fact, it deserves to be the watchword for every person who sees themselves living a gratifying life in this world: "A mind is a terrible thing to waste."

We would be wasting our precious time and minds if we failed to acknowledge how some of our most seemingly crippling encounters are the very ones that enable us to stand tall and appreciate the value of our own lives. In spite of what I believed to be a challenging life, I have come to embrace the idea of seeing past the immediate horizons and allowing the traces of life's promises to encourage me to live through every day.

One story that I have heard more than any other is that of Larry Walters. Over the years, he earned nicknames like *Lawn Chair Larry* and *Lawn Chair Pilot* among others, but his story was little more than a wild fable. The only thing that Larry Walters ever wanted to do was to fly.

Unlike some of us with much less adventurous dreams, Larry's was not to build a castle, buy a fancy yacht, marry a princess in a medieval temple, or any fanciful desire we can imagine. He just wanted to fly. Larry sat in his lawn chair hooked to large weather balloons he bought in a surplus store. He filled them with helium and proceeded with his plan to fly; packed his lunch, sandwiches and drinks, and also took with him a pellet gun.

Equally intriguing to me is the thought that he knew that just as it will take a plan to go up, he needed another plan to come back down. Sixteen thousand feet into the air, Larry Walters was flying into the airspace of the Los Angeles International Airport. What he had imagined to be a flying trip around his neighborhood had turned into a national news event. He was eventually rescued by the Los Angeles authorities and brought it down safely.

Upon questioning him regarding his motivation for such an awkward adventure, Larry Walters gave the world one of the most sincere and potent answers anyone could fathom, "A man can't just sit around!" The people who are lucky enough to find the magic in a trail of rainbows where none exist, who find the magic of living fulfilling lives on the most routine of days, have managed to convince themselves that the only guarantee life gives us is the moment we live in. What one person will find as a wild ambition may very well be the simplest thought that gives our life meaning.

Nyankoton is the Ashanti word for rainbow. In a culture and society where ambiguity surrounds every word and idea, there is no confusion in the wisdom that the beautiful colors of the rainbow take both sun's heat and rain's drench to appear. It helps to also know that the colors may not mean much by themselves, but together, they give us a clear picture of what nature can become, and what our lives can become even after the heavy rains and scorching suns.

There is too much to do, too little time to do it, and Larry Walters had struck that chord. We cannot just sit around eternally gazing into the sky while life passes us by. None of us can afford to breeze through life passively and yet expect that by some miracle, life will hand over the magic keys of success to us. I learned this truth a long time ago, that sitting around only produces one result, nothing.

Sometimes however, we see our well-thought-out plans go awry, even fall apart before we could start, and we face difficult choices of either trying again or pushing the cruise-control button. I am a firm believer also that there are many people who give up on themselves not because they enjoy failure or mediocrity, but rather because sometimes the hardest thing to do is give yourself a reason to even look up.

It is no easy task to shake off the disappointments and encourage yourself when everything else around you seems to be falling apart. How can you find a place to start when you feel either emotionally or mentally robbed, pushed so far down that giving up in that seemingly desolate state makes for a better option?

I don't have any easy feel-good answers, but I lived many years in my own extreme anxiety when somehow I had to clutch on to what seemed like *hope* to keep me from giving up. Whatever the basis of your reasoning to reduce the idle moments that negatively impact your dreams and ambitions, Larry Walters made a very vivid point through his actions and the belief that *a man can't just sit around.*

The real challenge is to see past the scars we have sustained through our individual journeys that remind us constantly of our painful past. A mind with all its capacity to engineer a way out of a hopeless situation is without a doubt a *terrible thing to waste.*

I vividly recall when I first graduated from high school I had a lot of determination but not a penny to pay for it. If you had asked me then who I wanted to be, where I wanted to go and what I'd wanted to be, even the sky would have been too low to have been my limit. There was no doubt in my mind that I could pursue the wildest dream in my heart.

I was a teenager with little regard for reality, so Georgetown University in Washington D.C. and Brock University in Ontario, Canada, were the only schools in the world I was determined to pursue for my undergraduate work. Why?

Even until this moment, I have no idea why I was so *locked in* on those particular colleges, but it was my dream nonetheless. I will admit to being stuck in my tunnel vision, but I will gladly take any moment of a mix of wild hopes and taking chances, any day.

Chapter 8: Still a Trace in the Horizon

If it wouldn't cost me a penny to dream, why not take a chance? In hindsight, I understand how the elements I had been exposed to, and had some prior information about, had inadvertently defined my frame of reference.

The reference to *Nyankonton* for the Ashantis in Ghana is often followed by *boshe,* which translates to mean *promise*. In their minds, there is always the subconscious reminder in the rainbow, one of reassurance and of hope. *Still a Trace in the Horizon* talks about how, without the wild Larry-like dreams and the power of our imagination, there probably will be nothing to tailor our inner ambitions to.

I contend that even when our dreams do not materialize in the precise manner we hope for, and we're in a *painted cave dark still,* having an aspiration for something to reach for in our lives becomes the essential glue that holds us together.

I never made it into Georgetown or Brock, I never accomplished everything I hoped for, but I am glad I held on to my dreams a little longer to give myself a fighting chance at least. Never will I live another day wishing I had thought bigger than what my limited conditions could afford. The compelling thought is how of all the schools in the world, those two had registered in my frame of reference. For whatever it was worth, they gave me a target to aim at.

A fact I cannot overemphasize is that none of us can afford to just sit around in rocking chairs wondering from which direction the next big break will come. Sure, luck may just find you where you are, but the greater odds are that it probably will not.

One Sunday in Houston, a preacher shared his insight about stepping out of our comfort zone and squarely taking on the challenges ahead of us. Since there is no guarantee for success, that leaves an equal probability for disappointment too. "What if you try and it does not work?" he asked. I will bet that you and I are not the first people to ponder this question, and that is the seemingly justifiable fear that many of us have.

It is fair to say that we live in a very convoluted society with enough people working hard to accomplish their ambitions, too. I hate to inform you that other people will not hesitate to run over you to achieve their own aspirations, but even that should not be enough to demotivate you. So should you just choose to play it safe and do nothing?

The Larry Walters story began when he was 13 years old, when he could not achieve his lifelong dream of becoming a pilot because of his poor eyesight. Call him crazy, but 20 years later, he decided to give himself a chance and do the one thing that has eluded him all his life. "What if you try and it does in fact work out?" The miracle of the rainbow, *nyankonton boshe*, is more in the effort we give to life than in what we may or may not have in hand.

There is always the temptation to go through the motions inertly and live half-baked lives because of our own distorted view of what is indeed possible. I lived in the experience that if only we could stretch our imagination into all that could be possible, none of us would be so quick to *kill our faith trapped in a winding maze.*

The inspiration for this poem was a challenge to myself to take a little leap of faith, one day at a time. Anyone of us can sit in rocking chairs and wish our lives into our destiny, but I am convinced that at some point the real players will have to jump onto the field and get into the action.

By the time I turned 17, I had learned this critical life lesson about *trying*. The truth is that if any event was not going to work out, sitting around doing nothing only guarantees that it indeed could never happen. All of us have stories of people we know, who spend their lifetime making excuses about why, where, when, how, what, and who. Almost to no surprise, most of them are still sitting around today reliving those same excuses. We have all heard of the truism, "Shoot for the stars."

Chapter 8: Still a Trace in the Horizon

Another popular thought suggests that you should "Shoot beyond the stars; in case you don't make it, you will at least land onto the stars." Our common-sense reasoning would cause us to prefer a much safer approach to life, especially if we can envision the end result even before we take our first step.

Many people will argue to the contrary, understandably perhaps, that it is safer not to set our ambitions too high in order to avert disappointment. The only problem in this kind of thinking is that we immediately define the limitations even before we take our first step.

When we were teenagers, my older brother Arthur coached a soccer team that I played on. He lacked every technical skill to coach any sports team, but that was something he always wanted to do. What was equally interesting is the fact that my brother happened to be one of the worst soccer players among our neighborhood kids; and instead of suffering the humiliation forever, he thought of an alternative that didn't require him to ever kick a soccer ball.

Never mind the embarrassing fact that Kaiser lost every game by a wide margin. Miraculously, none of us even thought of quitting the team. Those must have been some of the most humiliating events for teenagers trying their very best to compete. At that young age, I took the awkward performances with a grain of salt and didn't think much of them, but my brother Arthur was doing something he had always wanted to do.

A few years ago, we laughed about those embarrassing soccer events. I asked him what made him think about coaching a team when he didn't know anything about the game himself. In the mind of a 15-year old, he had come to terms with the fact that he was a below-average soccer player who never invested any effort into improving his own skill. In fact he never cared much about the sport except that he was tired of sitting on the sidelines watching other people run the show.

Even at the risk of ridicule and public mockery, Arthur was determined to not be just a spectator. Somehow, he had figured out that he didn't need to know how to play or coach. The most important thing was participation in the action. In much the same way, life is happening all around us and we can either choose to participate or just remain in the contentment of a bystander, and the indifference to our own lives.

The poem "Still a Trace in the Horizon" is about our individual dreams, conceived at one time or another, but which never saw the light of day. Perhaps they never saw the light of day because we have wasted precious time and energy sitting on the sidelines. It is a challenge about the hopes we abort before they could even take shape. It is also about enthusiastically holding on to our hopes and guarding our optimism, instead of sitting back and watching our lives flash before our eyes.

This poem was a reminder and a challenge to myself to jump out of the passenger's seat and take charge of the steering wheel in my own life. The beauty of rainbows in our lives is not about being fixated on the transient nature of life itself, that nothing is permanent, but rather realizing that every one of our life's challenges is within our grasp if only we can find the strength to lift our heads and eyes.

The line "treasures secure in a tranquil heart" speaks to the probability we channel for our lives, which we have to keep holding on to, no matter how discouraging the process gets. The roadblocks will show up; but instead of folding our lawn chairs, all of us will have to find the strength from within, a way around them and hook our dreams to weather balloons and helium tanks so we can fly.

I have always believed that our dreams are ours, and the unfortunate thing is that often times, even though we may believe in a project or an idea, no other person has to believe with us to make it happen. Our brilliant thoughts could even seem dim-witted to the next person, but that is why it is our dream. If anyone understands and supports your dream, count it as a bonus, not a prerequisite for its realization.

You may have heard of this story before· There were two men in a hospital that had been bedridden for months. They slept across a room from each other; and every day, one man would tell the other of how he could not wait for the morning to show up so he could look outside the window.

The second man curiously inquired about what he saw since his bed was far away from a window. The first man talked about the happy children playing outside, the beautiful flowers, all the birds, the dew on the grass, the beautiful sky, and on and on.

The storytelling went on for months until one day the second man was told that his friend had died. Like most of the people in the hospital, he was sad and was sure he would miss his friend, his storyteller, and all the enthusiasm that filled his hospital life near the hospital widow. They quietly wished that one day they would enjoy those beautiful sights together when they left the hospital.

The second man asked the nurses if it was possible for them to move his bed to the part of the room where the first man once was, which they gladly did. The next morning he woke up, and much to his surprise, he was sleeping next to a brick wall. He immediately called the nurses and asked why they put him next to a wall and not where the first man slept, but they politely explained that they had done exactly what he asked.

"Where is the window he always talked about? How come he could see the children playing, the birds, the beautiful skies, the rainbow after the rain, and the morning dew on the grass?" The nurse had a huge smile on her face, sat next to the man and said "Your friend was blind." She continued, "He saw all the sun, skies, birds, children, and even the colorful rainbows in his mind's eye." Some of us may need to be blind for a moment to appreciate the miracle around us, and cherish the hopeful reminders from other people's life experiences.

All of us can imagine the nurse explaining how the first man chose the images that he wanted to fill his mind, and instead of lying in bed feeling defeated and living the rest of his life with a sour attitude, he chose to live it on the positive side of life's fence. The blind man had chosen to live life, a gratifying one, when all he had to reassure his hopes was *Still a Trace in the Horizon,* but more importantly, in his own mind.

It took a series of devastating challenges and my face-to-face encounter with loneliness to acknowledge how our perspectives are the undeclared guiding thoughts that can either make or break our willpower. A person is bold or half-crazy depending on who is telling the story.

Deborah Goolsby, a good friend of mine, summed up her life's mantra in a single line, "The only thing someone can tell you is either a *yes* or a *no*. If we never stick our heads out, we may never know how many responses can be in our favor." A significant proportion of what we receive in life is linked to this simple principle. The crux of our individual happiness revolves upon our own outlook on life and it is in that viewpoint that we construct mental images to define our individual lives.

On several occasions, Deborah would talk of how we all ought to learn to be constructive and cheerful thinkers. It would be a lie to say that it doesn't take much effort, or that our hard work may not occasionally get disappointing, but all of us must venture outside our comfort territories and learn to live our wildest dreams, strapped to helium-filled balloons like Lawn Chair Larry.

Like most people, I also had many rude awakenings when I could not even find a reason to pursue what may seem to be mundane tasks. It was so hard to believe again. I felt so down on myself that I forgot everything that gave me an ounce of hope to climb up. For some of us, as we learn everything there is to learn about life-altering mindsets and attitudes, a sudden disappointment has a unique capacity to blow us off track, so much that we start to doubt the same reassuring images we once believed in.

Yes, there is power in positive thinking, but our willingness to pursue our dreams is what directs us in forming images where none exist. Thanks to what I considered to be the crushing defeats, I learned soon that it is in my own outlook that I develop prototypes for living a fulfilling life today.

As we walk through life, as baffling as this might sound, not everyone expects good things to happen to them; and moreover, some people actually enjoy living in misery. Then, there are some of us who enjoy our problems being validated by others to reassure us that we are not going nuts. We want people to listen and express sympathy for just about any misfortune. I will never think of that as an unreasonable sentiment, but as a potential trap of sitting around doing absolutely nothing.

In fact, Larry Walters also earned the nickname *"Larry the Moron,"* because he had done something he wanted to do. He could have even pondered over aborting his own ambition, or easily discarded it as crazy. Living with the victim mentality does us more harm than good. There are even some of us who find out that it is not sufficient for other people to validate our problems, so we drag them into our pity party.

Still a Trace in the Horizon is a hardnosed confrontation with a decision to make each moment of our lives count. With dreams of a victorious living, the setbacks are just temporary and it does not matter what other people think we can or cannot do. If indeed *a mind is a terrible thing to waste,* then we have to be determined to reconstruct the possibilities for our own lives and not abort our dreams, whatever they are.

There is a saying, "You have to learn to crawl before you can walk," except that the erroneous application is with some of us who get stuck in the act of crawling. As it is with the analogy, none of us can afford to be babies and crawl for the rest of our lives.

As painful as some of the days might be, I am a firm believer that at some point, the crawling child will have to grow up and will have to learn to walk. The happiest people in life are those who lose themselves in something bigger than their handicaps and chose to live life, not something like it.

STILL A TRACE IN THE HORIZON

1   Suns and moons are fathers to few
    Those whose tummies turn on slippery days
    The vacuum in a mind's eye once filled with glee
    And in cloudy traces of letting go,
5   Why the days roll by
    And nights downhill too,
    And the thoughts of how and why and how again
    A painted cave stays dark still.
    Heaven is right here beneath the stars
10 E'en with time lost to misery
    And killing faith trapped in winding maze.
    Like putrid flowers' pigments charming strangers,
    The stench kills me
    And the pricks too
15 But when the sting dissipates
    Nyankonton adawroma,
    The wait will be the calm in the faces
    Not a soul will know the prize of my value
    But comfort I'll find in the traces above
20 In the promises of rainbows
    And treasures secure in the tranquil heart.

PORCELAIN

Two days into my final semester in undergraduate work, my mother called my phone early in the morning. Her usual phone conversations lasted a good 30 minutes, except for today. I woke up, with a raspy and husky sleepy voice. She seemed surprised that I was still in bed.

"Are you still sleeping?" she asked. "Yes, Mama; it is five in the morning," I replied.

Without hesitation, her next words pierced through the phone, *"Wake up, time is not waiting for you."*

"What is that supposed to mean?" I mumbled to myself, partly because I was not in the mood to listen to a lecture that early in the day. I had heard the adage "Time waits for no one" many times before, but I was sure that even the busiest people in the world found time within the 24 hours in a day to sleep. I never thought it to be anything more than a part of life's many processes. However, later in my life I learned that my mother's idea was more than a challenge to nature's sleep cycles.

It didn't take much to ignore her advice and roll over for three more hours of precious sleep. Out of the clear blue, her words dawned on me again several days later. "Wake up, time is not waiting for you." The four years leading up to my final year in college had been strenuous and challenging, yet I had managed to survive every step of them. Just as it is important that the basic tenets of our life become our own internal definitions of happiness, none of us can afford to *clock out* of life while time marches on.

I am certainly not the first person to have eagerly begun a project, a business, a dream, a relationship or any adventure, only to have pushed the cruise control button halfway through it. I am sure I won't be the last either. Somehow we end up on a side street labeled Complacency Boulevard.

The interesting part of my college story is that I had mastered the craft of studying and comprehending academic material. Through my relentless effort at some point, excellent grades had become second nature to me. I never considered my attitude complacent, because I was actively pursuing excellence, although not with the same enthusiasm I'd had several years earlier.

Somewhere along the way, however, something dulled the intensity and calmed my zeal. I may have not only been sleeping in my bed that morning when my mother called. Perhaps her concern was that I had become one of the many people walking through life *asleep*. Maybe my mother knew that even the most determined hearts get weary, and that even a focused traveler occasionally needs a reminder to avoid *coasting* through life. The fact is many of us would have given up if no one had believed in us, and woken us up occasionally from what, over time, had become a mundane life activity.

Chapter 9: Porcelain

I am convinced that the most dangerous and potentially explosive part of our mental development is when we become smug and complacent in our endeavors. Before we know it, our once passionate life takes on a mundane routine. Complacency Boulevard is where dreams become humdrum and collapse. Mixed metaphor. "Jars of clay" doesn't go with boulevard image.

It is a false belief that our achievements to this moment are enough to carry us through the rest of our lives, and that all we need to do is to sit back and enjoy the ride. If anything, I was operating below what could easily be a maximum threshold of potential. I was asleep at my life's wheel, my ambitions on auto-pilot, and breezing through time with relative success.

So much of our life's activities can easily turn into repetitive functions, and even without our knowing, the best outlooks on life disintegrate into emptiness and a blasé lifestyle. I was drifting along, and that was why *wake up, time is not waiting for you* sounded an alarm. It is possible that like me, you too could have reached a comfortable place in your quest for a fulfilling life and have travelled on cruise control. I am living proof of how sooner or later we forget how slowly we may be moving, and some of us have come to a standstill.

I remember an incident from a few years ago. I worked with a group of older individuals who had worked for the company for many years. At a staff meeting, the managers were concerned with customer feedback on how employee performance was on a steady decline. We sought to find answers, and some of the older team members agreed that the reason for the apparent decline was external. So easily they took turns pointing to industry reports and growth analysis, and every other statistic to support their claim.

Then came my turn. Just before I could say a word, a man whose position no one knew, or even how long he had been there, uttered, "The problem is us." A few people turned to see who he was, as he explained that most of us had become so experienced at the job and the individual tasks, that they had become second nature to us. We were not rethinking our strategies anymore, and as we could all imagine, our effort and results were slumping as a consequence.

The room lit up with angry glances, and the older gentleman sitting next to him seemed ready to gouge his eyes out, but another coworker interrupted. She agreed. The lady went on to explain why she believed that we had hit a ceiling of productivity, and unless we redesigned the roof, and in essence reset our expectations, there was no more room to grow.

The man with the eyebrow-raising opinion did not make any friends at the company, but the management soon redesigned every procedure, introduced new metrics of measuring productivity, and even changed the personnel seating arrangements. Needless to say, the man no one knew anything about knew something no one had thought of.

Living our lives with a high degree of awareness averts the potential danger of our once promising dream ending up as brittle porcelain, at risk of being broken. In high school, I read about the concept of diminishing marginal returns. Early economists Thomas Malthus and David Ricardo in 19th century England were worried that land, a factor of production, was in limited supply; and as a result, it could lead to a concept known by many as diminishing returns in the overall productivity of additional labor.

Many years ago in college, I had several colleagues who could simply not wrap their minds around this concept. What could cause productivity loss in the midst of an increase? The misunderstanding of economic theory lies in the assumption that ignores the margins and extent to which productivity declines or grows.

No one questions the increase or even the decrease per se, but rather the rate at which the end result is affected. The concept of diminishing marginal returns, as it turn out, does not focus so much on the overall increase as much as it does on the aggregate, that extra unit of effort within a series of clustered actions.

Just as in our own lives, and with our hopes, there is ample room to push harder, and apply ourselves to whatever we are engaged in. How much are we adding or subtracting in relation to our optimum capacity? Have we reached a point where we've become complacent and happy with our station in life and forgotten how much more potential we have? I am cognizant of the fact that making some form of progress does not necessarily imply a commitment to the maximum output we can achieve if we use our talents, abilities and resources in the most efficient manner.

In our relationships, I imagine that we can all love more and try harder. With our careers, I imagine we can all learn more, try more and give our best effort. And for that matter, in any area of our life, I am confident that if we manage to kick complacency out of our attitudes, most of us can find the renewed energy toward living a fulfilling life.

I spoke to a group of friends a few years ago, some of whom have lived in the trap of assuming that they have found all the answers there are to living their lives. From their own stories, they had erected contentment camps and did not even know it. They could dissect any concept or scientific theory into a million pieces without trying. That sense of knowing-it-all, as one of them recounted a few years later, was the groundwork to their gradual downfall. They had stopped learning from their own experiences and from others around them. They had activated the cruise-control button and were gladly coasting along.

"Wake up, time is not waiting for you" was my mother's inadvertent advice to not let my guard down. David Ricardo and Thomas Malthus perhaps anticipated the complacency that potentially develops once all of us become comfortable in any activity, and soon we live in cruise control mode instead of forging ahead in earnest.

Porcelain is an acknowledgement that a chunk of life happens when we least expect it. That demands a constant reminder of a mission unaccomplished. In this thought, we encourage ourselves to hope for the best, yet plan for the worst. There are many so-called teachers of affirmative philosophy and authors of what have become known as *new age* thinking. Only you and I can make our life transcend any mental hurdle, regardless of what fancy definition we give it.

What matters most is for each of us to be aware of our station in life and how much more lies ahead to be done. If such an outlook falls under some fancy category, so be it. In our own way and from our own points of view, let us continue to seek to identify what more we can do to give our life more meaningful and fulfilling returns.

In your own city and country, there are countless bookstores abounding with endless aisles of insightful wisdom that has the ability to change life. I have seen hundreds of step-by-step recommendations to achieve just about anything. I have a sneaking suspicion that there could even be a 12-step secret to the most basic act of breathing if you look hard enough. The point is that none of these ideas will be of any value to you and me unless they make sense to our own circumstances.

I often make reference to how early Greek philosophers spoke to their audience in familiar stories and used relatable symbols to express complex ideas. For instance, it would be of no use to bakers to listen to lectures with neuroscientific analogies. It perhaps may not even register, and that would not reflect on the validity of the message, but rather on its resonance with the audience.

My story and perspective may very well be familiar to you. It is also possible that you may never be able to relate to the specific struggles anyone else may have. I am however convinced that the common strings that run through our lives are universal, and so are the fundamental attitudes necessary to assist us and to propel our own life forward.

In writing *Porcelain*, my simple but striking realization that time is not waiting for me can be an awakening message for you too. Fill your jars with hope, and expect brighter moments from unexpected events. That is my wish, that we will live our every moment with an enthusiasm to do more, to love more, to dream more, to give more, and to believe more than our present moment affords us.

Riding through life on autopilot is not only a dangerous approach; it is the toxic attitude that spills and kills the energy we radiate throughout life. I believe that the words of wisdom from the wisest person who ever lived are no more powerful than the simple affirmation from yourself, and to yourself. I pray that I am able to encourage you to wake up, be vigilant, and live your life with a transformed stance.

PORCELAIN

1 Two turns in a winding trajectory
My sticky heels pick pieces of sand.
Rain from my eyes, mud all over me, now
Closer to the ground my face is.
5 Days mixed in two distant basins
Happy here, sad here
Too little is what time gives
And molded jars of clay here I sit.
I am filled with craving to live
10 Racing with the wind
Through sweat and pain
And shifting trends of rain
A jar molded in life through dreary days.
I stand tall, but sand is less than few
15 The swirling water made me short, all clay I am.
My hope is sprained by disillusions
One pile of chances gone
A heap of fine sand of tomorrow's hope still here
So I'll block the distance and the sun
20 And not burn through freezing rain
Yesterday is long gone
But time is far and far to the wire
But shiny porcelain
From a traveler's trail.

10

FINGER MARKINGS IN FOGGY SCREENS

In the march 2008 issue of *Ebony* magazine, the cover story read, "In Our Lifetime." It was not just for African-Americans, but most people around the world did not anticipate the prospect of an African-American president of the United States at any point in their lifetime. As it was with many enthralling events in life, most people believed that such a hope was indeed possible, but in a distant future.

When a young black boy working in low-income neighborhoods on the South Side of Chicago ascends to office of the President, Barack Obama will be first to tell you that he was no accident. Years after the historic event unfolded, and the dust of amazement had settled, what once looked like happenstance to most of us was in fact a prudently orchestrated game plan. My guess is, it was one person's commitment, in his own world, to endure the hardships necessary to someday experience a winner's circle.

It was a calm night on a New Year's Eve when I pulled my car into an empty parking lot. It had been a long and eventful day, a snapshot of my year past. I recalled what a stressful year it had been, particularly so because with all the progress I had made in life's challenges, the trouble didn't seem to get any easier. I reclined my seat as if to take a nap in the empty parking area that on any other day would have been filled with cars of all sizes and noise from all directions.

In that moment as I rested my head, it was as if the whole world had gone to sleep, and life itself had come to a standstill. There would be no sounds from passersby, no car engines humming, and no sirens. The moment was as quiet as any perfect night would be. I must have dozed off for a few minutes. The windows were foggy and looked white and cloudy. For a moment, it was impossible to see through the damp screen, not even a sign of the loneliest star in the sky.

Without much thought, I touched the window with my finger, dragging it slowly, partly as if to scribble something, and partly to find a clear space and see the life outside. Just as my finger moved down to clear another space, the glass was covered with fog again.

Over and over again, one finger line after another, my slow scribbles would not last long enough for me to see through screens. As if a neon sign flashed across my mind, I sat upright, made one more finger mark on the window, then used my palm, and I moved a little faster, wiping more, and the quiet blue sky was in sight again.

In our own lives, there will of course be many people with posters and signposts along the way to remind you and me that we are only dreaming our lives away. We may even hear the unenthusiastic voices as the fog fills the clear screens of our lives. Circumstances may build a fog around our ambitions. I have however learned this all-important fact, that opposition to any cause does not involve wasting effort on

Chapter 10: Finger Markings in Foggy Screens

fruitless adventures. The presence of the posters and signposts should be a cue that we may very well be on track to our winner's circle.

In a journey filled with foggy screens, any attempt to bulldoze our way through the naysayers will require us to wipe the dampness off the screens so we can see our life's true promise beyond the blue skies. Most of the energy-sapping and optimism-dampening people, those I call Gloomy Gusses, do not bother with people doing nothing or going nowhere in life. It is nice to know that the mere presence of opposition should be a reminder that we are perhaps on our upward climb.

The lesson in my inadvertent experiment wasn't about how quickly the clear windows turned white; rather it was how the more we manage to wipe our damp moments with a finger, even if that's all we have, it gives us a chance to clear the fog to see the skies again. The finger's mark is only a start. We ought to find the faith to do more than unflappably cruise through life. Ask President Barack Obama and he will probably tell you that the price of his imagination was nothing.

For me, the lesson beyond that is the fact that carving ourselves into exactly what we desire for our own lives requires much more than imagination. The preliminary *dreaming* step is worth everything and luckily costs nothing. That is where it starts, a dream to make a difference in our own lives, but we must do something beyond the ordinary.

In 2007, America witnessed a daring proclamation. That same African-American boy who had a dream to become the president of United States of America was living his dream. It was not part of a Saturday night comedic routine, but it was difficult for many people to take his words beyond a very nice idea.

I recall a conversation one evening with my brother Arthur, who lived in England at the time. He asked if I thought that Barack Obama had a chance to become president. Based on the historical accounts that had shaped the political expectations, up to that point, I couldn't see that happening. My reply was no different from that of Ebony magazine's declaration, *"Not in our lifetime."*

My brother, who was full of beautiful expectations, went on to tell me how much of my doubt was tied to my being in America. In the midst of fellow African-Americans, with a checkered history of racism and a stigma of second-class citizenship, it was almost impossible to imagine the prospect of a black president.

Even worse, this possibility had been a common punch line for a comedian's joke; and the mere thought of it invoked laughter. It was as if every hope in our minds had been discolored by unpleasant experiences, thus forcing a process of self-doubt and sub-par expectation upon ourselves and anyone we could think of.

The question to ask is how much of our perception had been clouded by the *painful vapors* irrespective of how valid they may have been, and our many restrained thoughts. If the dream came to pass, it would make Obama the first president in the United States from any minority ethnic group. He had a plan to connect to his desire, the action to make it possible, but most importantly, the nerve to change American history.

He graduated from Columbia University in 1983 and Harvard University in 1991. Among his accomplishments, he became the first African-American president of the Harvard Law Review. Through those very feats, he became aware of what impact his every decision had on his future. After winning the election to the United States Senate in 2008, Barack Obama set his sights on the supposedly impossible goal of becoming president.

Of course, Obama had a vision, and it is also noteworthy that such a tenacity to overcome incredible odds did not just appear out of nowhere. Our life events are far from a mumbo jumbo of coincidences and wishful thinking. He did not come from a royal family, neither was he born into a socially-connected community. In fact,

Chapter 10: Finger Markings in Foggy Screens

President Obama often joked about having come from the same side of the street where most of us found ourselves from day one; but whatever that side of the street was, there was absolutely no substitute for pushing harder, one *finger marking* at a time through the damp window screens.

I will bet my last penny that many people like President Obama heard the same *impossible chants* that some of us have heard all our lives. The challenges he faced during his boyhood and his teenage years were not enough to subdue his passion. The big difference lies in the strength of mind that creates a relentless fighting spirit in people like Barack Obama when most of us give up. He called it, "The Audacity of Hope."

"Finger Markings in Foggy Screens" asserts that how we achieve individual successes and fulfillment may be individual, but as clichéd as it may sound, ultimately all of us are only capable of achieving that which we are able to imagine. If there is any trick to life's puzzle, it has everything to do with how we define our own targets, determine to commit, and most importantly visualize an end point in our mind's eye.

Why is the visual so vital? How is the perception of a tangible product or goal able to facilitate a journey towards achieving it? I believe it is because our imagination clears the foggy uncertainty, recreates an image of what is indeed possible and connects our thought processes all the way to the point of fulfillment. When we are able to envision a clear objective, the path begins to make sense in our own minds. The timeless truth is that we cannot sell any idea to anyone else if we cannot first convince ourselves to buy into it.

The story of President Barack Obama is the same for many of us who in spite of seemingly insurmountable odds, find a hope for our purpose in life. Sure, he became the president of the United States; and contrary to what most of us had thought, it happened in our lifetime. He dared to see the alternatives to every step, even when stuck between a rock and a hard place. We saw overwhelming odds because that's how we chose to define it. That was our reality, not his.

When the winds are taken out of our sails, those of us who want to win badly might jump into the sea and swim. That's the mark of a person who would rather take his chances than sit aloof in the middle of life's seas, waiting for a life jacket before he begins to swim.

Those people who find sanguinity, even in places where no one else finds such optimism, are unambiguous about their purpose when they are surrounded by dark windows and *foggy screens*. We find one more reason to keep hanging on. I am convinced that people who defy the odds and determine to change their own history do not allow their thoughts to become a kiss of death to their dreams.

Unlike *momentum*, which is the strength of continuity, we derive something from an initial *inertia*, the sluggish state when we lack power to move forward. It is during such lethargic moments that we dig deeper for our own *audacity of hope*. I define that as the shamelessly bold decision to fix our attention on our objectives, career goals, relationships, or anything we hope for.

I am inspired by the thought that we all have within us, the bravado to continue pushing even in such moments when we find our energy depleted, psychologically scrawny and on the verge of falling apart. Some of the most fulfilled individuals in the world subscribe to the simple life truths that have been told over and over. Getting to the point where we are able to articulate and emphatically state our own purpose is the tricky part of life's adventure. I believe that there are several routes to any particular destination, but most people with a compelling vision use their gusto as the sound formula to achieve their goals.

In my junior year in the school of communications, a man named Randy Polk explained a model he had seen at work throughout his career in Hollywood. We were television production students and like most untrained beginners, our arrival at a final product followed a simple outline. We planned, we executed, and let the chips fall where they may.

When most of us plan to do something, we set out to accomplish it on some unconscious linear timeline. There is nothing wrong with that. In fact sometimes we may even be lucky and hit a jackpot. However, there is a fascinating process in television production known as the preproduction model. The idea is based on the understanding that the best way of organizing the intricate details from an idea to the concrete finished product is to work backwards.

There is a popular phenomenon called Murphy's Law. It is perceived perversity of the universe when everything that can possibly go wrong, goes wrong. For people who have come to accept this as a fact of life, the object of working backwards with a defined objective is to minimize random outcomes, some of which may not be in their favor.

The overwhelming view is that the preproduction process, which involves the planning and outline of every creative step, is the most crucial of all. If producers plan well and thoroughly, the ripple effect is an almost effortless process the rest of the way. The reverse is also true. Creators of television programs invest time and energy in what is called the *program objective*.

Program objectives define their *desired effect;* what they want their audience to think, feel, learn or do after watching their program. It is interesting to know that no one sits inside a television studio, puts a show together in the hope that their viewers may like it, and by some coincidence, connect with their message. If that is not true, then I gladly stand corrected, but I will assert that getting the utmost fulfillment in life takes a little more than just luck.

In the case of television producers, their final objective becomes their guide at the starting point. It is only then, that they proceed to gather the essential requirements to facilitate reaching that target. It is by no accident that programming intended to make viewers cry or laugh achieves that effect. If any of us can live our lives as in a Hollywood show, the first step is visualizing the end-product, having a clear image of what we want our life's final product to be, and then searching for the necessary accoutrements to help us on the journey.

The most important part of this exercise is that all of us, like producers of our own life's script, will have to invest the time in our own preproduction process. Whether we have a story or dream similar to Barack Obama's, or are simply striving to live a rewarding and successful life, the crucial stride is in knowing what our unique satisfaction point is, and then working our way backwards to accomplish it.

The poem "Finger Markings in Foggy Screens" is about dreaming the seemingly impossible dreams and giving life to our heart's ambitions. I have learned also that there are no automatic light switches to change our lives overnight.

Anyone can wake up, sleep, eat, and live. In fact, anyone can have a wish and a desire to be or have something other than who they are or what they have. Maybe all of us can learn from the fact that the resolve to withstand the *foggy screens* of life requires more than casual finger markings, one slide after another. I contend that knowing about a helpful idea or inspirational concept only adds to our library of information. It does nothing in itself to change us. It is my hope that our subtle realizations will become the proactive inspiration to nudge us along.

One memory that will never fade in my mind is of a morning when I sat in a lecture hall. My college professor said he was going to tell us a secret that would perhaps change our lives forever. To our disappointment, it was not the winning lottery numbers for a million dollar prize. Instead he said there was something that Ivy League students knew that the rest of us may never find out.

The professor went on to explain that there is no guarantee that a person simply drifting along on the Ivy League campus will become any more important than the next person who never made it to such

Chapter 10: Finger Markings in Foggy Screens

an institution. He had graduated from one such elite school years ago; and in my professor's own observation, the reason why most graduates from the so-called top schools in the world succeed in life is not because of the friends they make or the politicians who roam the hallways, but rather, that someone took the time to give them *a view from above*. A different way of approaching life.

I share an interesting occurrence from my childhood. All throughout life, we are trained to look up at life. We look up for our first toys, our first instructions and unfortunately spend the rest of our lives *looking up*.

I often get one of those flashbulb moments when in talking to my father. My head accidentally wanders and my eyes stare at the floor. My father, without skipping a beat, would say, "Look up." The trouble with perpetually looking up is that it eventually affects our angle of perception. If indeed it is true, looking up gives us a narrow view of any concept, any idea, or in this case, a look at our own lives.

However true, my professor had explained how he believed that Ivy League students are trained to look at life from the *top down*, not the *bottom up*. One of the first ideas that those students learn in their prestigious business schools is to see life from the perspective of a CEO, the decision maker. Just as it was in President Barack Obama's story, it is so in all of ours, too. How far we travel in life is directly impacted by our own angle of perception, and what becomes our vantage point.

As long as a person can see life from above with the view from the top down, he or she sees the whole picture and not just part of it. The presumably impossible and unreachable goal becomes clearer when the "sun's rise clears the foggy screens." I take comfort in the fact that our *top-down view* is remarkable in shaping our understanding of fear, failure, responsibility, duty, and fortitude.

It bears mentioning that the process starts when we are able to see ourselves where we desire to be. "Finger Markings in Foggy

Screens" is doing what not everyone is willing to do, that which in turn separates the dreamers from the daydreamers. It is the *"audacity of hope"* that gives people who intend to forge through life a lifeline when all of life is clouded by misty days of doubt and ambiguity.

A good friend once told me that people who have a goal in life often have a *"je ne sais quoi"* around them. It is that *certain something* that allows us to embrace life's truths and live decisively, passionately and completely although often that *certain something* can't be adequately described or even expressed.

Foggy screens are the lenses of life through which we have to persevere to find meaning to our own lives. It is where the mental picture loses its clarity and we're left with the choice either to proceed or retreat. In those moments, even when all we have is a *finger's mark* to give us hope, proceed anyway. People who get a panoramic view of life don't see the clammy screens at all. When the rest of us are fixated on how life has treated us unfairly, they chose to be naïve, and keep wiping their damp screens a little faster.

One day I made a conscious decision to stop counting the number of people who told me to turn away from the sky because there was no way the sun was going to shine my way. How many of our friends and family members killed our enthusiasm, questioned our hopes, and gave us reasons to wonder if we ever could see past the physical obstructions and the mental hurdles? Even worse, how many times have we talked ourselves out of our own ambitions because of our myopic viewpoint?

I was determined to ignore the people who did not believe that I could rise from my humble beginnings and change my own future. I am still learning that my life is no accident, neither is even the most piercing misfortune. Remember that the most important piece of the puzzle is what we tell ourselves and the consequent image we see of ourselves on the other side of the foggy screens.

Finger Markings in Foggy Screens

1 Leave a tiny streak for nostalgia
And a smudge if need be
But clean so you'll see
Painful vapors filling times and screens.
5 A moment to breathe fleeting air
When hope is the bolt in a misty glass.
The dreams we have
Before the night falls
The cloudy stars, and the ones we scare
10 Are the imaginations to arouse a fragile wit
And undying faith in spite of poking fears.
I give spirit to memory's time
To dream aloud
And walk in wonderland
15 In the sludge and the dirt
And the doubts and the fears
And the many blessings in foggy screens.
Wipe the windows clear you'll see
What many in eternity never see
20 To give soul to a prying heart
Beyond the vapor, beyond the shallow
Beyond the ebb and beyond the flow.
The shrubbery dies when no longer carry seed
And the dreams die when we cease to believe
25 And when fresh breeze ceases to poke a giggle.
But for a distant faith
Truth live behind the misty glass
When the sun's rise will clear foggy screens
And our filthy dreams be clean as new.

A HUMMINGBIRD'S RIDE

I learned a gripping and enthralling fact about a hummingbird. The longer I pondered over it, the more it made sense to me. It is a well-documented fact that hummingbirds have surprisingly small wings compared to the size of their bodies, which logically would mean that this affects their ability to fly.

Occasionally the hummingbird would fly across long distances, far into regions which it never knew existed and would make its home somewhere new. The unique ride of the hummingbird is among other things an illustration of courage on a long and lonely journey, and following its inner guidance to do the seemingly impossible.

In Texas, my friend Larry was a big talker, and occasionally almost annoying. Even worse, no one we all knew ever saw any of the luxurious accomplishments and wild ideas he talked about. Often I would lose my patience and argue against his chatter with a logical flaw that made his story one of delirious and wishful thinking. He would smile, shake his head and walk away, as if I had said the most amusing thing to him. Many years later, most of our peers were taken aback by Larry's entrepreneurial endeavors and wondered if he actually worked out a plan, or stumbled into a pile of business luck.

Today, Larry is a successful web designer and barely utters a word unless it has something to do with his clients. By his own admission he "faked it, 'til he made it," but also worked diligently on his empty talk to be sure that he would not be blabbing forever. I had previously heard of such attitudes, but I saw Larry talk his way into his aspirations.

It was then that he told me the story of the hummingbird's ride. We would often exchange our tear-jerking stories of perseverance, and how our seemingly insignificant journey was evolving into our own heroic rides. In our own small way, every achievement gives us another wing on the presumably improbable journey.

As a young boy, Larry was diagnosed with dyslexia, a learning disability that manifests primarily as a difficulty with written language, particularly with reading and spelling. Earlier in his life, he accepted an elementary school teacher's recommendation that his brain would never have the ability to process complex information, thus he would be better off finding a profession that did not require much complex reasoning.

For many years, Larry convinced himself that dyslexia was his legitimate excuse to cruise through life and do nothing. He tells of the day when a friend told him that although dyslexia was the result of a neurological difference, it was probably not an intellectual disability.

My friend Larry had problems with the simplest math but was excellent in creative work and graphic design, even with the most complicated software applications. It was during one of such artistic moments when it clicked for Larry. He may not have been the smartest kid in his math class but that did not make him dyslexic.

Larry perhaps just did not like mathematics as much as he loved art, literature, or any other subject. He was not sick. For 15 years, he believed a story that turned out to be untrue. He thought to himself that he would find his own radical way to change his circumstances. That is where he got the idea to *fake it, until he made it*. He talked to himself until he started believing in what he was saying. He told his story and with a smile, and asked if I had ever heard someone say, "Find the difficulties in your life, and make opportunities through them." I simply replied "No." Without skipping a beat, Larry replied, "Now you've heard it."

A hummingbird starting out its journey with impossibly small wings is like our venturing into life with incredible disadvantages. Irrespective of what our intrinsic inabilities are, we all have to somehow find the faith to begin. I learned of how the hummingbird has learned to fly close to the waves of the oceans, so that the headwinds will not impede its movement but rather help it. Somehow it finds the heart and nerve to follow an inner guidance and keep pressing forward.

I am sure that the hummingbird instinctively knows he must do whatever it takes to make it to the other side of a long and lonely ride. The most presumptuous assertion would follow my thinking that we are all somewhat like my friend Larry. All of us, nevertheless, have a *hummingbird* inside of us.

In the past we may have given ourselves excuses or listened to other people tell us how inadequate we are in performing some activity. The size of our wings may not measure up to the size of our bodies, and our ambitions may be bigger than our resources to achieve them. Whatever the nature of the excuse we give to ourselves, it often takes the same amount of energy to say a "yes" as it is to say a "no" to any undertaking. I contend that our predicament will not vanish mysteriously unless we make a determined attempt to change it, even if it means *faking it 'til we make it.*

Oftentimes we find ourselves at a decisive junction and the critical point is when we must decide what kind of response we are going to give to the headwinds blowing against our path. Our resolve may very well be different from Larry's, but as in his case, our victories would be nothing to cherish if we failed to keep our heart fixed on our destination. It is tragic how many of us never recognize that our scholarly disabilities are the limitations we allow ourselves to buy into.

As you read this book, my guess is that somewhere in the world, there are some brilliant psychology gurus computing the statistics on how many times a person fails before he formally becomes a failure. There are people measuring our chances of making it across the oceans. The good news is that until that research shows up, there is no reason why we cannot live our lives, and live fulfilling ones.

The hummingbird flies alone through different conditions and many circumstances beyond its control, towards an end that is fixed in its imagination. The journey will get difficult; windy with troubles, and wet with frustration, but neither is good enough reason to give up.

I recall my own opinion of the city of Houston before packing my bags to live there. All I knew about Texas were the images in Western films with cowboys and gunslingers on horseback. I knew my skewed picture could not be precise, but the idea of warriors, cowboys, and fighters seemed attractive to me. Years earlier, I wanted to go somewhere different and start my young life over.

Not sure what it was I looking for, I sought to find my true self and redefine my unique identity and thought that in faraway Texas, there was an answer. Among the many character traits which I would gather from some of the people I met was this inconceivable sense of belief that even the most unimportant person could become a *somebody*. The caveat is if we manage to hang in there and not give in.

Chapter 11: A Hummingbird's Ride

I often joked about some of the distinct actions of people in Texas, especially as the first group of people I met admitted that in their part of the world, no excuse was good enough. True or not, a colleague once pointed out that in Texas, there is a do-it-yourself and a come-what-may *cowboy mentality,* a conquering mindset that an unimaginable event could begin from the most insignificant quarters. Anyone could win if they followed their inner guidance with a sense of purpose.

Writing "Hummingbird's Ride" was a striking reminder of my own experiences when I moved to a new city. One day my brother called, curious to know if my new home was any different from the places where we had grown up.

In my opinion, the city and the people may not be any different from any other city or people anywhere else. Luckily for me I had been fortunate to have stumbled into a few people who lived life with the impudence to give it their best effort. They grabbed life by the horns, or so it seemed, and I could say they were *guys who just thought differently.*

The belief that all of us can indeed achieve the seemingly unattainable and fulfill our life purpose by pushing just a little harder was an *"aha-moment."* I embraced this mindset and for as long as I could remember, I used it as a centrifuge for redefining my own self-concept. Just as with the birds on a desperate flight across vast oceans, it was a positive impetus to forge ahead in my personal aspirations. It is the hope, expectation and conviction which strengthen our *weak limbs,* and shed a guiding light on a "Hummingbird's Ride."

I once told a story of day laborers who would stand at a major intersection waiting for menial job opportunities. Most of them were illegal immigrants from Mexico who had crossed into Brownsville or Laredo, Texas, just to find a means to survive. Controversial as it was, their argument was that they also needed to find a way to make their own dreams, no matter how small or different, a reality.

I drove past one of their usual gathering points every morning on my way to school. Almost like clockwork, the sight of other people just like me, unsure of where their next meal would come from, forced me to reflect on my own life.

Sure, they were undocumented immigrants, without the authorized resources and the wherewithal to fit into the legal economic framework, but so were another 25 million people in America, but certainly not all of them were waiting with signs on the street corners. It is intriguing to think that there were no symbols or labels on their foreheads showing what they could or could not do. I wondered to myself on one such morning if anyone told them of the hummingbird's story.

In college, I met Vincent who also had an impossible journey which began from his poor village in El Salvador. For seven years, he had worked on orange farms in Florida, worked long hours in dusty factories in Tennessee and washed dishes in what seems to have been every restaurant in Arizona.

Seven years later, Vincent was studying medicine at a university while working as a day laborer on several construction sites. His colleagues from his past are still working on the same orange farms, have accepted the sequence of life as they live it, and as he puts it, "They are still waiting on a miracle."

When he first told them his idea of going to college, they called him a "fool living in a surreal world." Vincent had the same aspirations that most of us have and he seized on that sudden moment to fly into *the improbable* to change his life forever. I listened to Vincent, knowing that he not only heard the story, he lived it; he was a hummingbird. He recalled one afternoon on the orange farm when his supervisor noticed him whispering something quietly to himself.

Curiously, the supervisor asked what the mumbling was about. Vincent told him he had always wanted the chance to go to a university someday. The supervisor smiled and asked, "So why are you sitting out here wishing?" He knew that the adventure could be lonesome and tiresome, but he did not measure the size of the young man's wings compared to the size of his dream.

Vincent had *sixty-eight dollars for a million dollar ambition.* The supervisor did not assume that the young man's present situation was the ultimate destination for the rest of his life. Unlike the elementary school teacher who had prescribed mediocrity for my friend Larry, he understood the power we all have to rearrange the odds if we want anything badly enough. He continued, "Don't tell me about it, go do it."

That was the last of Vincent's days in the scorching heat on the orange farm. The sudden jolt was the reminder of how far he had traveled and how much farther he could go. He smiles today in his recollection that the choices were not easy to make, and that if it wasn't for the word of a stranger in the orange farm, he might very well be sitting on the same stage still.

For most of us, one difficult choice precedes another. I will argue that the difference in what prompts a poor illegal immigrant to risk his own life, choose to enroll in a university, while another person sits back and *waits for the sun to shine,* depends on something I have come to identify as *relative exposure.* This is what I believe defines our parameters of possibility.

Our adventures in life, our beliefs and perceptions paint an image of reality in all of our minds. It is for that reason that we define one action as possible and another as impossible. What we are exposed to, in relation to that which we are not exposed to, affects our judgment, enthusiasm and confidence. Whether we forge ahead to create miracles out of our modest starting points or sit around in the hope that a miracle will be on its way, largely depends on what we envision to be doable.

Two birds will attempt to fly across the same ocean, but one will see the waves and rushing tides and become fearful to fly. A few more will be stopped in mid-flight. The others would imagine a flight through the air and over the oceans; the same rushing tides and forceful winds could be the same headwinds that would push them farther. Some people acknowledge the high costs of success and others fear the shame of failure.

Some of us never ventured because we did not even know what was possible. Others knew what was possible, but the expense became a deterrent. Either way, amazing journeys of people like Vincent, who had every reason to live a mediocre life, challenge us all to stop rehearsing our ambitions and actually get out there and do it.

In the same way, we can choose to either be cheerful about the little joy we have in our hands or keep on recounting the agonizing memories of what the wind blew away. The *hummingbird's ride* is not devoid of loneliness and heartache. No matter how much time is gone and how many fights we've lost, all of us are still able to complete our fulfilling trips past the turbulent oceans of life. Psychologists believe that one of the key reasons why a single loss often possesses the aptitude to trigger a series of losses in a chain reaction is because we never take the time to see that despite the setback, the advantage has not shifted or tilted against us.

I am a testament to distressing moments when our personal dreams and timelines may not have turned out as we planned. In fact the winds of life may very well have driven most of our aspirations into another realm, but it is never too late to reassess and gather what is left. In so much as we have life, we are never wiped clean. Jokingly, a good friend suggested that the fact that we are alive gives us one leg-up on many people who did not make it out alive today.

I have seen my own life take sharp detours from time-to-time; but through it all, I am learning to master the art of holding on when everything around us is shaking and falling apart. The *pro-choice* attitude is making the choice to hold our chin up when there is nothing but a cheek bone to grab hold to.

Chapter 11: A Hummingbird's Ride

It is easy for us to smile in the good times, but our genuine temperament is unveiled in that instant when nothing seems to be going according to the charming script we wrote for our lives. You and I may be stuck with feeble wings for a seemingly improbable journey, but that is when we need the most in-your-face optimism to fight through.

At every turn in our lives, we all have to make a conscious effort to keep on fighting forward. My friend Larry had to tell himself a counter story to what an elementary school teacher told him. Vincent ignored the obvious stop signs and quit rehearsing his life outside the orange farms. The flight of a little hummingbird takes lonely, tedious and uncertain routes, but makes for an extraordinary ride. As with the many people I met who inspired me to hang in and not give in, my life was no longer illusions, delusions or figments of a little bird's imagination.

With every new day's challenges, I am certain that my flight is far from over, but it is uplifting to know that I am becoming the person I hoped for. With every feeble, trivial, and tiny step, I walk an inch closer to the other side. Recently, I discovered that the hummingbird, apart from its unusual ability to flap its wings as fast as 80 flaps per second, is the only bird that can fly backwards.

In a world where everyone is desperately learning to follow other people's footprints, it is incredibly important to acknowledge our unique gifts and talents, even as we live through our unique sets of challenges on our own journeys. Let us strive to give our faith a fighting chance, and I am confident that the *quiet songs of a gentle breeze* will possess the energy to guide us into a gratifying and fulfilling future, just like a hummingbird.

A Hummingbird's Ride

1 Right here is the sunny side of time
The joys across the high
And the stars
There is grace before morning,
5 And before the impossible
All grown and two wings shy of able.
A hum and sound in split seconds here
Squeaking calls
And songs of ache
10 Grace fills my beak and weakly limb.
The bird's lane is muddy in space
Bony and dying
Through a wandering cloud.
Away I fly to save my hope
15 I promised my heart for the other side
The shining sun I finally see
When my world had spun across the seas
Almost home,
Will never know too soon.
20 In the quiet songs of a gentle breeze
Blowing by in perfect tunes
My ride is but a long and glowing fly
A hummingbird's ride.

TEARS FROM THE GRAVE

Years ago I read about how a person's life flashes across his eyes in his final moments. Different schools of thought share differing and strong opinions on whether the occurrence is a myth or in fact a filmstrip of one's life literally flashed by.

Obviously I haven't died yet, so I cannot tell for certain what is involved at the end of any neurological function. Whatever an individual's interpretation of this phenomenon, in which I have no vested interest, I imagine there is some complex dialogue even in the final seconds of what we think to be a desperate life.

My childhood friend, Josiah, always talked about a man from very humble beginnings who became arguably one of the bestselling poets in world history. When Khalil Gabran died in 1931, the Lebanese-born philosopher and theologian had left a remarkable portrait of thought that will affect later generations. He was born in the Mount Lebanon Province of the Ottoman Empire and he did not receive any formal education until he went to the United States during his teenage years.

Gabran's life story and his many accomplishments hinged on a single premise that "Desire is half of life; indifference is half of death." The poet's imagery of death prompted me to wonder if an unfinished life can ever pass on unfinished dreams and hopes to the friends and loved ones left behind. How much then would all the missed opportunities or the passionate attitude be worth to a life? How will the memories of our lives impact the people whose lives we have touched along the way?

If life is anything like a proverbial battle, the craving and *desire* to confront challenges, as daunting as they may be, will be half the battle itself. The lack of impetus and passionate impulsion is the recipe for losing our foothold in the battle, long before it starts. In much the same way, indifference and apathy to our life's events might as well be counted as a kind of death. Sooner or later we would have combed through life as if on a window-shopping trip, and done no more than anyone in a grave.

Josiah died in a horrifying car accident in the summer of 2001. He would be quick to tell you how much he lived every day to the fullest. Our last conversation was brief, as if we were both in a hurry chasing a moment in time. It seemed as if we had lost the value of simple smiles which gave our friendship true meaning many years before.

In our own unique ways, we were both living in overdrive, fervently pursuing all the ambitions we could imagine. We would spend the rest of our lives in two different countries, separated by miles of oceans, but connected still to the lofty ambitions we signed on for ourselves as teenagers. "You can always count on me on this side," he would say.

Chapter 12: Tears from the Grave

Three weeks later, *this side* meant much more than two countries thousands of miles apart. We had managed to hang on to the bond of friendship and the passion we learned from each other growing up. At some point, we believed that in spite of the different trajectories we pursued, we would often come back to the *happy starting point,* and to the very things that had kept our childhood smiles together in the first place.

But until then, we wanted to dream bigger dreams, strive harder, and challenge ourselves to desire much more out of life than our circumstances afforded us. Unlike children, whose innocence of a future becomes a protective shield against constant anxiety, most adults miss the precious messages in every step we take. It is only after a heartbreaking transition of death that most of us take the time to re-evaluate the simple things that matter the most in life. I believe also, that central to our existence is the often missed thought that we are not alive forever.

If we could all have the chance for a repeat, we would perhaps endeavor to live fully, whatever that truly means to us. Some of us will completely love the people in our lives again, and others will dream much bigger dreams. A lucky few are exceptions to this, but I am sure many of us will never get a chance for do-overs in our lifetime. Whatever you tend to call it, whether the final sleep or ultimate awakening, we are all on some intricate journey, and having a burning desire to give our best stab is half the journey itself.

The reflection in "Tears from the Grave" is my hope that all of us would have endured every moment in life in our best efforts and with a sense of urgency for ourselves and others on the *other side.* They may be the true owners of an unfinished portrait, but we owe it to ourselves to let the fickle nature of life itself urge us to live every moment in full blast.

There are countless lessons to be learned from the grief of losing a friend, and a challenge to live the rest of our lives with genuine gusto and hope is one of them. Now that my friend is no longer around, I have the pleasant burden of dressing up for two, living my life for two; one for me and another in the constant memory of *my friend who died.*

Like the poet Khalil Gabran, many people I knew from humble beginnings learned to identify the true meaning of *life as a stage,* where our acts tell a story beyond the spaces we occupy. It also marks the trail of our lives for people to see what we have done with the gift of life. In our conscious effort to not casually drift through life, it is imperative that we give ourselves every reason to commit our moments to those things of true value to us.

In writing this poem, I recall the many bus rides with my friend Josiah through the busy streets of Accra. We visited everyone we knew, considered every plan there was to ponder, and searched for the humor in every image, every person and every event around us. As if to convince himself and to recharge his energy, Josiah said "There is more sleep after death." The logic in this statement only rings true for people who choose to live in overdrive, and work overtime to see their passions come to life. What friend, grandchild, colleague, mother, son, or neighbor will say you lived well, and that you gave life your best shot while you could?

On a Saturday morning, I was driving alone on a highway when I came close to something resembling a paranormal activity. I felt empty and trapped in what must have been one of the lowest points of my life. As best I can remember, my life did not flash before my eyes; instead, a distinct voice reminded me that I was still capable of *fighting on* and that the essential life lessons can in fact show up at the lowest point of our lives.

I was driving down the busy U.S. Highway 59 in Houston, Texas. I pulled past a pile of cars on the left shoulder of the road. The long line of emergency trucks and police cars indicated a horrific accident and possibly a loss of innocent lives. A small black car had smashed

Chapter 12: Tears from the Grave

into the back of a truck, and emergency crews were desperately running around to save a young woman trapped inside the small car.

Immediately, I thought to myself how some of the onlookers would see the same tragedy, and even for a split second, imagine a serene life for the unfortunate victims. Such a desperate thought will assume that the frustrations of a very unsure life and future could suddenly disappear, as with the young lady whose life ended in that awful accident.

The sad thought however is how many people are mostly full of life, but wishing to trade places with a lifeless woman. Something difficult or a pile of desperate moments must have brought them to this point. I have been fortunate to not harbor such split-second negative thoughts, but there are people around us for whom the many years of difficulties and the copious heartaches have slowly piled up into a quiet sense of dejection and sadness. Most people joke about this, and imagine that life could not get any harder in the afterlife, and nothing could get worse than it was in the hard-hitting moments of the present.

In my almost surreal experience, it was not so much a filmstrip, but it was as if someone juggled my memory and served it to me with the small victories bouncing to the top. A split-second flashback of many people who had turned their backs, the long days of uncertainty, and many sad stories finally vanished. The pieces of my life were soon juxtaposed with every one of the triumphant days when the simplest accomplishment had given me some hope. I was tired of being stuck in the same rut, but my life was definitely far from over.

All of us have at one time or another heard about the possibility of disappointed souls whose best ideas are lying next to them in their graves, unable to see the light of day. Those ideas could have touched a life, changed a heart or even affected a world; but will not do any of those. It was from that thought that the poem "Tears from the Grave" was born.

One of the most powerful detractors of human nature's desire for ambition is guilt. The emotion that brands itself as a feeling of not being good enough, not having done enough or lived well enough. Time wasted, moments gone and feelings of helplessness are enough to make us feel like giving up on our hopes and dreams.

It wasn't long after my years of research for this book that a startling thought crossed my mind. Yes, life is unpredictable. Sure, life is full of disappointments, and the journey for most of us is no less frustrating than feeling trapped in a maze, full of winding roads leading to nowhere. Sure, all of that is true. What is true also is that life perhaps is not as complicated as we force ourselves to believe.

The daily grind of striving for accomplishment is enough to make us lose sight of the fact that at the end of the day, nothing new exists under the sun. When our plans fall through the cracks, the first people to jump on the guilt train are you and me. Our circumstances may be new to us and have shock value only to us, but I will bet millions more have lived where we are, or been where we have been, in their own way.

Our complicated internal dialogue deconstructs and reconstructs our circumstances *nine ways to Sunday,* to make sense of it. I learned later, that it may be our vague definitions of what we strive for in life that complicate our pursuit. Did I say vague? Precisely.

Guilt is that emotion that pokes a hole in our life's potential, and the hollow twang of hope over reason. Even worse, as if in a conspiracy, the feelings of underachievement and inadequacy often show up in droves, and also from all sides. Sooner or later, it is those feelings of dissatisfaction and inaction that compound, and make us the uninterested and passive onlookers to our own life's events.

When I wrote "Tears from the Grave," I imagined a symbolic mother's displeasure with her son who is on the verge of giving up on life. The poem would be a rejoinder from a concerned mother whose son is seconds away from waving a white flag of surrender. The intriguing thought for this poem recalls an image of a son standing

Chapter 12: Tears from the Grave

next to the deceased mother's grave, a wreath in hand and tears running down his face. He talks about his lonely days, his unsure life and losing his faith. He then wonders to himself, *"What if she could hear me? What if she could talk back?"*

What if the *mothers* of our lives could hear our disgruntled hearts' plea to give up on what seems to be a difficult life? What would they say? Who can she trust to comfort her lonely son? "Tears from the Grave" is a mother's words, a friend's encouragement and an inspirational urge for us to keep on moving even when we have almost nothing to move on to.

For some of us, it is impossible to understand why another person could feel so dejected, ignoring the fact that there may very well be much more underlying pain of which we will never become aware. I remember the story of a good friend who lost everything but his own life in Operation Desert Storm. My friend Steve returned home from the war with numerous symptoms of post-traumatic stress disorder. Accidents and the traumatic events of the war were one thing, but the intrusive thoughts and the dissociative flashback experiences made his life unbearable.

The morning Steve left the veterans hospital, it was six months later, and he learned that he was paralyzed in a part of his body. I can't even begin to imagine the feeling and heartbreak at such news. He would often remember all the simple things that he had done, all of which he took for granted as routine parts of life, but now he could no longer do. Steve explains that it wasn't any one particular incident that pushed him closer to the depression cliff, but rather a cumulative effect of the grief and the emotional hurt built up over the years.

I have heard experts explain how a true self-image is developed through an exchange between self-concept, which are the *thoughts about self,* and self-esteem, which are the *feelings about self.* I believe that there is a constant flux between these two intimate parts of our human existence.

The real self, ideal self and experiential self in turn translates into how we are, how we would like to be and how we interpret our survival. My own set of personal hurdles had unconsciously affected my *ideal self*, hence it didn't take much to appreciate Steve's desperate search for answers.

Every action and activity we engage in directly affects one of the component parts of *self* directly and perhaps another part inadvertently. Our circumstances in life have a way of refining and shaping how we perceive the simplest acts; and very soon it leads to the question of what our value in life has become. At the lowest point of my emotional journey, "Tears from the Grave" seemed to suggest to a lonely man that his life wasn't as empty as he imagined.

From my own experiences, I contend that in spite of our individual differences and unique challenges, there are times when we all come full circle and face-to-face with the snowballing effect of life's choices. We are forced to account for them, even the unpleasant ones. It is in that moment that we have the chance to either regret the things we should have done, or praise ourselves for the things we've done well. We can look back at our own lives and see the trails of how differently our lives could have ended up if we went one way or another.

My friend's lesson was no different from mine and perhaps from yours, too. I would assume that not all of us will hear the voices of our mothers, nor see filmstrips of our lives flash in the critical moment before we give up on our hopes and ourselves. *But morning still left in you, and my memory will push you on.* Our waking up today gives us an extra lifeline which millions of people across the world will never have.

A few years ago, I was riding in a double-deck bus in Central London. It was an unusually breezy evening and many of the passengers sat in the upper deck admiring the sights in London's Piccadilly Circus. The sights along the streets were overwhelming, just as the billboards were countless; from Virgin Records to Coca-Cola, Panasonic to Big Ben.

The many glaring lights had unique messages of their own, ultimately with the sole purpose to pull your attention to the product being advertised. Some of the billboards overtly described products and events, while others used more subtle messages wrapped up in cute imagery to convey an idea.

Into the distance stood a much smaller signpost, hardly noticeable among the giant advertisements parading the main street. It simply stated, "Life is best with you in it." Amidst the plethora of billboards and huge signposts along one of the busiest streets in the world, the most powerful message lived on the seemingly insignificant one of them all.

It is amazing, just as it is sad, that most people live their entire lives as if they are merely spectators to their existence. My best guess is that it would be sad to hear the *final buzzer go off*, only to look back and regret all the things they could have done with their lives.

Country music recording artist Tim McGraw wrote a very popular song he called, "Live like You Were Dying." What more would we do if the next second was indeed our last? An obviously unpleasant thought to carry through life, but if we appreciate the seemingly inconsequential seconds we have, only then will we understand that nothing else is guaranteed.

Often I reflect on what more I could have talked about with my best friend, and where else we would have gone together, if we had had one more day. It is my humble opinion that none of us have eternity to live so we might as well let today be the one we make count, the opportunity of now. Death ends life but never the connection between the people we once shared our hopes with and the lessons they have taught us.

Losing someone we love to the grim specter of death is the reminder that none of us will escape the clutches of nature. Many people I know share their own stories of losing a mother, a father, friend, or neighbor. That is the one inevitable sadness all of us will have to deal with at some point in time. The challenge is to transform the pain of grief into an elixir of hope, and I will be first to admit, that is no easy task.

The inspiration in "Tears from the Grave" is the memory of a friend who passionately believed that "life is full of punch lines." It is the kind of memory that teaches us to rethink how much of our lives can become stale simply because of our *indifference* to it. Punch lines are often the final parts of a joke or story, usually a word or a thought, intended to be funny or provoke a thought. Even more striking, punch lines add meaning.

I am forever humbled by the realization that the real tragedy is not the ones we lose to death, but rather how so many of us are still alive but whose actions very well qualify us as the *living dead*. If we ever can *live like we were dying*, it will demand us using the time and opportunity we still own to take full advantage of today's air while we breathe. If indeed "Desire is half of life; indifference is half of death," then the decision to either live or die starts with a much simpler decision to either try or not try.

How many of us often wish we could turn back the hands of time and close the chapter to an unfinished life? How many of us would search harder for a dream we once held close to our hearts but which had slipped away with time? The enlightening and encouraging thought for us is to relive every day to our utmost potential and within the limitless possibilities.

Life, indeed, is full of punch lines. It will take a conscious desire to give life our best shot to discover the truly happy turns in all of them. I suggest that all we have on our side is *today*, and an unrivalled opportunity to make it count.

The poem "Tears from the Grave" is not only about my complex web of emotional roller coasters, but that of many people who stood on the verge of saying *goodbye to life too soon.* How do we find the strength to hold on when we envy the peace in the lifeless? The reassurance in the poem is especially for those of us who gave up on our dreams and ourselves, and walked away. It is the words for an untapped potential laying waste within us, when we still have all the time and opportunity in the world to fulfill our heart's ambitions.

I wrote this poem as a deeply reflective monologue of a voice from an unexpected place, a grave. My challenge to the many people I met over the years has been that there is no such a moment in time as too late. Of course, there are no quick fixes or overnight reprieves. We may someday find a way to reconcile with whatever we have done, but I am sure that there is no way to reconcile with those things we never did. With the latter, we may never be able to forgive ourselves for missing the opportunities while we still have life, and we soon realize the grave can wait.

As I wrote "Tears from the Grave" the desire for adventure and success had sent me thousands of miles beyond anything familiar from my childhood. I stood at the edge of a desperate emotional cliff. I sat in the dark by a mother's proverbial grave to tell my reasons for my despondency. It was then that I heard the voice, the reassuring nudge, and was full of tears.

It is a fact of life that when we devote our energy to weeping over moments lost, we lose even more of our present and the here and now. The most important thing for us is to live the best we know how; someday we will look back and be grateful we did not bury our dreams a little too soon.

In memory of Josiah N. Ennin

TEARS FROM THE GRAVE

1 Welcome to no one nowhere, son
    I saved your soul in my silent womb
    Long days with my aching hands and knees
    And you show up at night in desperate tears.
5 You calm my grief with fancy hibiscus
    And songs of how much more you hurt.
    The son I once had,
    Who lived but leaving now
    A goodbye too soon, before the sun and the morn
10 I was there once,
    In whitewashed veracity.
    I saw virtue turn blue,
    And a heart's search for truth
    Son, the earth below is blinding dark
15 So welcome to nowhere, not even here.
    If living is bizarre, dying is a mirage
    Don't pick a plot here,
    Lest the shade fool you.
    Sadness in time comes in a hurry, when life is brisk
20 A heart drifting through millions of wishes
    Running through hope and grace's moment
    All the burns through the walk in the sun
    Only if time changes sequence eternal
    Before death's misery invades like rain.
25 I lost my hair to age,
    My hands withered from strain
    Never killed my faith to sail ashore
    Wipe your tears and save your strength
    A guest I won't call my own

30 No one sees your dreary cheeks,
    No one wants you here.
    The souls next door are fast asleep below
    But a morning still left in you,
    My memory will push you on
35 In search to save a miracle
    In the sun's rise and calming set.
    Save the flowers and smell 'em again
    A welcome song I have none
    For my son will live again
40 The satin on ego is precious still
    And a birth of soul in teary joy
    Goodbye son,
    Your mother's grave has a voice
    Your mother's love is a marvel
45 Live!
    Son, live!
    Hear my heart
    And live through today too.

SAVING RAINS

One afternoon I had the strangest feeling during what turned out to be a terrifying dream. I had taken a very out of character afternoon catnap as I was still dressed in my long-sleeved shirt and a neck tie. I did not intend to fall asleep, but tired as I was, I thought to just shut my eyes for a few minutes. After what I imagined to be an hour later, I found myself struggling with a very physically powerful hand that had gripped my neck and appeared to be squeezing it.

I wrestled to pull the hand off my neck. For a moment I could not breathe and felt myself choking. In what must have been my tossing and turning on the bed, I suddenly woke up, sweating profusely, frantically gulping for air and wondering what had just happened in my dream.

It was certainly a bad dream; my neck tie had wrapped twice around my neck and it seemed like I was out of breath from suffocation. I was struck by intense fear as I lay down on my bed to replay the sequence of events in my mind. This was the second time I had such a strange dream, both as if I wrestled for my life. It bore every resemblance to our real world encounters, in that every day was a tussle for some form of progress in each of our own lives.

I have often said that our instinctive reactions to any life sequence are a true assessment of our core personality. Some of us live actively, just as well as others casually pace through life with a come-what-may attitude. In real life the alternative to wrestling the *strange hand* is the road often traveled. A chunk of us live by the maxim, "It is what it is." Fortunately, it isn't so, but rather what we make it.

Occasionally, I take a moment to think about my true worth in life; and for that matter, why all of us are here. Without struggling for answers from the supernatural, I even wonder if our lives are hanging in some space with a grandmaster running a puppet show behind the scenes. Any such grandmaster must have given you and me way too many options and freewill to control his intended ending. So I imagined that "it is what it is" probably isn't the case. I am convinced that we all have a say-so in our future, and we might as well micromanage every step along the way.

As I made notes on "Saving Rains", I was engaged in a futile argument with a colleague about fate and how an individual resolve is connected to it. One of the worn-out but fairly understandable questions we all ask is, why bother if this is all a script? What difference then does our individual tussle and wrestling with the *strange hand* make if all we are doing is acting our parts in a play?

Those are fair questions; I do not have the most convincing answers to either of them. Frankly, I never took enough time to delve into any substantial research about fate and providence. For me, "Saving Rains" is about our quest to control those elements which we have power over, instead of sitting back aloofly to drown in the downpour of chaos all around us.

Chapter 13: Saving Rains

Not long ago, I read a story about two construction workers, Tom and Dave, who ate their lunch together every day at work. They had been friends for many years and each day they would sit in the shade of the building project and open their lunch boxes. On Monday, Tom carefully unwrapped his sandwich. Picking up the top layer of the bread, he peeked.

"Peanut butter again?" he said with a look of disgust.

Dave continued to eat without uttering a word. On Tuesday afternoon, Tom took his sandwich out of the lunch box, stared at it with a puzzled look. He furiously yelled, "No, not peanut butter again!" Again, his friend Dave refrained from any comment as Tom went on to eat his lunch. By Friday, the same thing happened and as Tom screamed about the peanut butter sandwich, Dave could not help himself, *"If you don't like peanut butter, why don't you tell your wife?"* he said. *"Now listen,"* replied Tom, *"You leave my wife out of this. I make my own sandwiches!"*

Wait a minute. How dense and strange can anyone be to fix his own sandwich in the morning and passionately complain about it a few hours later? I know what you may be thinking. Tom makes his own peanut butter lunch and whines every time he gets ready to eat it. He is probably not as clueless as you and I may imagine, but there is certainly something about Tom which I believe is emblematic of all of us. If the story continued, I would imagine Dave's response as "Dude, you've got to be kidding me."

Like Tom, most of us spend time and precious energy digging tight spots for ourselves, creating avenues to inconvenience ourselves and then complaining about it. The fear of an uncertain consequence forces us to make some of the same mediocre choices we have made in the past. Our instinctive tendency is to stick to the same process even if it has yielded the same lukewarm results. I call that a tragedy.

At a little girl's eighth birthday party, it came time for her to make a wish and blow out the candles. We had all gathered around the table for the routine act, which most of us have done throughout our lives without much question. The little girl closed her eyes, and as if in deep thought, she slowly turned and said to her mother standing behind her, "Mama, do I really have to do this?"

The mother explained that she didn't have to, but was curious to know why she decided suddenly against something she had done several times before. The little girl said the last time she made good wishes on her birthday she had a horrible time at school, her dog died, and her best friend moved to another city all in the same year.

In her mind, all the bad things happened to her after she made good wishes and blew out the candle the year before. She would rather do something else, anything else, so she decided unquestionably not to do the same thing. The rest of us gathered at the table looked puzzled as her mother pulled the candles off the birthday cake.

My friend's eight-year-old girl inadvertently had figured out a remarkable secret to life that Tom never found out whenever he prepared his lunch. She was determined to avoid repeating the same actions and following the same routines, especially when the end result was not the kind she hoped for. In her mind, she did not want another horrible year at school, another dog to die and her new best friend to move to another city.

Surely most of us thought the little girl was connecting dots in her mind, in places where none existed. The interesting twist was that it all made sense in her childish mind. For that reason, I ask myself how much of our present situation is a result of fate? What fraction of life is our own peanut butter sandwich that we have carefully prepared from home? I have said before that no one can clearly define where we plan to go in life or determine those things we desire to achieve, except each one of us.

Ultimately, you and I will have to take responsibility for every one of our actions, no matter how minimal. Our methods could be conventional or unconventional; but the people who survive the

Chapter 13: Saving Rains

rains are those who, instead of sitting back *with open arms dipping down,* see a *reflection of hope in the water's mirror* and determine to live even in the *drench* of life's difficulties. Whether we decide to blow any more candles or fix something else apart from the same peanut butter sandwich is our own prerogative. In most cases, no grandmaster running a puppet show will force us to an alternative choice.

One time I was helping my friend Jason on a final presentation for his architecture diploma at Cornell University in New York. I noticed that the other sample projects had several different designs in any one presentation, all cautiously drawn and elaborately designed. Jason's work was somewhat different.

Out of curiosity, I asked him about why he had invested so much time on only two elaborate pieces and relatively no time at all on the others in the middle. He laughed. Jason explained that he is daring to try something very different from what he had done for the past four years. "But isn't that your sample to follow," I asked pointing to the board on the table. He nodded, and without looking up at me politely reminded me that it sure was a sample but definitely not a template.

No one required him to follow that exact model, and he would rather take his chances by doing the best he knew how. He had a sense that something was always lacking in his final presentations no matter how much time he devoted to all his drawings. Just as it is with the many people who are never content with mediocrity, they gather their experiences like raindrops and save them as invaluable lessons for the next steps of their lives.

My friend Jason's plan would be to put the most elaborate pieces on the top and bottom and work out an unusual strategy. He knew exactly what he had in mind to say about all the pieces; but even further, he had something intriguing for only two of his presentations. He said, "I will knock them dead with the first piece, so much that by the time they wake up, they will only have room in their mind for one more."

Such a confident student, I thought to myself. Isn't that too risky a preparation? What if the first design is unable to *knock them dead,* then what? Too many things could go awry. As a well-intentioned colleague, I reasoned that all it took was a shuffle in arrangements and Jason's grand scheme would fly out of the window.

"Too many things have already gone awry," Jason said. "I have done the same thing for four years and maybe it's time to do something different, anything new," he continued. We spoke again several days after his final presentation. "It worked like magic!" he said. Then with a sigh of relief, he admitted to being scared more than once that something could go wrong, but kept on telling himself that nothing would. *"I just wanted to do something new this time."* The most powerful message in listening to Jason wasn't the fact that he put his faith to work, but that he *expected* it to work.

An ancient Greek myth involved Pygmalion, a man who attempted to create the ideal statute of a woman, whom he named Galatea. The moral of the story was the *expectancy effect*. Also known as the *Galatea Effect,* it is the perception that high expectations ultimately led to high performance. The *Galatea Effect* is a compelling idea which works also in management psychology just as it does in our lives. It is understood as the power of self-expectations, how a person's belief in himself and his efficacy remarkably alters his performance and achievement.

Of course, there are countless contributing factors to individual accomplishment, but we cannot eliminate the crucial element of our own perception of self-worth. My friend Jason would admit that he was far from an overachiever, but he later talked about how he has learned to apply this attitude of affirmative anticipation to his life, not just his architectural presentations. His expectation of a rather favorable outcome inspired his altering belief in a new line of attack to approach a simple school presentation, and now his entire life.

Chapter 13: Saving Rains

Ever since I could recall, my father had planted a rather fascinating mental seed in me that some fathers craft in their sons. My father would address me as *sir* and *Mr*. By the time I was five years old, every child in my neighborhood could not help but call me by my *proper* greeting. This line of thinking is no different from the affirmations we believe as children, in societies where a child is pumped with the belief that he can accomplish just about anything he wants.

Inasmuch as I will argue that no amount of vocal coaching can turn some of us into world-class singers, and that inbuilt belief in our abilities springs us to achieve anything else we hope for. As insignificant as my father's actions were, it was no coincidence that they gradually developed into other intriguing personal traits which in turn affected my self-assurance.

I was five and, even in my naiveté, had convinced myself that I was smarter than my friends with whom I played in the sands. It probably came out of the principle that unless a person believes in who they are and what they possess, no one else will. Many years later, jokingly I would say to myself, "If you don't say I am, no one will say thou art."

"Saving Rains" is about a conscious reliance on our experiences and life crutches to rethink our methods, rewire our attitudes and reignite our hopes for a fulfilling future. With every day, the renewed expectations of our self-worth become the unsuspected boat which keeps us afloat in our own unique journeys.

In my freshman year in college, I wanted to apply to Rice University, one of my favorite schools. Somehow I managed to shortchange myself and talked myself out of the application process. By the time I found out that my own expectations had become the mastermind to my presumed inability, it was too late.

The consolation for me was that I never forgot that lesson, and will use that experience to rewrite my expectations for the rest of my life. I had learned the fine line between sheer arrogance and confidence supported by tangible substantiation of a dream. If one hope falls apart, we use that energy to carve another.

Over the next four years, I took a few minutes before every exam to silently whisper to myself that I never made it to Rice University because I was broke, and that particular exam would be my nice revenge and proof that I was right. I did not only pass the exams, I actually *broke the curves* every time. I knew very well that the two circumstances had no connection per se, but I somehow used that affirmation to ensure that I was never stuck in a rut, merely getting by through school.

Deep inside, there was that simple idea my father told me, that made me latch onto my own anticipation of either turning rains into insignificant raindrops or turning raindrops into floods.

One morning I decided to make a list of every possible obstacle that could derail my ambitions. There were several of them that I assumed I could not think of; but the more I wrote down, the easier it was to identify a strategy to overcome them. Somehow I was using a simple process to outline a laundry list of problems to see how different my reactions would be to each of them.

Like most people, I discovered many things that I had done over and over again, the cost of which I blamed on fate. In turn, "Saving Rains" expresses our renewed energy to move past our own mental status quo and avoid marching to the same tunes as we have done repeatedly.

From the earlier story, it is strikingly interesting how Tom, the construction worker, always ate the peanut butter sandwich he hated so much, despite his complaints. Oddly, his realization and dissatisfaction did not change his subsequent action and it is sad to know that he would repeat the same process again.

As you read this, a new wave of refreshing thought should challenge you to expect the best for yourself and even confront the painful resistance of change. In "Saving Rains," it is easier to hang on to the familiar and the comfort of what we know for certain, but the central focus of our lives ought to be a discontent with a current state that has failed to produced results for us.

In my own small way, I lived in the experience that our anticipation and the expectation for a rewarding outcome is one of the finest elements of our human willpower to venture into the unfamiliar.

Saving Rains

1 Down it comes,
Sunny skies in erratic flash
In my world,
Even shady twirls and waves bear chance
5 So I will change fright to sanguinity
Starting here,
With wells filled in rainy nights.
When nothing is well, drops make me slip
The cloudy skies shun vague rays
10 But with open arms dipping down
Drop after drop,
All that matters is tomorrow.
Down it comes,
A kid's eyes glistens in shock
15 Will be gone in time and another day
The tiny pieces of broken records and dreams
Will save our starve and drying heart
And live in the drench itself.
Now I know why it pours
20 Why the changing times and dim truth
Holds the odds of life's ambiguity.
Down and down it comes
Sacred secrets and the will to win
Is sinking sand on desolate tracts.
25 Voices I hear in the deepest souls
Reflection of hope in water's mirror
Healing rays of morning sun,
Hides beyond the night before.
The joy is a drop,

30 Then a drop
    Dreamy eyes to save my panic
    Echoes of promises fall from clouds
    To hope more and save my rains
    And save my self,
35 Only if the sky above will let me
    Not to fall in water's pile.
    And a heart's cry in the rain.

NIGHTINGALE

A greek myth tells a story of Philomela, the daughter of an Attic king. After she had been treated cruelly by her own brother Tereus, she was compassionately changed by the gods into a nightingale. She spent the rest of her life in the woods lamenting in mournful and sad notes on her fate. Intertwined with the myth of the nightingale is the bird's leaning its breast against the thorns when it sings, as if pouring out a melody in anguish. The nightingale is popular as the *singer of the night*. In my mind, I wondered, why the night?

The poem "Nightingale" reflects the emotionally challenging projects I had undertaken, as every word recalled my many long nights and endless bumps in an uncertain road. My best guess is that all of us have had our share of glumness and loneliness. All of us are logical and emotional creatures, from the most powerful military generals, presidents, renowned scientists, to the strongest of individuals.

None of them are any different from you and me. I am sure that there are days that they felt alone, downhearted and down in the dumps. In the same way, the nightingale's song may not be too different from the other birds' cheeping and chirping; but the darkness of the night perhaps hides the tears of a nightingale's cheerless notes.

I imagine all of us cry sometimes, but would it make a big difference if we did in the dark, in a brief moment, so that we can rise up the next morning with fresh hope? *Nightingale, teach me a song before dark. So I don't see my own heart cry in the morning light.*

Many years ago, I read an excerpt from an article that talk show host Oprah Winfrey had written. She said, "I act as if everything depends on me, and pray as if everything depends on God." Her resolve and steadfastness revolved around a belief in God and the anticipation of reprieve through the most difficult of circumstances. She also had downhearted days, perhaps many more than most of us. My guess is that Oprah Winfrey may have cried to herself for many nights in the quietness and in the solitude of feeling alone.

It's also true that she did not take a back seat, press the cruise control button and wait for her God to send her an emergency relief crew. I would guess she cried her fair share of *nightingale tears.* As with Oprah there are many days when the constant grind of life's grueling problems sends us all crashing face first.

In some of those moments, what matters the most is not what we are made up of, or how much we can handle before the world caves in; what matters most is that we choose to push past the obstacles in our lives so that we can ultimately sing inspiring songs about our lives as we reach our next victory lap. We cry sometimes because our human nature is not constructed of steel, but rather intermittently filled with the heaviness that consumes our thoughts.

"Nightingale" was a memo to myself. It was a reminder to *sing my song* when life hurts the most and to continue to sing even when I was unsure of where the next crossroad would lead. I had to pull myself by

Chapter 14: Nightingale

the remainder of my bootstraps, with a subconscious tenacity in spite of my fragility. I had to determine that no matter how wearisome the passage became, I would hold my head up high and face it head-on.

In my own naiveté, I asserted that the surest way for us to give up on our ambition is to stop trying. The *nightingale* is a loud and persistent singer who may cry all night, yet manages to find the joy and elation to smile in the morning light.

Researchers over the years describe how the bird continues to add new notes and songs to its repertoire and perhaps expresses its pain in song deep into the night, only to smile again in the morning's sun. A metaphor might help; as long as we are in the game, we still have a chance of winning; but by all means, cry if you have to. When you feel crushed and bogged down and the tears are forcibly dripping down either side of your cheeks, go ahead and cry. The important thing is that when the morning comes, we will be geared up to live again.

September 1996 is a time that many tennis fans may never forget. One of the greatest players of the sport, Pete Sampras, was in a match against an unrelenting opponent, Alex Corretja. A defining moment occurred when Sampras was exhausted to the point of sickness and was barely able to move. He vomited on the tennis court in the middle of the fifth-set tiebreaker and there seemed no plausible way he could compete any further.

The people who saw Sampras wobbling dizzily did not anticipate him staying on the court even for the next minute. How and where he found the power to keep playing is a marvel to many, even until today. Sampras survived one of the most daunting games in U.S. Open history to defeat Alex Corretja, but I believe the overriding principle was far from extraordinary. Once he stayed in the game, he still had a 50/50 chance of winning. We can take a treasured lesson from Sampras, who may have thought to himself that anything could happen; but in order to know that, we have to stay in the game.

Successful people in every aspect of life endure difficulties like all of us do. In fact, successful people fail more than unsuccessful people. Thomas Edison may have failed a thousand times before creating a light bulb. I imagine every step of the failing effort was demoralizing, but he eventually did create a light bulb.

How many light bulbs have you attempted to create lately? I am of the opinion that successful people who live a fulfilling life to their utmost potential have mastered the art of living beyond setbacks. Like a downcast bird singing deep into the dark night, they all cry sometimes, wipe their tears and keep on fighting. It is not a coincidence that most successful people we all know, often have lengthy stories of adversities to share.

The nightingale songs and enduring stories are a part of their process. I learned a lesson from my grandfather many years ago that life does not owe any of us any favors. We are not entitled to lucky breaks in life. What is important is seizing the opportunity and shaking off the sad nights, the sad songs and the misfortunes, however they come.

I read an old fable about a man who was riding across the desert at night. As he crossed the riverbed, a voice came out of the darkness ordering him to halt. It was too dark for the man to see his own feet, or the little gravels which he stood on. Then the voice said, "Now get off your camel." The man did just that. Then the voice said, "Pick up some gravel from the riverbed, *as much as you want.*"

The man followed the instructions carefully as he picked up just enough gravel to fill his bag. It was too dark for him to choose between the smaller gravel and the much larger ones, so he picked up just a few in obedience to a strange voice in the desert. Finally, the voice said, "In the morning, you will be both happy and sorry."

When the sun came up, the man looked at what he had picked up the night before only to discover that is was not gravel, it was gold. As the voice told him, he was happy because he picked a handful but also very sorry about the amount. He was happy he took a chance and listened to the voice in the dark, but sorry that he did not grab more.

There was no way for the man in this story to go back to where he heard the voice, and *his regret was in his caution.* I have always believed that what we have in our hands, the opportunities and the life we have is much more valuable than we may care to see. Even in the face of the most devastating setbacks, we can find a silver lining in the darkest clouds if we persevere long enough. The lesson from the nightingale crying in the dark is that when the morning comes, no one would have seen its tears, neither would it have stayed in the dumps where it found itself.

We may have all heard of this funny story where a man, tired of his life, went to God to exchange his problems. God was just as kind as the man had hoped so he asked why the man wanted to exchange his life's problems for another. "This is too much for me," he told God. "If only I could change it for another set of problems, I promise I will never complain again."

The kind God obliged and asked the man to dump all his problems into a white bag. He did. God then threw the bag into a room below, and shuffled it together with all the other white bags in the room. Then the kind God said, "I will give you the choice of picking any of the bags in this big room. You can pick any one you want."

The clever man walked across the room and soon he saw a tiny bag sitting on a huge one, so he asked God if that was also part of the deal. God said, "Yes son, you can choose that tiny one if you want." Happy and relieved, he came back home with his new tiny bag of problems. To his surprise, he opened the white bag only to find out that they were the same problems he had before and a note included which read, "Just in case you thought you had problems, imagine being the person whose huge bag your tiny bag was sitting on."

There is no comfort in the thought that none of us are problem-free. We all have different magnitudes of heavy hearts when life gets tough, and it probably wouldn't be such a good idea to switch our problems for another person's problems. Most of us have occasionally thought to ourselves how different our lives would be if only we could trade lives with the next person. What is true is that all of us still have the ability to make our lives rewarding by accepting who we truly are and appreciating the unique circumstances that come our way.

While I wrote "Nightingale," I had lived what I believed were many frustrating years in different parts of the world. The important turning point begins with our learning to deal with the most intimate fears. There is no shame in crying sometimes when the weight of our load gets much heavier than what we think we can carry. What is shameful is when we never give ourselves another reason to wipe the tears and live a fulfilling life beginning with this moment.

Anyone who did anything unforgettable to change the course of his own life has had to resort to similar principles. There is absolutely nothing magical about sticking-with-it, dusting off the filth, and starting over. People who aspire to live fulfilling lives give themselves a reason to keep on believing with a *gentle belligerence.*

Just like the *nightingale*, I believe that they cry in the dark if they have to, but wake up in the sunrise, shake off the tears and push past their own heart's cry.

NIGHTINGALE

1 The nights will fall longing for dusk
   A dawn of a day no telling what next
   Behind the mask, nightingale here you are
   Sing one more song and count the time.
5 When burnt and crushed and eyes have ceased to cry
   Sing a soul a song when the sun stands still
   Closer, so I see your face
   Autumn's here, flying back from Africa.
   My ears clogged with melancholy and distance
10 Nightingale, come to me in the summer
   And find love in a fool's mythology.
   Your beak still far from tail feather
   In the morning sun, your beauty will glow.
   Nightingale, it's full moon again
15 Your crumbled heart will soon be gone
   So please sing me another song
   A hurting noble mockingbird fell at night
   Dead leaves were home near the ground
   But in the sound of joy
20 Through the winter woods
   I heard your tear drops fall at night
   Bliss again, and now you are.
   Nightingale, where are you?
   The forest's watching your flappy wings
25 Their hearts melt with notes and melody
   Teach me a song before dark,
   Long after the night
   And in the morning's light.

15

A REFUGE FOR
THE BURNING CANDLE

In my sophomore year in college I met Ira Black in a public speaking class. He was a professor who often talked about disappointments throughout his own life. In fact he had come to accept the reality that the frustration that comes with the freefalling days was an inevitable part of life.

The disappointment is often born of the seasons where everything within is dry and withered, when friends are gone, when hope leaves us to comfort ourselves, and with nowhere to turn to. Ira Black would even argue that even God the creator, in his infinite majesty, perhaps gets disappointed every now and then, often with us humans.

In our first day of lecture, he quoted Mark Twain, "God created man because he was disappointed with the monkey," and spent the rest of the semester explaining what it meant. I dismissed his joke as purely witty and comical until it dawned on me one day that Ira Black may have inadvertently cautioned us to do something we were often not so good at.

The "burning candle" in this chapter refers to the raging storms that rattle our faith, and the wild rides of disappointments that life drags us on through a street we can safely call *Chaos Avenue*. More often than not, we have no vote in the matter.

I thought to myself, maybe the point wasn't to poke fun at a supposedly disappointed God, but maybe tell of how a supposedly disappointed God reacts to the presumed displeasure. Whatever its purpose, it perhaps serves well because disappointments have a unique way of sending all of us either into the deepest doldrums of life, or of becoming a valuable lesson on what to avoid in the next lifetime.

As I wrote "A Refuge for the Burning Candle," there is nothing more crushing than when the hope on which our lives hang seems to have caved in on us. The *burning candle moments* are when the events or unfortunate circumstances have left us in the middle of the road in despair, lost in the shadows, and we look back to see that the only set of footprints in the sand is ours. To find refuge in the middle of the raging storms and the disappointments, my proposition is for our hope to be the driving force behind any activity we engage in, which is our faith.

When our life events are filled with strings of disappointments and the foundations on which we stand have crumbled beneath us, refuge is often born out of redirecting our attention away from the caved-in roofs. My safe haven would come from a sudden realization that I was not alone.

I am a strong proponent of praying for *open doors,* but I have also learned that there is nothing wrong with looking out for a window of refuge that our faith provides until the door opens. In fact, sometimes

Chapter 15: A Refuge for the Burning Candle

while we are busy praying for open doors, we can easily miss the crack in the wall, through which refreshing winds of new opportunities may indeed be blowing our way.

Growing up as a curious little kid, there was nothing more fascinating for me than to discover how the simplest life events occurred. I woke up one morning to notice that the hencoop was filled with little chickens which were not there the previous night. I marveled at the event the rest of the day and started my mornings checking to see how many more chickens would miraculously appear. I counted chickens to start my day, and a natural curiosity was born.

It wasn't long before I observed the dry patch on the front porch that stayed dry after the rain. I could never understand why everywhere would be wet, except this small circle of an area. It was even stranger because there was no roof directly hovering over it. Other times, I saw lizards crawling on the side of vertical walls but never once fell off. I also wondered why some flowers withered during the day and appeared full of life at sunset. Little did I know that I was slowly nurturing a mind-set of wanting events to make sense. I was also setting the stage for disappointment. I observed more, noticed odd occurrences about almost everything, but my biggest surprise was yet to come.

Every night my mother would ask my older brother to light up the lantern on the porch. The lantern was often bulky, needed more kerosene, and the glass covering sometimes made it more tedious than it was worth. The alternative was a homemade candle. It was called *bobo*. *Bobo* was a large empty can with a circular opening attached to the lid. It was filled with kerosene. A threaded rope pushed through the opening and the remaining rope was left to soak in the can.

When lit, the homemade candle would be brighter than the lantern. The wind blew from all directions, and that which would often dim or put out the light from the lantern, never put out the *bobo*. I was particularly stunned as any 5 year old kid would be. How is it possible that the light in the sophisticated lantern, with the glass protective coverings, was smothered, and the *bobo* with its light exposed to all the elements survived?

Refuge in the midst of storms of life, and in the middle of winds blowing in all directions comes from drawing upon our energy to endure life's uncertainty from a faith beyond the raging events encircling us. This resolve is starkly different from temporary fixes and feel-good wrong turns that may come with fleeting satisfaction, and in no time send us back to *Misery Lane* again. When it comes to living through the distress and disappointment, it is easy to get our eyes glued to the door we hope for, that we forget that we could just as easily climb through a window, or even a roof, if only we look hard enough.

Even as a little kid I saw how the wind would sway the light from the candle from side to side. The light would dim and dull, but would prop right back up seconds later, never going out. It is entirely possible that just as it was with the lantern, we can also get comfortable in our seemingly protective covering, glass shields, and temporary fixes only to expose ourselves to disappointment when we least expect it.

In the wave of the weariness and the hurt, I turned to the faith that I know. Alone and desperate, all I had to do was to manage to keep my light burning, just like the *bobo*. Sure I would be disappointed sometimes, lights get dim other times, but the kerosene is a deeper source of energy that reminds the rope to keep its flame alive.

It is the kind of faith that desperate souls in the wilderness hang on to and not sit back *hoping* for someone to make their hopes come alive. This is when we learn that no matter how downcast we are, or in which direction the winds of disappointment blow us; no one will do the heavy lifting for us, but ourselves. The safe haven in the chaos around us may not be in the faces of friends, in the heart of families, or live in the walls of churches and religious temples.

Chapter 15: A Refuge for the Burning Candle

"A Refuge for the Burning Candle" is where we find the hope to expunge our pain and soothe a desperate heart. The often unsaid part of disappointment is the fact that it permeates much more than the outward emotions we exhibit. In the midst of our storms, with no resource to bank on and no recourse to turn to, all I had was a faith to lean on.

The same is true, I believe, for any idea or action we employ as a response. It is very easy to dismiss one disappointing event as a non-issue, and we all do it. It doesn't take much to see how a series of non-issues turns into one of *big issues* for all of us. Not having those things we want, or the failure to accomplish the simplest tasks we hope for is capable of producing further depressive thoughts. That is why I believe that miracles happen to those people who by their actions find the fortitude to put themselves in line for a brighter day, rather than allow displeasure and regret to snowball into overwhelming troubles.

I learned something intriguing from a television show which profiled prison inmates in a California penitentiary. The individuals behind the steel bars shared their stories on what they had done wrong, why they did or did not deserve their sentences, and also what they expected from life behind bars. I particularly never cared much about prison shows, but on this occasion I found something interesting about their outlook.

Two striking observations stood out for these individuals. First, the longer a person was sentenced to live in the penitentiary, the dimmer his view on life outside and the opposite view for his expectations in the jail. For them, adapting to the environment was a no-brainer, no matter how violent or unstable. It didn't take much to notice that the real sentence was the one they had handed themselves in their own outlook. They had defined their options, sealed their fate and thrown the keys away.

The second observation was the words of the repentant convicts and often the newly-arrived inmates to the penitentiary. They hated themselves, hated their actions and would have given anything for a second chance to relive those fateful moments. Life outside the penitentiary was fresh on their minds, so they remembered every bit of it, as well as the freedom they'd just given up.

Some cried, others stared as if in a daze, and the rest slumped into deep thought. All of them saw one thing—the precious moments of time slipping right in front of their eyes. One inmate stared at the camera and reflected, "My biggest fear is that I will get used to this situation."

Throughout this book, I acknowledged that how we deal with the negative events and sentiments are completely independent of what the next person would do, and that is why I cannot offer you any shortcuts. There is no greater mandate than for us to do all that we can do in our power, and let God do what we cannot do. Most importantly, it is critical to not get comfortable in our disappointment.

Like Mark Twain, "Create a monkey if you're disappointed in humans," but there is nothing more dangerous than sitting back drooling into our mishaps and missteps. The real danger, like the inmate summed up, is getting *used to this situation*. Assuming Mark Twain was right, and that God did in fact create a monkey because he was disappointed with mankind, what stops you and me from creating whatever will work for us in order to quash our disappointments? That, for me, was finding a refuge in a faith I knew of.

I can imagine all of us at different points in our lives would have made plans for triumph and envisioned our own *paradise*. I know people who can tell you every detail of their dreams except how they will pay for them. One thing is certain, they are not putting their dreams on hold and counting their disappointments. They are living in spite of them.

The truth is that no matter how lavish or meager our aspirations may be to others, our goals are our own. The disheveled heart will have to dig deeper to find a reason to believe again. It is true that the

Chapter 15: A Refuge for the Burning Candle

smallest *sanctuaries* of hope add huge chunks of confidence to our desire to keep moving on and to try even harder. This is probably a good reason why any setback or deviation from our hopes should not overwhelm our innate ability to overcome it.

Waiting for the pieces to come together before we act on our hope may mean eternity, or in most cases, never. I am confident, however, that we all have the ability to pursue the portions of our dreams that our talents are sufficient for. The interesting part of our life's story is how every disappointment exists even more in our own minds and hearts, than it does outside of them.

I have found that no one really knows what we feel unless we explicitly state our crisis. By that same token, our individual interpretation of the event and the consequent response to it can translate into what was supposed to be a crushing defeat into a life-changing victory. It is no coincidence that we hear over and again that life is 20 percent what happens to us, and 80 percent how we react to it.

A long time ago, I read the words of Charles Spurgeon, "Many men owe the grandeur of their lives to tremendous difficulties." Whether it is in everyday life, our business dealings or our interpersonal relationships, occasionally we are dealt the cards whose chances of winning are slim to none. No predictions, no magic wands, just running against the odds. Let me be first to say that this is no easy position to negotiate from. The cards may have been dealt, sure, but the outcome is still undetermined.

Rather sadly, most of us write our closing chapters even before we turn the first page. I have heard of many people who will argue that disappointments in life are directly related to the level of our expectations. That also, is a perfectly logical argument to make, and even correct in most cases. There may be commonsense truth in that statement, but the potential danger comes when that becomes our barometer for living a fulfilling life. So what if I expect more and don't get it all?

Many times, in searching for a hope to cling to, and a refuge in the midst of our burning candles, logic won't get the job done. Logic adds up the known elements we can conceive and comprehend. Logic does not account for the uncertainty and how the odds could very well be working in our favor. I can bet that any one of us has a much better chance than the next person who didn't hope for much, didn't work for much, and in turn didn't get much.

The poem "A Refuge for the Burning Candle" is a cherished reminder to me and the many people I met over the years that disappointments are a part of the natural cycles of life. What for? I am not exactly sure of the answer, but if we can manage to keep our dreams afloat through our actions, I am confident that we will give ourselves a chance to live a fulfilling life amidst all the chaos.

If Mark Twain was right, God did not halt the creation exercise because of one disappointment; rather He created something other than man. As loony as this quote has always sounded to me, I have in different points in my life had to find the most *ridiculous* responses upon which to build my own fortitude, enlarge my vision, and keep on living. If we had a roadmap for our lives, navigating our paths would be much easier. Maybe we wouldn't have learned anything in the process, and perhaps that is what the storms, the lonely days and the disappointments are all about.

One of my favorite authors, Charles Spurgeon was born in Essex, England, and would later become a late nineteenth-century Baptist preacher, who until his death shared the message of identifying and understanding the woven intricacies of life's subtle messages. I read many of Spurgeon's work over the years, but nothing has stuck to me more than, "Many men owe the grandeur of their lives to tremendous difficulties."

The storms have been many, and the burning candles may have had their share of furious winds from all sides. I am fortunate to have discovered that life can be a roller-coaster event when our individual hopes collide with unexpected reality, but there can be a refuge in the midst of it all. The answer lies in our conscious effort to not curb our hopes, but rather in an active engagement to make our hopes come alive.

Professor Ira Black's recall of Mark Twain's witty remark was his inference to our individual ability to put a positive spin on setbacks and see our lives refined through some of life's grueling fires, which none of us are immune to. Real refuge is not slapping a band-aid on our heartaches, or temporary numbing of the pain, but the giving of courage to try again.

As you read this book, I will imagine that you will form your own opinions about every one of my stories and subtle messages, and I expect you to. I believe that our individual values have a unique way of either bolstering our personal filtering network, or finding the connections from one person's life to our own.

With every crippling defeat that has inspired me to write "A Refuge for the Burning Candle," I use my life stories as a very modest invitation into an experience I have termed *re-constructive thinking*. There probably are no speedy remedies for our disappointing moments, but once we learn to deconstruct our instinctive responses to them, only then can we possibly begin to make sense of them and move on with our fulfilling lives.

Griping and grumbling about our setbacks hardly cure any heavy burden caused by our frustrations. I have never been fond of living in that mindset that "Life is like a box of chocolates, you never know what you're gonna get."

I won't know how every waking moment will play out, but I am not content with sitting back and letting every aspect of life hit me like a brick from unexpected angles. I am sure that all of us can deal with surprise tastes in boxes of chocolates sometimes, but none of us can afford to live our lives completely oblivious of what it takes to prepare for our next turn.

I remember a conversation with a group of friends one Sunday afternoon. One of them described himself as staunchly spiritual, and not too long ago, had lost his mother to ovarian cancer. He was mad at the world, disappointed with God and fuming at everyone else. I reasoned he had every reason to be angry. Two of his friends had different opinions however. One of them suggested that he should never be angry with God, while the other passionately disagreed. Both asked what I thought about the matter.

"Do whatever makes it easier to move on with life," I said. I admit to knowing a lot of things, but knowing what God is thinking isn't one of them. I don't know the right answer for a man whose heart is heavy with a loss and not sure if it was worth the effort to keep his hope and faith. The two friends burst out, "Never mind, he is one of those positive thinkers." I should have expressed my appreciation at that remark because there is absolutely nothing wrong with *thinking positive,* especially when a disappointing event is become a roadblock to our moving on in life.

Anytime I tell this story, I am quick to add, that my friends certainly were not *negative people,* neither were they any less insightful than my *positive friends*. In finding out our individual differences of opinion, one fact is paramount. It is possible that the life ideas that have been of remarkable help to many people unfortunately may not mean anything to you and me. That also is perfectly fine.

Although the stories may be different, I am confident that we can all take a page from each other's play book and learn from them. Ultimately we have the task of dusting ourselves off and moving again, irrespective of how crushing the blow has been.

I am cognizant of the fact that some of us dislike the arduous task of living through the bumps in our roads. The first impediment is the last one we would ever want to see. Unfortunately we will continue to hit the bumps in the road, continue to make our mistakes, and have to manage to use them as valuable learning points towards a future.

English novelist Jane Austen once advised her readers that there will be little rubs and disappointments everywhere, and if one scheme of happiness fails, human nature turns to another, thereby finding comfort somewhere else. That *"somewhere"* begins in our decision to not stop living.

It is finding a window to jump through when all the doors to our hopes are shut close. It is what we do next after we have spent all the night praying, and hoping, crying and wishing. If only we can fit our personal circumstances into the same framework of relative impermanence, that not everything lasts forever, we will learn to live in the moment the problems we shoulder will seem lighter.

Every thought in "A Refuge for the Burning Candle" is a constructive reception of the ever-changing moments, which has the tremendous capability to redefine our anticipation for tomorrow. If today is not what it should have been for us, there are many more *todays* that lie ahead, any of which can bring the change that we yearn for.

Think about this for a moment—just as we cannot sneeze with our eyes opened, or lick our own elbows, we cannot waste precious time on the things our human nature is not designed to do.

Our perpetual despair about events that have disappointed our life's goals and ambitions will not change a thing. Somewhere in the thick cloud is a rainbow, the *change* to *erase* our *stormy* days. We can all find comfort in the timeless wisdom in the poem "Footprints"— that the moment when we looked back and saw only one set of footprints in the sand, that was when God carried us the rest of the way.

A Refuge for the Burning Candle

1 The sharp edge of change pierces harder
When the troubles in today
And everything else a blur
Change itself is changing fast
5 The shuffle of seconds in blazing speed
And still not a stripe to prove my worth in war.
A sense of time,
No reason to fret
Spilled the vague and hope unsure
10 And the feelings in a gut bleeding pain.
The times will change, for this I'll pray
I will soon be the friend I seek
A scuffle and bruises for wasted moments
But time precious
15 Never gone for naught.
I am rising past the sharpest edge
My hope cut through the morning storm
Through mystery's slashes in tattered faith.
I was dampened dull but bright again
20 In a changing day that I'd pay with hurt
Tomorrow's long,
But awake still I'll be
Engraved in beauty and time
Taking refuge through the storm.

16

SIDEWALK

A well-liked saying that most of us are familiar with is that "A journey of a thousand miles begins with a single step." As clichéd as it may seem to many of us, it is nonetheless no farther from the truth. The meaning wouldn't take much to decipher. The saying did not add a caveat that warned —"Except on the sidewalk." Even there, it still begins with the step.

One evening over a random dinner conversation, I made reference to the thousand miles statement in that, the most important thing is to be repeatedly taking a step, moving. In a general sense, that doesn't seem too difficult to accomplish. My friend Marc thought of something in response. He put his fork down, smiled and said, "You realize also, that a journey to nowhere also begins with a step."

We both laughed over the plain but powerful thought, and took turns sharing our personal experiences on to what extent the idea resonates with many different stories we knew of. One common and fundamental flaw in our understanding is that we make progress by virtue of an action. The misconception often expressed is that we tend to equate an activity with automatic improvement. It does not work quite that simply.

I often thought about a trip along the famous Mount Everest, the highest mountain on Earth, with a height of about thirty thousand feet above sea level. Mountain climbers from all over the world take turns in enduring physical activity for many days and weeks just to get to the mountain's top. They push themselves beyond their physical and mental limits so that they can look back someday as being among the few people to reach the summit.

None of the climbers will tell you that every step is of the same value. That I believe, just as in my friend Marc's response, certainly a step forward is remarkably different from a step backward.

I have read about how Mount Everest is often believed not to create considerable technical climbing difficulty on the standard route, but the many inherent dangers such as altitude sickness, weather and wind are what make it a climbing feat. In spite of all this, the climbers keep on moving. I imagined to myself that halfway through the journey, if a climber decided to retreat, it would take another substantial effort just to descend.

Like mountain climbers on an upward slope, our life's journey often increases in the level of difficulty as we gradually mature in some aspect of life. The tired hands and the weary feet are no excuse to turn back halfway into the sky. What is most important is moving forward.

The poem "Sidewalk" is a reminder that the same universal rule applies in all of life's journeys, even beyond the highest mountains, and our most challenging adversities. A mental image of anything we set our minds on begins the difficult climb, but it is only through those images that our steps will begin to make sense to us. On many occasions through my own troubles, I had found that having an outline and path to how we get to our destination is critical to whether or not the process survives.

The proverbial *sidewalk* is not the path of least resistance, but rather a path next to the main lanes that ensures that we are still pressing forward and trudging along. Many statistics and researchers have well-documented facts on how many individual goals are accomplished once we are able to translate a mental picture into a realistic outline. Our concerns become key deciding factors in every action. Like the mountain climber, if any map can show us how far we have come, and how close we are to the summit, no reason under the sun will be good enough to cause us to start sliding backwards.

It would not make much sense for a mountain climber to give up twenty-thousand feet into the climb, in spite of the daunting physical conditions the rest of the way. I am sure of this also, that for those who persevere, reaching the summit makes sense of the entire ordeal and they are even more appreciative of their most difficult strides.

Another interesting premise to the poem "Sidewalk" is a question I wondered about, that after a person reaches the summit of the tallest mountain, *what next?* Surely the satisfaction will not end upon taking pictures atop of a mountain. True, but even more powerful is that the accomplishment teaches the mountain climber that anything is attainable. Isn't it interesting that the same individuals who make it through one challenge find another to overcome?

In our individual lives, and along our own unique paths, the tasks may be exhausting, uncomfortable and even seemingly not worth the pain. For the man who travelled on the sidewalks instead of resorting to the comfort of the main lanes, his satisfaction will reside in the fact that no matter what events pushed him off the main tracks, he did not give up. For the mountain climber, the sense of accomplishment makes the thirty-thousand foot journey worthwhile.

I believe that if we have managed a trip this far, looking down or looking back at the *grassy fields* where we once stood would not do us much good. Our lives should not stop when we believe we have gone as far and high as we can go, because until the day that we no longer can breathe, all of us will have to rid ourselves of the self-defeating distractions and keep stepping forward.

It is just as important to identify the distracting obstacles as it is to overcome them, because no one made it atop Mount Everest without sweat and many excruciating memories. I live in the hope that our lives' most fulfilling rewards sit behind our daily struggles and our tedious climb along a never-ending slope.

I learned early on in my own life that the obstacles in life are very different depending on which direction we are heading. Even those of us who browse through life casually and clueless, may find ourselves with some bumpy hills to overcome, except that they may not amount to much unless they force us to make some progress. The harsh truth is that sometimes, whether or not we are moving at all may be clouded by the fact that we may have been stuck at the same place for a long period of time, thus confusing aimless movements with advancement.

As I recalled my own life's events and the many nights when I wondered why I was unable to pursue the "main lane" desires which many of my colleagues did, something intriguing came to mind. There are no consolation prizes for the many people who set out to reach the mountain tops, but never do.

Ten years from today, no one will feel sorry for you because your journey took wider turns. Those who stretched themselves to keep moving one step at a time can peacefully rest in the fact that they gave it their best effort. I believe that there is a lot of real work involved in our daily existence, *just being there* and breathing is no security deposit for a rewarding life.

Chapter 16: Sidewalk

Somehow we all manage to convince ourselves that there were no good reasons for pushing harder, and effectively crash our own confidence even before step one. It is no wonder that in our moments of frustration we start taking steps backwards, unlike the mountain climber who hangs on the edge of the cliff, catches his breath and keep his eyes on the summit ahead. The difference is that he recognizes that he has made a twenty thousand foot trip, and cannot afford to go back down empty-handed.

Over dinner, I listened to a friend share her disappointing marital story. Ten years of personal investment had come down to naught. Even after years of emotional drain in the relationship, she had been hesitant to call it quits. Soon she had developed health problems relating to depression and anxiety, and she was on a medical freefall. As we talked that evening, she described how she would often feel like a heavy load was weighing her down, with every step being harder than the one before.

During one of her medical screenings, a doctor who was almost certain that her problem had a root cause beyond the medicinal origins, asked if she cared to talk about her personal life. Her doctor listened very carefully and with a gentle grin. Halfway through her story, the doctor almost playfully began to rip the prescription form into little pieces. My friend stopped talking and asked, "Why did you do that?"

Her doctor smiled, "You don't need this. Your only problem is that you are piling on diseases with your decisions, and no amount of medication can make you well." She told the story of the doctor saying, "It's not your health that is in jeopardy, your life is heading downhill *because you are allowing it to.*" It took several months of conversations with herself, replaying the words of the doctor as she sat in the consultation room.

Out of nowhere, she would have a random thought regarding her choices, her situations and the consequent stress. Then something else rang in her mind, a bible quote she didn't even know she could remember. *"Lay aside every weight, throwing away all that so easily entangles us, and keep running with endurance the race before us."*

In that moment, the quote had every meaning, as it had been as a religious message several years before. My friend would be quick to remind anyone of how non-religious she was, but in that *blank-thought* moment, she knew that the weight that entangled her was the everyday decisions and negative consequences which strapped her into positions she never imagined would be. She was allowing her life to disintegrate before her own eyes, and worst of all, she had every power to avert its course.

My friend's turnaround would start from a bold decision to take charge of her own life by ridding herself of the pile of weight in which she was bogged down. I contend that she probably would have been in the same position ten years later if everyone around her had told her she needed medication.

The essence of her story was not to belittle the challenge of enduring a rocky marriage; instead it was about how she labeled the events in her own life. A wrong label to a prescription is a recipe for disaster, so it's vital that we recognize, i.e., correctly label the snowball effects of our actions or inactions. The moment we fail to properly identify the pieces which make us perform a task, behave a certain way or exhibit certain reactions, we may very well be moving, except in the wrong direction.

Unless we make a conscientious effort to rid ourselves of the erroneous *"It is what it is"* approach that justifies our retreat, it may take a lifetime for us to find that we have been making some progress in our daily lives, except it had not been in the right direction.

The people who travel past incredible odds and find reasons out of nowhere to persevere manage to envision the rewards on the *sidewalk*. For them, it is not enough to just pace through life when they could be forging ahead and making strides with every small step. Whatever it is that we seek in life or hope for, nothing kills our enthusiasm quicker than living another day in hyper-diligence and hyper-vigilance, but with nothing to show for it.

I remember in college, I had friends who just could not wait for graduation day. Their mind was so fixed on leaving school that they forgot all about being in school. Their least concern was grades, whether they went to school or stayed at home, or anything involving the rigorous school work. There was nothing more interesting than how for them, every assignment was the one they could do without and still graduate.

As expected, they all made it to the finish line just like anyone else, but one such person would be the first to admit that a mediocre outlook did not pay quite the same dividends as our best effort. In my friend's own words, she wished she could have tried just a little harder instead of standing at the end wondering how fulfilling life could have been.

It is true that a journey of a thousand miles does begin with one step, and it happens to be one of those universal truths that none of us can argue. In much the same way, climbing life's tallest mountains requires the unequivocal understanding of what the goal is, as it is in running the longest distance, and taking a first step.

I shared a story of former South African president Nelson Mandela with a group of high school students. After twenty-seven years in prison in Robben Island, Mandela became president of South Africa, not because of where he had been, but rather who he became as a result of being there. He had spent all his life as an anti-apartheid activist and sacrificed his life for it even when he had no idea when his freedom would come, or if indeed it ever would.

After his release, Mandela advocated a policy of *reconciliation and negotiation*, which helped lead the transition to multi-racial democracy in a previously divided South Africa. One of the most inspiring underpinnings of his determination was how much the oppressive status quo and the social obstacles along his path didn't sway him to backpedal. He pursued a diligent course.

People like Nelson Mandela faced adversity with dignity and still managed to make every one of their steps a remarkable memory. It is the same as how the words and thoughts we conceive especially when we are trudging along the *sidewalk* have enormous potential to either move us closer to or farther from our goal. The simple logic is that affirmative thoughts give us the extra impetus to a more fulfilling life when the climb gets unbearable.

Sure, not all of us may have the same motivations as people like Mandela, or can manage to catch our breath living through one challenge after another. I have learned that the option to run through life looking forward and fighting onward prevents our having to make strides leading *nowhere*, only to realize our negative progression further down the line. None of us want to cruise through life in a boatload of *missteps* but sometimes life will throw us off our comfortable and ideal path, and sit us on the sidewalks, and challenge us to keep moving.

I like to think that sometimes we make our lives much more complicated than they ought to be in the first place. A phrase often thrown around very easily is, "You have the power to change your life," but we all do. With one step after another and a conscientious effort to live a more fulfilling life, we can redirect our energies into activities that build, rather than break us. There is plenty of evidence around us pointing to the fact that how far we are able to travel has every bearing on how much superfluous weight we allow to *oppress* us.

If life is indeed a journey, it is hard enough going through it trouble free, let alone with heaps of problems, distress, discontent, resentment, hatred, frustration and unresolved failures. In some of my most difficult moments, I learned to shake off as much of the mental weight as possible, no matter how small.

Chapter 16: Sidewalk

This principle is no different from the advice the financial guru gives people on getting out of financial debt. For instance, even the most knowledgeable financial planner is quick to remind his client that nothing in his suggestions are magical.

Relieving oneself of the unnecessary load is more commonsense than it is scientific. A so-called financial guru's first suggestion is always to get rid of the little debts which are almost insignificant, yet very consequential. As you would imagine, the smallest unpaid debts are just as significant deadweights as the larger ones. The guru will tell you that the elimination of the little debts restores self-confidence, which in turn happens to be the crucial element to facing the larger debts.

This reasoning is far from novel, and certainly nothing magical. Often we experience it in our everyday lives, unaware of how much a relief from one drawback pushes us a little farther. No amount of prescription drugs can propel us any faster than our own decision to affect an aspect of our lives. The only tried and tested formula is to keep moving on, beginning with one step. There are probable outcomes in every action and the best reward we can give ourselves is to focus our attention on how we can shift the advantage to our side.

Just as there is ample opportunity to fail, there is an equal probability that we can all succeed at whatever we choose to. Problem is, we place the wrong labels and wrong emphasis on the wrong attitudes. Sure, we may be travelling on a thornier and more uncomfortable *sidewalk*, but some of us often are stuck in familiar territory, tied down in the weight and pain of mediocrity, rather than venturing onto unfamiliar grounds, to take our chances.

There is nothing more important in life than having our thoughts and actions in sync. I write extensively in other chapters, that not only does that help in appreciating the ultimate destination we seek to reach, but our ability to visualize the result is the only way we can truly appreciate the *why* we perform any action.

The seemingly difficult steps should have a lot more practical significance to us. Our life's hurdles, the tallest mountains, may well be over thirty-thousand feet, but a simple step to the fore is exactly what it will take to make any kind of advancement, no matter how small.

Our journey along the *sidewalk* is but a step at a time. One day, I am confident that we will all be able to afford to look back at every moment, no matter how thorny it seemed at first, and appreciate our sacrifices, as we stand thirty-thousand feet into the sky, and thirty-thousand miles into our destiny.

Sidewalk

1   So heavy a pound on a happy soul
    How did I get here?
    The tip of victory from soaring high
    Weight after weight is my trip and splash in a valley
5   Changing the tide in plunging drops
    Now my joy is letting go
    And living here, on a sidewalk.
    The giant in open fields of green
    Is tiny still from above, even in the winter snow.
10 The valleys are dark
    The paved concrete is no ease to footsteps
    Yet the flowers will bloom
    Like the hearts that sail the odds of wither
    Mountaintop is far
15 The beauty of a cloud is a traveler's friend.
    Rocky climbs in steps and blocks and chunks of ice
    Frozen feet through the cracks of time.
    Up I go in open earth,
    From dry valleys to slippery peaks
20 Day after day in my crying skin.
    The gift of a mile is posh with filth
    Heavy and dirty, feels like hell
    Of streaks of tears and cricks within
    Into butterflies, someday my soul will fly.
25 The sad instant's gone with the wind
    The foe of the faith trapped by resolute soul.
    I am here at the shoulder of lasting turns
    The end of a struggle at a man's core
    Like the blooming buds of moments before

30 The pace was mine, the frozen feet too
     The steps of burly giants
     Carve resting hopes on slippery slopes.
     I walked in open fields
     Past wooden fences in valley's deep
35 Below is far from mountain's top
     The lasting calm of soaring on
     Is high with God,
     Next in line to the rising sky.
     The distant is far, below in green
40 One more mile, another clasp
     My soaring soul be home
     My soul will be home.

THE COLOR OF DREAMS

When I first learned about how an aircraft navigates its journey, I wondered how many people would comfortably ride on an airplane if they knew the widely publicized reality of *course correction*. The very complex action of a plane cruising through the air involves having to balance its course, and to repeatedly bring itself in line. The plane veers to the left and to the right constantly, a fact only the pilot knows of. The path through space deals with many factors ranging from individual pilot skills, to wind force and the direction itself.

One such example is how thunderstorms and thunderclouds abound in the sky, and could be extremely dangerous to an airplane. The presence of rain-forming clouds cumulonimbus for instance, signals to a pilot to avoid them at all costs. My guess is that a heavy cloud presence would require having to take an entirely different route opposed to what the initial plan was. By that same deduction, a pilot wanting to risk flying through that cloudy obstacle will probably be just as clever as a *Titanic* ship captain determined to sail through an iceberg.

"The Color of Dreams" reflects on my own difficulty in finding balance in life, and a clear path sometimes. I believe that for most of us, our struggle is to find the perfect sense of balance, just the right thing to do, and the magic combination to discover our life's meaning. For that reason, the gaps we feel in our own lives are the direct result of veering from one lane to another and from one ambition to the other.

In the absence of the clarity we seek, we are willing to do anything to get anywhere, as long as it offers some gratifying perspective. These spinning elements of life, and our attempt to make sense of our endeavors, make our simplest days complex. Like the plane in the air, the unanticipated natural barriers and the wind force make it imperative for pilots to continually adjust in the course of the flight. In aviation, the repeated changes to the initial and ideal track are known as *course correction*.

As I mentioned before, airline passengers are seldom aware of this subtle deviation because the plane eventually reaches its destination, in what our minds interpret to be somewhat of a linear path. In any event, I believe that what matters most is that the airplane comes back on its original track regardless of how many times it veers off its course. What is your guiding benchmark for staying on course?

The semblance of this pattern to our own life's journey is twofold. First, the same pressures that a plane in flight has to succumb to or overcome, are much like what we encounter as we march through our individual life's ambitions. As a result, finding the sense of balance to *stay on course* will demand a harmonious coexistence of our minds with our fundamentally deep-seated beliefs.

Chapter 17: The Color of Dreams

Second and more poignant, is that of our roles as the pilots of our own flights. The pilot metaphor elicits an image of our hands on the steering control units, our eyes fixed on what lies ahead, and our hope to reach a certain destination no matter what unexpected barriers and hurdles fall in our path.

It is amazing the creative ideas we all feed ourselves to rationalize actions, but none of them come to mind when we need to *psyche* ourselves to overcome a hurdle. Most of us would agree that in many aspects of our lives, our health and happiness are too valuable to leave to chance. That which guides us to psyche ourselves is a belief and faith upon which we have planted our hopes.

As opposed to impulsive decisions, carefully listening to our intuitions is key to a life beyond passively marching to any tune and drifting along. Over the years, I learned how much we are all running different races, and live within very unique frames, in spite of how similar our dreams and passions may be to others'.

Navigating our paths is ultimately an individual exercise. From my own experiences, we forget sometimes that life is not a dress rehearsal, and if we are to sit around and live our lives in the future tense, we may never make complete use of the opportunities in the present.

Like most people, I had my long list of personal misfortunes and gradually, the weight of the tons of distress took its toll. My only hope for making any progress and saving myself from the emotional tailspin was to think of myself as the baseball player who never forgets that he can always return to *home base*.

Maybe one day we will all get that dream job we have been working hard for, or buy that dream house or car we have been planning for, or travel the universe, or do whatever it is that we set our hearts to accomplish. "The Color of Dreams" is in knowing that postponing our lives until that happens will not make those dreams come true any sooner. Sitting around in search of clarity and waiting for life to happen to us is not failure-proof.

There is a tale of a man who decided to stay inside his house forever for fear of his own safety. He believed that there was too much chaos in the world and too many things that could possibly go wrong on the world outside, so he locked himself in his house. One day the wind blew the shingles off his roof, and the rest of the ceiling caved in. He died.

The point is, had the man known that he would die anyway, I bet he would have given himself a reason to step out and take a chance. Rather than fold in our little corner and wait for a rescue mission, we may have to sometimes dig deeper, and trust in our inner guiding force to continue directing us to stay on course.

We are not cats, and none of us certainly have nine lives; disaster can find us wherever we hide and exercising caution should not be the same as a fear of taking action. We are in control of every aspect of our lives and no one else can make that choice for us. Whether we decide to live a gratifying life or simply exist and inertly roam through life is an individual preference.

Whatever the *color of your dreams,* there is no better time than now to begin any adventure, regardless of the baggage from yesterday and the experience we have today. The decision to step out on my faith and act out my dream started when I embraced the fact that I was not the victim of a bad script, and the sooner I dusted my tears off and started living, the sooner I would reach my destination. Whatever the nature of my baggage, there was no one coming to my rescue anytime soon, but rather I had been equipped with enough grace to ride through tumultuous times, and come back on track even if I should swerve off my course.

As effortless as it may sound, I would reiterate that the process begins in our mind, and you and I are the majority stakeholders in this investment. The resources around us and the people in our lives

Chapter 17: The Color of Dreams

only serve as tools towards this path, if only we pursue life with a purpose. One thing is certain, if at the end of the day I am unable to use my talents and follow the inner desire of my life, no reason or excuse will suffice, and the justifications will not redeem lost time.

From the airplane analogy, one thing I have found out as a critical difference, however, is that while the pilot in a plane is aware of *course correction* and has made provision for any such deviations, most of us have no idea of this phenomenon in our own lives. "The Color of Dreams" is about how our living in constant reactionary mode can throw us off-track farther and farther away from our intended plan for our lives.

Life is filled with many reactionary demands, and many problems which over time could push us so far off our intended course that we soon forget what our initial starting point looked like. Irrespective of the wrong turns that we may have made in our own lives, I contend that what matters at the end of the day, like the carefully prepared pilot, is to know when and how to *course correct* back on track.

Throughout this book, I am certain that the scope of my story is no different from most of yours, at least in the meaning we deduce from them. Somewhere along the way, some of us strayed from the many things we once believed for our lives and depreciated our once beautiful ambitions. In my own life, I grew up in neighborhoods that I no longer enjoyed living in as I grew older. I had made friends who were not adding any value to my life. I had cluttered my life with habits and attitudes which were not helping me in any way, but rather piling on extra dead weight. No wonder I was stressed out, burned out, and washed out in more ways than one.

One of the most colorful turns of events in American political history would be the day a man in the highest office of the country found himself having to answer difficult questions in front of a nation. It is heartbreaking to imagine such an influential man standing in front of his wife and family and being forced to relive the consequences of his indecisions every time the television news came on. Here he was, President of the United States, caught in a sex scandal that would give any journalist seeking his downfall a field day with the headlines.

For a split second, we can forget that the most influential people in the world have the same blood running through their veins as we do, and that power they wield does not make them immune to the pitfalls we all have to be on the lookout for. I imagined how he got to that moment—a decision to compromise one moral action after another. I can only imagine that something that had probably begun with a thought, left unchecked, had become the biggest scar of his career and life. It must have not happened suddenly and overnight. He must have had plenty of opportunities to right the emotional slip. After all he was the most powerful man in the world, with several people watching his every move. Didn't he at least have one person who stood next to him and who probably could have pinched him in the moments he was making a wrong turn? I cannot imagine that a man of his stature who fully knew the impact his actions would have on his family and his position, would throw everything away for a moment of pleasure. Many years later, it is hard to imagine someone would do so, yet it happened.

And it happens every day in our own lives, too. Maybe our moments of questions, actions and decisions may not earn a front page tabloid headline, but in our lives, they misalign us just enough that it probably seems insignificant. Just as little drops of water someday fill a bucket, sooner or later the little wrong turns will have shifted us so far from our true center that if we are not careful, we may not even recall where we started from. Taking stock of the seemingly most inconsequential things is the only way we would know how far we have veered off the path we are supposed to be on. For President Bill Clinton, the challenge for the rest of his life will be coming back to a point where his own internal compass will be

Chapter 17: The Color of Dreams

in tune with the self-image he has created. He will have to pick the pieces of his shattered reputation and patch them together one day after another and one event after another.

Looking back at my own walk through the years and the myriad of choices I have made thus far, I believe there is a greater propensity to invest valuable time and energy in avenues that we should instead avoid. I recall the many years when I worked in jobs that I hated from the very first day I signed on.

We all do what is necessary for our survival, but unless we set parameters of how far we are willing to bend over or how low we are willing to stoop, it would take a lifetime to discover how much of our actions have been futile, at best. A candid conversation with our own selves may help expose our Achilles' heels, and those thoughts and attitudes which made us drift away in the first place. There are many such points in my own life, all of which I consider deviations from what had become my core value system and my objective for living.

It is a never-ending struggle reshaping and redirecting our genuine ambitions every step along the way. All these pieces, however, become a valuable resource for finding wholeness and a sense of fulfillment in life. "The Color of Dreams" does not have any shortcuts to simplify our lives or direct them towards any steadiness in our endeavors.

Rather, they are the colors we paint for ourselves. That is a job which each of us will have to do on our own. I am sure that when we take honest stock of our own lives, we engage in the most powerful dialogue with our true selves into the life we want. There is no greater truth than this: we know ourselves better than anyone else, and I will assume that we know when we are off track sooner than anyone else.

Often, we are fortunate to have other people help us in that discovery, when we are too drowned by our troubles to stay on course. The key to knowing whether we are on or off course and have drifted off our original path has absolutely everything to with our *knowing where we are going*. When the lanes of life are spinning around us, and we find ourselves in panic mode, unsure of where to turn, how high or far we go depends on this awareness, and it is that mental map that guides us back on to the right tracks.

Years ago I had a colleague who will argue to his death bed that the words *passion, mission, purpose* and *vision* were essentially the same thing, and distinguished as merely a play on words. This conviction simplified a significant portion of life for him, which is certainly a good thing. For most of us however, I will imagine it is not that simple. I never bothered to challenge his technical mastery of grammar, but I was sure that any one or all four words were essential to living a fulfilling life.

What exactly is it that I wanted to do with my life? I thought to myself that of all the things I have done in my life, if only I can carefully reposition every single one of them, it may then be easier to weigh my relative enthusiasm for all of them. My guess is that most of us have bounced around in different lanes, some of which we have no control over. Finding our passion is often not one of the easiest exercises in the world.

The remarkable task of fine-tuning our own sense of purpose is how we keep our hope alive and come back to *center*. Every new day is our opportunity for *course correction*, and it is my hope that we can go through our days sentient of how our presence at any moment creates a kind of magnetic field that affects our ability to stay with our dreams.

As we interact and move through life, a rather understated dimension exists to this concept. The exchange with each of the people we come across also has the energy to build us up and keep us on track. They also have every potential to shove us off our paths, either with an alluring idea, or even well-meaning suggestions.

I have learned that it is important to understand the value of our associations and the relationships we form, in that hopefully our innate sensors will alert us when we cruise away from our own goals. I believe also that we cannot *course correct* if we are completely oblivious to when we have veered. Our actions ought to have some purpose, for the art of living itself is a balancing act.

With every hurdle, I have forced myself to keep the spotlight on the hope which has inspired me to have come this far. For many months and years, I had several conversations with myself as I would in any other exchange with another person. Inasmuch as none of us are immune to life's countless stumbling blocks, we fear the possibility of missing our mark in the "cloudy" world of unpredictable events. "The Color of Dreams" is a challenge to use our own values and value system as the guiding platform upon which we make our daily choices.

Two years after the talk with my colleague, the crux of the words *passion, mission, purpose* and *vision* had changed from being a play on words, to their being entirely different points on a linear map to accomplish a task. He explained that the words may mean different things for different people, but by his own admission, after a series of wrong turns, he had learned to follow his intuitive desires, which he called *passion*, and now was on a *mission* to accomplish something he called a *vision*.

It is impossible to overstate that assigning meanings to words is a tricky deal. One of the most pertinent life lessons for me was that the implicit and explicit definitive values which guide our lives are actual tools that can channel our every action to a destination. Our mission in turn becomes the tangible hook that arises out of our having a clear purpose. Even if we have made the wrong choices at some point, having that sense of purpose is enough to redirect us back to the *straight line* we ought to be traveling on.

There is a desire in all of our hearts today for a fresh start and a new beginning. Yours could be a new venture, a crazy adventure, a healthy lifestyle and relationship, a selfless act, or a bigger self-image. The harsh winds we confront could very well be our self-engineered prototype that results from our individual choices, all of which has the power to change the course of our own future.

There is no excuse good enough to derail you from doing what you know in your heart to do. If you believe there is no way out of your current situation, you are definitely right; there will never be a way out. There is an overused saying, "Where there is a will, there is a way." There is a reason why it has been around for so long. It is very true, and it is our resolve that guides us to confront the barriers, and keep moving on.

As I wrote "The Color of Dreams," I thought of all the many dreams and hopes that I let die because I could not see past the dense fog to the bright spot on the other side. I remembered the many ambitions that I had successfully watch drift away. I remembered how my faith had waned and I had talked myself out of my passions.

Whether we choose to be happy or sad, win or lose and live or die, is all a personal choice. The only prescription worth any result is in our own minds. At the end of our journey, we look back at all the thorny moments and realize how much of who we are, is who we thought we were. If only we can have a *guiding light* and a point of reference for *course correction*, even the most difficult challenges may become the nuggets of wisdom we can cherish somewhere along the way.

The premise of a triumphant existence revolves around a constant examination, reexamination, and the discipline to stick to our decisions. In case you are wondering, I do not assume such a reflective exercise is trouble-free. Of course not! Otherwise everyone would have done it with little effort. It takes an undying sense of determination to come back to *home base*, to rebalance, and to reach our desired goals.

There is a philosophy underlying everything we do, whether we recognize it or not. I believe that it is very crucial for us to be mindful of the *little veers* and seemingly inconsequential compromises we make to our dreams, because over time that is who we become. There is always a tendency for "The Color of Dreams" to change, but it is that honest appraisal of our efforts that keeps us on course, no matter what personal narrative we tell ourselves, or whatever fancy rhetoric we make up to justify our choices.

I challenge all of us to live alert, and be mindful of the fact that the stakes in our lives are high, and that we possess every opportunity in every waking moment to make every day count. It is our responsibility to be honest with ourselves in spite of how much our values are challenged or our faith is rattled. I am confident that it is through this logic that we are able to make what I often call *'now decisions'* with a true sense of how they fit in a bigger context.

The Color of Dreams

1 If I fall before the sun will fall
   My eyes were filled with blinding rays.
   If my perfect world leans away
   Must have taken thirty years
5 And shade more to fall asleep.
   Life spins right around in blustery motions
   And desire is warped in a fainting man
   How far wide is too far
   When color is all faded pale?
10 When all doors made of bars and steel stay shut
   And signs of life come with mounds and hills
   The color of self is painted in strength
   With reels and reels of sacred prayers
   Backwashed into ponds of derailed dreams.
15 How many clouds can fill my lane?
   The whirling sound and or my dizzy dream
   In the same unsure skies where my faith found a way.
   If I'm a miracle
   I'm not who I am
20 I am lost in a resolute sky
   A future with no grace and face
   And the woozy feel killing my feet
   Spill malignant fears of my father
   Into a vacuum and now the sun in my eyes.
25 I am center here
   My mind locked in circles of different shades
   Falling in my dreams to live in perfect color.
   The sound of a song will fill my world
   My dream leads me through the windy sky

30 To a lane in line in perfect swirls
     In brighter colors and brightest memories
     Nothing is golden
     When gold is turned to stone
     All the things that never die
35 My wishes are two more steps away from them all.
     Until the sun breaks in my watery eyes
     To see dreams the same as were before
     When desire had no end
     And fear had no home
40 And too late never lived
     And dream before the blinding rays
     And just before awake in a trail of joy.

SMILES AND CRIES

One of life's simplest acts that we soon forget how to do is to cry. Even when the pressure from every side is heavy with pain and one tumultuous day flows into another, maybe the tears we hold back needed to run down our cheeks. Once we had all been babies and crying was the only language we knew. It was easy then. As we grow and navigate our way through life, shedding a tear becomes one of the most difficult things to do and the restlessness that comes with dealing with discomfort and frustration finds its way into every area of our life. Because every inch of our being does its best to become an antidote to our tears, we muster the courage to stand, and very seldom deal with the pain as constructively as we could.

There is nothing more central than to live with integrity with our feelings. It is acceptable to shed a tear. It is acceptable for a person's heart to be heavy, and filled with tears. The lesson I have learned through it all is that even when our smiles turn into cries, we cry with a hope. In doing so, maybe we can afford to hold our head high with a God-given courage, and by allowing our hearts to drain themselves of the heaviness, to be better even in disappointment.

In the long seasons of our lives when we have almost nothing to cling to, and the outcome of our days is much different from what we have planned or imagined, we ought to let that strength in the small victories we have lived through provide the affirmations for the days ahead. When it seems like our entire world is ripped into shreds, we cannot remain stuck in the grief and disappointment, because even in that frustration and anger in the cry, we may very well be at the cusp of one of our brightest moments.

As a little boy, I had been curious to understand the atmospheric glitch that caused a sunny day with heavy rain coming down from the still blue skies. In my childish mind, I thought that was unusual but never ascribed any myths or legends to it.

Years later, a friend told a story that had been told to her while she was a little girl halfway across the world. Someone had told her that when the sun was shining while it rained, it meant that the *devil was beating up his wife*. To this day I cannot quite make the logical connection among the sun, the rain and the devil, but it makes for a fascinating tale for little children nonetheless.

Not long ago, as this thought crossed my mind, I thought of something much simpler but essential to our everyday lives. I imagined for a moment the significance of the *sun* to our lives, as a symbol of the triumphs, the many successes and the joyfulness. The *rain* may very well be symbolic of the hurting moments, the disappointing spoils and the heartaches we all live with. The simple event of the rain and sun seemed to be a subtle welcome of our human nature to whatever came down from the *sky* above.

Chapter 18: Smiles and Cries

The imagery of these natural elements in our lives is fairly simple. Sometimes the sun will shine and with that come the blissful days and the many *smiles*. There may be other days where our heart will be laden with heaviness, and the rain will have poured on our peace, washed away our hopes and left us with many *cries*. The poem "Smiles and Cries" is my reflection on life, that in our perfect world, all of us would like the rainy days to give way to the sunny moments, and let the bright dazzling days last forever.

Unfortunately for most of us, we have seen the heavy days and the joyful times appear in the same moment *drenched and wet in the shining sun*. Our constant worry may become too overpowering for us to acknowledge the presence of a *silver lining*, a shining sun. Our *sun* and *rain* moments will give birth to our *smiles* and *cries*. Then, I thought also about all the different points in our lives when most of us will find that the people and the events that made us smile coincidentally have become the authors of our tears.

I found that it is in these moments that we learn through our own resilience that the same *umbrella* saving us from the drenched day could very well be providing the shade from the shining sun. In my own experience, and those of many people I met, what is astounding is how our cries create a sort of defensive shield by molding our character in such a way that we are unable to see our *sun shining* when its moment arrives.

Truth is, in our attempt to adapt to the complicated and thorny moments of our lives, we are pushed into a mental corner and barricaded by our own actions in response. My fear has always been that such a condition could make it almost impossible to understand that we still have the potential to *swim upstream,* no matter how far down the heavy rains have pushed us. For this reason, I would learn to take some comfort in the truism that "April showers" in turn, bring "May flowers."

Often, when our hearts are filled with tears and we are stuck on the ropes of uncertainty, it is difficult to find a reason to be hopeful again. All of us can only afford a *smile* after we decide to make the most of our scanty resources, acknowledge where we are and be determined to seize every moment. If indeed our "Smiles and Cries" pour down from the same sky, it is not completely irrational for us to remember that there is always a sun above the temporary dark clouds.

In time, the sun will shine again and the fascinating thought is that it had been sitting there all this while. The instant when the proverbial *rain* pours from the sky may very well be the ideal moment to move to action and to keep working at our ambitions, rather than sit back with our arms folded in self-pity.

Even with the wildest individuals we know of, for whom life seemingly never has a sad moment, along the way the *cries* will expose their human weaknesses and make dull their strengths. This *stains the depths of joy within*. Unless we are vigilant in our own thought development, our ability to sharpen our strengths and improve on our weaknesses will be gravely diminished by allowing the misfortunes and hardships to mold us into something that we are not.

As I share different and difficult moments in my life, the lesson through them have been that just as it probably will always rain, and the sun will always shine, all of us will have the chance every day to get off the sidelines and dig ourselves out of the most uncomfortable days. Many times we will have to use our life's resources, our own experiences and the stories in our hearts as our *umbrella* to keep fighting on.

The poem "Smiles and Cries" seeks to encourage all of us that in the smallest details of our own lives, it is imperative that we learn not to marginally get along, mired in our comfort zones and allow the *heavy rains* to push us into mediocrity and an unaccomplished life.

Not too long ago, I shared a joke with my younger sister. There was a phrase we used for people who we reckoned were living their lives from the edge of their seat. Such people were never drenched in the heavy downpours and sadness, but rather their minds were fixed on the sunshine in the horizon which had every power to erase their dismal moments. Those people listened to their hearts even when the sounds were faint and pushed past their innate limitations. We called such people and their actions *going postal*. This expression described a person becoming extremely and uncontrollably angry, often to the point of violence. In a rather lighthearted way, it was to mean describe a person willing to do whatever it took to accomplish a task, in the good sense of being spontaneous or daring, even when it appeared they would drive themselves crazy in doing so.

The word *unusual* is often a hallmark of someone who is pushing beyond his own drawbacks, and gone *postal*. Then there is *pushing the envelope*. The interesting truth I believe is that a person pushes the envelope when he redefines what is possible and lives life with a different, often wilder sense of urgency. The connection between the two phrases, however, is that it will take an individual who is "Willing to go postal to push the envelope."

Many years later, my sister would remind me of the need to stay sane at all cost whenever I told of how stuck I had been in a rut. Even so, I was still pushing. Whatever our personal inadequacies may be, there will perhaps be opportunities that we can all excel in, if only we make the time and the investment to explore them. *A shining star is a heart's comfort* and that was ample reason to push beyond my constraints, and dare to be a person living with a renewed sense of gusto.

When I first learned about how much power our words have to become self-fulfilling prophecies, I tried a crazy experiment. As inconsequential as our words can seem to us, we will end up believing anything we tell ourselves if we say it often enough. I had piled on many years of incapability, one setback after another. My mental database was packed with cheerless events. I recall the final straw being my migrating to different countries where adjusting the nuances of social life was not the easiest exercise.

Gradually, the stress compounded into sadness. The brief spells of misery and unhappiness evolved into despondency and bleakness. Life was all *rain*, and inadvertently I was too busy worrying about personal setbacks to acknowledge the sunshine moments. In fact in the figurative "Smiles and Cries," I did *cry* more than *smile*.

Then one day, out of nowhere I thought of something unusual. I did not call a psychologist, a religious guru or a life coach. In fact I decided not to tell anyone who could understand the magnitude of my problems. My idea would be a drastic deviation from what most of us do instinctively, to go in search of people who understand our plight and *cry* with us. I had to *go postal*, willingly.

Over the next several months, I spent some Saturdays with two little friends while their parents worked all afternoon. We would visit a local ice cream parlor and sit on the benches nearby in the sun watching other kids on the playground close by. They were six years old. So I would begin my conversation about the many adversities of my life and how I planned to squarely confront and live through them.

It didn't take much to notice that the little girls had come along for the ice cream, not my theories on life. It was only fair that since I paid for the ice cream, they listened to everything I said without interrupting or questioning my opinion. In fact they never did disrupt my thoughts probably because they didn't have the faintest idea of what I was so passionately talking about.

Occasionally, I would pause and ask, "Do you understand me?" Without missing a heartbeat or a drop from their ice cream, they would both nod "Yes" to my question. They nodded "yes" to everything I said. The unusually reassuring part of this exercise was that my two little friends were exactly the kind of listening ear that I needed, unconditionally understanding and naïvely comforting.

Chapter 18: Smiles and Cries

During one such conversation, the more attentive of the two suddenly burst out laughing heartily. I had not said anything funny so I was baffled for a moment. Then she pointed to a little boy running through the water sprinklers nearby. This little boy had no shirt on, and definitely had not a care in the world. It was a hot sunny afternoon, and most families had brought their children to get ice cream and to sit in the cool shade. The sprinklers on the sunny day seemed to their innocent minds like a rainy day under the shining sun.

The little boy was full of joy and life, and kept running in a circle as fast as he could. He stopped running, looked up, and with his face to the sky he stretched out his hand as if the embrace the best of both the sun and the rain. I thought to myself how different our own lives would be if we could manage to keep our center of attention on the *shining sun* even in the midst of the *rain*. How different would my own life be if I could cultivate that sense of calm and sanguinity in the midst of the pouring rain?

Why the conversations with the two little girls? Why would I engage in an almost pointless dialogue? I found out that oftentimes, most of us want to articulate our thoughts without the fear of ridicule. Most of the time we even have the answers to the questions we ask others, and what we need rather is a listening ear, not a psychotherapist.

Of course, I told myself many reassuring stories and recreated affirmative images to sustain my enthusiasm to live. A good friend with whom I shared this thought wondered, "Isn't this crazy?" We both laughed, but I had to remind him also that *the craziness was what has kept me sane*. It is the *lasting grin through the fleeting cries* which turns out to be the *lingering smiles in a sunny day*.

The blunt truth is that no one is going to do the heavy lifting for us and there are no emergency crews coming to our rescue with a blueprint for a fulfilling life. How we manage to smile through our *cries* is our own making.

All of us will have to navigate our paths through the winding roads of life, and *push the envelope* in our unique strengths. By telling myself affirmative stories, or as in my radical chatting experiment with six-year-olds about complicated life scenarios, I may have done myself a huge favor to see past the cloudy skies.

I contend that perhaps the craziest ideas could very well work to our advantage, because it indeed makes a big difference if we tell ourselves positive, affirmative, encouraging, and self-motivating *stories*, then use this positive energy as impetus to challenge our own roadblocks. I am not advising you to employ any of my so-called *avant-garde* methods, but I will imagine that there are elements in all of our gloomy days which can be turned into an arsenal. There is *grace through the drizzle and the pours,* enabling us to cling onto the hope and give our best effort at every turn.

It goes without mention that beyond innovative views and actively exercising our imaginations, there is more action needed to making our pursuit a pragmatic venture. For instance, it would be nice to be an astronaut tomorrow morning if that were possible, but you know as well as I do, that a person cannot wish himself or herself onto the moon. That is being practical, and you will agree that no measure of hope can turn you and me into brain surgeons overnight.

If they were to tell, we'd find that the greatest artists, most successful athletes, renowned scientists, and the most fulfilled individuals we can think of had many attributes in common, including cultivating an elevated outlook. I would guess that none of these individuals began their journey completely unaware of the odds of accomplishing their tasks. They knew the problems, understood the complications and yet determined to override the odds.

It bears mentioning again that cultivating a point of view is not the end game. It is an essential catalyst. As it is with anything else, just having a frame of reference is different from having one that consistently uplifts us and puts our mind in winning mode.

Chapter 18: Smiles and Cries

One important idea in the poem "Smiles and Cries" is that somewhere in all the chaos, and in our *cries*, there still exists *the* energy to recreate our own *smiles*. I have often mentioned how with every thought and word we utter, we sell an idea or belief to ourselves. Eventually, we will buy whatever it is that we sell. Most people who fail to live life with a sense of hope may have never had the knack and the aptitude to recognize the opportunity in some of our most unpleasant circumstances.

When the rain falls in the same moment when the sun shines, what we choose to focus on will inspire the predominant emotion that drives us to expect more sunshine, or dread the rains. In fact, when both are present, there is a tendency to allow the sad turns to rule our day, instead of seeing them as temporary events that should not have any consequence on the moment that lies ahead. The uplifting news is that while the rains leaves a host of puddles behind in all of our lives, there may very well be plenty of opportunity to reorient our inner compass and set it back on what we ought to be focusing our energy on.

Not all of us will have the luxury of cheerleaders in our lives who urge us to give life our best even when nothing is going our way. Indeed, in the middle of the smiles and cries, we may not have anyone reminding us that we can never drown in the puddles of life. Sure, we will get dirty with mud y now and then, but we still can stand tall and follow our hearts' ambition with a good attitude. The rains cannot wash away any progress we made along the way, and only our guarded minds will continue to be open to the sunshine.

I genuinely believe that we can all find missed opportunities in our lives, which perhaps might be a starting point to learn through them and desire much more fulfilling destinations for our own lives. It ultimately is our responsibility to tune in to the chance to *smile* rather than live on the avenue of misery and *cries*.

We will all have our *smiles and cries,* but all of us still have the business of living to do, and the success of that is paramount to overcoming any shortcomings that we may have, or think we have, even if they are nothing more than *two buckets full of teardrops.*

SMILES AND CRIES

1 Some two buckets full of teardrops
Falling from the distance
And from the stars
Drenched and wet in the shining sun
5 One second of gloom spoils the dazzling sky.
Trying hearts in a blanket of heavy ache
Wonder what stains the depths of joy within
And leak the strength in time to begin.
Smiles and cries,
10 Together they fall
Grace through the drizzle and pours.
A heart of man heavier than stone
When clouds made the days blue,
Darker yet in just a moment
15 The colored rays have changed its tune
And the shining star is a heart's comfort.
The solace in the quiet
And moment serene
Like a mystic hand holding cover
20 In the swirls of the clouds above.
It dries the tears,
For the drench is over now
The lasting grin in the fleeting cries
Be the lingering smile
25 Born soon in a sunny day.

THE LOUDEST WIND THERE

Hope is the indispensable virtue inherent in the state of being alive. If life is to be sustained, hope must remain, even where confidence is wounded, and trust impaired.

—Erik H. Erikson

During a speech in Paris at the Sorbonne, United States President Theodore Roosevelt said:

"It is not the critic who counts, not the man who points out how the strong man stumbled; or where the doer of deeds could have done better. The credit belongs to the man who is actually in the arena, whose face is marred by dust and sweat and blood, *who strives valiantly, who errs and comes short again and again, who knows the great enthusiasms, the great devotions, and spends himself in a worthy cause, who at best knows achievement and who at the worst if he fails at least fails while daring greatly so that his place shall never be with those cold and timid souls who know neither victory nor defeat."*

Roosevelt's speech had the same weight in 1910, as it does today. The simplest translation of it is that it is only the person who has repeatedly fought in his own battles, and suffered the wounds thereof, who knows the price of his victory. In that same vein, it is only that person who struggled for his survival who knows the worth of each sleepless night and dreary step along the way.

Anyone except the *doer* of the act can only imagine your challenge, can only imagine your fortitude, and may never appreciate your tenacity. Onlookers and observers can only imagine and envision the pain, but their assumption of our true worth cannot, and should not deter us from our engagement with a rewarding future.

It does take much more effort to run a race, than it does for bystanders to judge a performance. By some coincidence however, it is amazing how every person in the audience thinks someone else's performance is subpar. I use this example: how often have we attended a sporting event only to hear everyone in the crowd give an *expert analysis* on what the coach or a player ought to have done?

It is just as easy to forget that the man in the trenches is perhaps also giving it his all. There are many spectators who will imagine that the runner may not have tried hard enough or even had given up too soon, yet they forget that if they could run the race, they wouldn't be sitting in the stands in the first place offering their insight.

It is interesting how everyone else would be excellent at someone else's life, often without taking a moment to see where that person came from, and without having traveled a second in their shoes. Despite

Chapter 19: The Loudest Wind There

everyone else's best intents, only you and I can correctly appreciate the hurt and the sweat we have invested at any juncture of life.

I have found that the most effective way to shut off the *loudest winds* and the unsolicited distractions in our lives is our own ability to live in a proactive mode, planning and forecasting what we want our next steps to be, rather than living in a constant reactionary mode.

Waiting for the noise from the sidelines to force us into our next decisions also introduces an undue stress into our lives. Anyone can ridicule and criticize; all it takes is an opinion.

Many years ago I told a story of the popular television and movie critics Ebert and Roeper. They were neither film makers, nor were they actors. They had no part to play in the films they scrutinized and dissected, but Ebert and Roeper were critics whose job was to watch films and rate them on their arbitrary scale.

Roger Ebert and Richard Roeper probably worked in different roles in the film business, but all their collective experience could not override their skewed interpretations of human nature. Their opinions were subjective, but the reason why they were celebrated critics in the film business is that they had spent enough time analyzing other people's work to be experts at it. They were excellent at showing the rest of us how the film could have been better, how the actor could have tried harder and why the story earned a thumb down.

Did Ebert and Roeper know the intricate details of how the scripts were developed and the cinematographers ran through mud and rain to get the perfect picture? Perhaps not, but Ebert and Roeper were hired to do only one job, critique. Sure enough, I know many people who believe they can do as much critiquing, and would gladly do so for free. The truth of the matter is that it is in our human nature to observe and criticize. I would have paid anything to see Ebert and Roper act in a film.

Inside my favorite Italian restaurant, a mirror in the restroom had a big red sign across the top. It read, "Accidents only happen to the other guy." At the bottom of that same mirror was an even bigger sign, "Meet the Other Guy." The meaning: all of us are the *other guy*.

Coincidentally, it was that same day that I saw the writing on the mirror when I heard of David J. Pollay's *law of the garbage truck*. He tells the life-changing lesson he would learn at the back of a New York City taxi cab. The driver of another car had made a wrong turn, and although almost causing an accident, he began hurling insults at the taxi driver who had every reason to be fuming. Instead, the taxi driver just smiled and waved at the peeved driver.

David Pollay was stunned. "Why did you just do that? This guy could have killed us!" The driver was calm as he explained how *many people we come across are like garbage trucks. They run around full of rubbish, frustration, disappointment, anger, and all kinds of junk. As their garbage piles up, they look for a place to dump it. "If you let them, they'll dump it on you,"* he added.

The taxi driver's analogy couldn't have been any more outstanding. *If you let them, they'll dump it on you.* Unfortunately there is also the garbage we pile up in our daily frustrations and disappointments that could be showing up on other people's front lawns. Even in our most insignificant interactions, in much the same way as the *law of garbage trucks* happens to us, let's be cognizant of the moments when the junk shows up, and when it so easily piles up and turns into a crisis for us.

As I wrote in "The Loudest Wind There," the problem with most of us is that we panic when we find out suddenly that there is no one jumping in the ring to fight on our behalf, and that we all have to endure the intimidating task of hauling off the junk by ourselves. The noise, the uncalled-for advice, and the unconstructive insights from bystanders may be the garbage truck we ought to be on the lookout for.

In many of my conversations, I would often say that just as we ought to be watching for the garbage trucks, we are responsible for our own trash and we should not carry it around ruining other people's day. All of us are the *other guy;* we could just as easily be the source of the garbage as the recipients of it.

None of us are immune to the unexpected *wrong turns* from strangers but I believe that our enthusiasm is not only a positive mind-set, but also the starting point for renewed vigor to keeping our focus. Through the turbulent currents every day, a person who is passionate about life is happy to take responsibility and welcomes the challenges as part of the cycles of nature, instead of allowing the sour strangers to affect our days. That person hears the critics and all their reasons why they *can't,* but they remind themselves of one good reason why they *can.*

Enthusiasm gives us the ability to look for the silver lining where everyone else is looking for a reason to find the closest exit door. Why is the law of the garbage truck so intriguing? Avoiding the unflattering and downbeat piles of garbage around us is what guards our zeal to take a chance, to find alternatives, and to be willing to live in the best way we know how.

"The Loudest Wind There" is also about finding the scattered pieces of dreams and passions, once blown away by the winds of fear and doubt. From our births to this very moment, we have picked up many desires, and an ever-changing list of ambitions along the way. We have also, rather unfortunately, left behind many aspirations at every turning point.

We have every reason to bring our dreams back to reality, but not everything that falls into the heap of garbage and dwells there over time, can regain its worth. The caution, however, is to be sure not to spend the rest of our lives digging through the garbage for lost time and missed opportunities. I look back on my own life and see that many lost moments slipped by because of my focus on another person's spill of anger and frustration. I let another person's junk ruin my smile.

I once had a grumpy neighbor with a talent for ruining other people's days. Here was a young man, always depressed and who looked as if the burdens of the world were pinned onto his shoulders. He had a pessimistic version of any good report. Tell him an uplifting story, and he would give you a good reason why the bottom would surely fall apart soon. We called him *Bad News Santa*. What was worse, he would go around knocking on doors with a sad story, a piece of gossip, or a useless rumor that had every ingredient to dampen your day. Life was unusually gloomy for him, and he made sure that all his neighbors shared his discontent.

One afternoon, I saw another neighbor and asked if he knew of the *Bad News Santa*. He did, but he had never talked to the grumpy young man and was particularly careful to avoid his depressing stories. My neighbor added that he had a sick mother to take care of, and had enough sad stories of his own to worry about. His words, "That guy has convinced himself that everything in life will go wrong for him, so he is living his belief." There is priceless significance in that some people choose to dwell on the most inconsequential and negligible issues to give meaning to their lives.

It is amazing how many garbage trucks live next door to us, could be our friends and people we relate to everyday. They, sometimes unknowingly, could be "The Loudest Wind There." Avoid the voluntary bearers of bad news at all cost if you can. If everything in life was of equal use, there won't be a need for garbage cans and definitely not garbage trucks. My humble proposition is that some of life's events are inconsequential because we can do without them and not miss a step. Wasting precious energy on them is making room for unnecessary junk.

A long time ago, I was pouring my heart out to a good friend about an overwhelming predicament. I was stressed and stuck between difficult personal choices. There weren't too many voices cheering me on, but rather every sound and echo reminding me of how my efforts weren't going to amount to much. Every day had a new set of frustrations and even its own pile of garbage. My friend interrupted my sad monologue and said, "I hope you know that some things don't matter much, and most things do not matter at all."

Wait a minute! Some things, even most things, don't matter at all. The ability to distinguish between what does or does not matter is emotional intelligence. The author of *the law of garbage trucks* learned his lesson from the taxi driver who understood the secret to a rewarding life with every moment. You can bet he is not driving around New York flipping middle fingers at unruly strangers in the street. The rest of us will be reminded by President Roosevelt's crucial warning that, *"It is not the critic who counts."*

As I wrote in "The Loudest Wind There," most of us will expend precious time soaking in other people's filth and ruin our own unique journeys. Even worse, some of us do an excellent job wasting the remainder of our lives beating ourselves up for what we do not have. I often said that there is a deliberate reason why the United States Marines indoctrinate recruits with their mantra, "Be all you can be." To *be all you can be*, not what the crowd on the sidelines says you can be.

Not to be like the next person, or the famous person you admire, but rather to strive to become the very best person your individual potential will allow. Ebert and Roeper may give you and me thumbs down, but as hard as we may try, spending the rest of our lives in a boxing gym will not make any of us a Rocky Marciano or Muhammad Ali. We have more important things to spend our energy on, than debating irrelevant issues, piling up and cleaning out other people's garbage.

None of us can afford to be recipients of strangers *outsourcing* their misery. If we fail to decide what is important to us, I bet there are other people who will be glad to dump their junk on us, perhaps to help us figure out what is indeed important. In my own observation, no two people will probably evaluate you and your life's purpose on the same scale. Just as there is the subjective assessment of individual talent, it is important to not allow other people to determine our self-worth.

For some of us, if other people measured our potential, we would never make the cut. It is no surprise that living our life by someone else's benchmark is the surest route to eternal frustration. This unfortunately is the surest way to invite junky thoughts into our own lives, even from unsuspecting garbage trucks.

At the very least, it is a potential recipe for self-defeating thoughts. Albeit a difficult exercise, avoiding the garbage trucks and the negative sideshows or sour attitudes is the passport to keep dreaming about the future we want.

It is not easy to have or maintain a three-dimensional view of our own circumstances, one that lets us truly appreciate the benefits of our darkest nights and challenging moments, but perhaps keeping the *violin quartet* far from our little strides is not a bad start. I will argue that people who seems to have all the answers to our lives' problems are those who have never lived our unique lives, and thus find it much easier to transpose their own interpretation of us, unto us. Remember Roosevelt's words: *"It is not the critic who counts."*

There are many times when we set our minds on a goal, and work relentlessly to achieve it, but sometimes our strategy falls short. Without fail, there are many people waiting in the stands to evaluate what we could have done well or what we ought to have done differently.

There may have been times when we have mentally, physically, and carefully planned our prospective course of action, but disaster strikes once we set out to execute the plan. You know as well as I do that hard work is no panacea for the disappointments in life, but once we yield to the naysayers on the sidelines, we shortchange our own investment and our potential.

Chapter 19: The Loudest Wind There

A friend told his story as a young man joining a band on tour as a guitarist. He had his dream job traveling across the country and entertaining fans. When the tour came to an end, he was surprised to find out that the band's apparent success was only a promotional tour without any contract offers. He had left his steady employment and his secured lifestyle to pursue a passion.

Almost immediately, everyone he knew who had previously celebrated his successes jumped on the other side of the fence. They had all become experts and life coaches, and my friend saw the axis tilt against him from all directions. Friends poured in their suggestions on what he should have done and what they thought he had done wrong. Although the pieces of his dream had fallen apart, until this day, he still asserts that, "You have to want something out of life to get anything in life."

My friend admits to never wanting a reason to regret not making a decision, and to rather trust his own passions and instincts. Furthermore, he will be the first to tell you that the people giving you instructions from the sidelines are usually those who need their own advice the most. Just as it happens to most of us, there were naysayers against his ambitions. However, he understood this—that he was the only person with the ultimate decision on what his next move would be. Lest we forget, oftentimes the "Loudest Wind There" is just *noise*.

The inspiration for "The Loudest Wind There" came from my own realization that no matter how many times we have seen ourselves lose the figurative tug or war, ultimately, you and I make the final call and own the veto power in our life. What if that *something* we want out of life never happens? What if we have done all we can, and yet we have nothing to show for our hard work and undying tenacity?

When I first listened to the garbage truck story, one peculiar thought which came to mind also, was that not every garbage truck stinks around us. If every unconstructive action was indeed obvious to us, none of us would have much to worry about. My father would say, "The unmarked junk is the worst of all."

It would be fairly simple if we could readily identify the unwanted *bad news Santas* of our lives, or the strangers who own the *beautiful trash*, disguised as ordinary life happenings. The poem "The Loudest Wind There" traces the pressures which have the tendency to pollute our progress, and rob us of the energy to listen to the voice in our hearts just as we do to the voices in our head.

What do you do when the bottom of your dream falls off after all the faith exercises? How do you find a place to start again, especially when the critics are so busy giving us thumbs down? I suggest keeping on believing. My only suggestion will be to tune out the distractions and the discouraging chants, whether from our friends, strangers or even from ourselves, and believe again. At least we would have given our dreams a fighting chance and maybe another opportunity in our lives to be able to tap into that same experience.

The poem "The Loudest Wind There" is about how we manage to fight one more round when the *Monday morning quarterbacks* are standing behind us waving banners from our past failures. They are all the people who jump out of the woodwork after the fact to give us the winning formulas on how best we could have won the game from the night before. The good news is that their opinions don't count.

Throughout this book I have mentioned how easy it is for us to lose our perspective, especially when our plans and hopes fall apart and we question ourselves. The truth is that excellence in life is about doing our best, and there is nothing more important in this exercise than our own definition of winning and happiness. Our default setting is to look over our shoulders and see our lives through the eyes of the next person, without having any clue of what that person is living through.

A few years ago, Lakewood Ministries' Joel Osteen was speaking to a congregation about our human tendency to dissect and decode

Chapter 19: The Loudest Wind There

every event we encounter. Then he mentioned the "I don't understand box." The resonance to my own life was how we have built-in expectations to know the answer to every question and everything that happens to us.

That is how we are probably wired, or how some of us have been trained to function. From our infancy, we are programmed to always ask *why?* As good an idea as it is, it turns out that most of us struggle with the puzzling events when we cannot rationalize an answer for them. Even when we try to push the heavy thoughts aside, the voices from the sidelines gives us a boatload of reasons to fret again. So we keep asking *why*.

The Osteen suggestion was just as intriguing as it was very simple in its acknowledgement of a powerful truth. "Sometimes things happen to us, or our loved ones and we do not understand why," he said. Common sense, logic and a critical way of thinking may not answer the questions. In fact logic may end up confusing you more than it could have helped. In his own life, he had learned about putting such events into a compartment he called the *I don't understand it box*.

Sometimes when we do not readily comprehend why an event happens, we find it even more baffling to process, let alone know what we should do next. By the same token it is equally important to not allow the critic's voices to drown our enthusiasm. In writing this book, I will not have tailor-made answers for any one of life's situations. As I suggested earlier, when it comes to those pieces of the puzzle which I am unable to figure out in my own life, I am also learning to stash them away in my own *I don't understand box,* and keep moving on.

When I met Frank in East London in 1997, there was a film that he thought was so important that I watch. From his interesting ideas on life, his fascination with history, to the handful of video tapes on his coffee table, my first guess was the 1987 film *Escape from Sorbibor*.

That film recalled the site of one of the most successful and extraordinary uprising by Jewish prisoners of German extermination camps.

Instead, we would watch a story about legendary boxer Muhammad Ali. Frank's idea was to get my attention to a very simple, yet incredible way of thinking through images that I had known all my life, but never paid any attention to.

In one of the many subtle messages, people reminded Ali how his skill and experience was insufficient to match his competition. While his critics hashed on his apparent weaknesses, Ali was busy reminding himself that he was too fast and too pretty to lose. The more people told him he would lose, the more Ali reminded them that he was the champion. The longer his critics told him who he wasn't, the more he told them who he was. Interestingly, Muhammad Ali had declared himself a champion long before he set foot in the boxing ring.

At the height of his success, Muhammad Ali wrote that, "Life is a gamble. You can get hurt, but people die in plane crashes, lose their arms and legs in car accidents; people die every day. It is the same with fighters; some die, some get hurt, and some go on. They tell themselves that a winner ought not to allow his mind to believe for a minute that it could happen to them." The wisdom of this belief rests in the kind of information winners feed themselves with.

In spite of the negative reports, all of us can find a little spark, and perhaps a tiny jolt to recharge our hopes, and to put a little pep in our step. For some of us, this task may be a little harder than others, but it is definitely worth giving it a try. From Muhammad Ali's vantage point, anyone can lose in a boxing match or in life, except the people who are bent on winning.

I contend that Ali developed his loud talkative and even boastful stance to drown the voices of his critics. He may have known that the way to the winner's circle would demand him to silence the Eberts and Roepers who never stood in a boxing ring a day in their lives, but had all the expert analyses on how to score a knockout punch.

Chapter 19: The Loudest Wind There

I am also certain that Ali reminded himself countless times that *it is not the critic who counts* but that what matters the most was doing his best in spite of the *noise*. He was not perturbed by what the critics saw in him because he knew a lot more about his own fortitude than any critic would ever find out. The Alis of this world examine the payoffs to their hard work and focus their mental "limelight" on their own goals.

I have learned that once we illuminate our life's big picture, all the pieces become clear, and the fact that we don't have any *friendly faces* in the crowd will not blow us off course. The strangest part of this is that when we learn to put those events we wrestle with into our own *"I don't understand it box"* the background noises and the *Monday morning quarterbacks* turn into cheering sounds in our advantage. I will be first to admit that in the same light, the obstacles become clear also, yet our task is not to entertain the compromising thoughts that might derail us.

All of us know of people whose dreams seemingly came to fruition in a blink of an eye, or at least such is the impression of it. They struck gold without much effort, or won the lottery by some luck, so the same rules may not apply to them. However, I am sure that there are many others busy working on their ambitions, and even more people in the audience preparing a banner to announce their failure.

In the end, a naysayer's voice is just one of the many in the crowd. I can never overemphasize that ultimately, we possess the final say on what voice we will allow to supersede all others.

How we exercise our freewill and inner strength is a matter of personal choices. The subtle message in the poem is the reminder that every inspiring thought we find along the way is just that, a thought. If positive thinking were the only recipe for success, there would be no need for the millions of self-help books in bookstores around the world.

An old adage says "You can force the horse to the river side but you can't force it to drink." All of us will have to do the extra work of drinking the affirmative thoughts for ourselves, and even more so when there are a myriad of voices telling us how inept we are.

On many occasions I have said that only you and I have ownership of our dreams or our ambitions. It is only ours for a reason. That does not mean the rest of world will or should follow you, understand you, or even listen to you. I hate to disappoint you, but not too many people care about what your hopes are. I believe that there is a reason why our aspirations live in our hearts instead of the billboard along the highways. I encourage you to listen to yourself and your heart, especially when it is so difficult to understand why things turn out the way they do, not the voices chanting "No" in the crowd.

I also challenge you to remember that sometimes, although we aspire to things and persistently pursue our ambitions, the unforeseen contingencies that can derail them are often more temporary than we imagine. There will undoubtedly be the many Eberts and Roepers to remind us of how high we could have jumped or how far we should have run. The good news is that indeed *it is not the critic who counts.*

There are many faces standing along our life's path with glaring signs and wild opinions on how many thumbs down we will get. There are the detractors who will critique all our efforts, skillfully belittle and deride any of our hard-fought achievements. I like to think that they too, have a job to do, but in Roosevelt's words, *the credit belongs to the man who is actually in the arena, whose face is marred by dust and sweat and blood.*

The next time someone tells you what they would do if they were you, kindly remind them that they would do exactly what you are doing if they were in your shoes. I can only imagine how much better each of the naysayers would have performed if they had lived your life, and walked a mile in your shoes. Despite all the loud noise, the bystanders are the least important part of our life's equation.

Chapter 19: The Loudest Wind There

Steering our way through the daily grind and unsure of what our future holds can be so daunting a challenge that we could even find ourselves tempted to throw in the towel right where we stand. Even before we take a step. Every stride in our journey may have come along with its own set of bruises, so much that we have become dazed by the range of possibilities we have to choose from. Angst keeps us from stretching our faith and trusting our God-given strength to carry us through. For every voice in the crowd we pay attention to, all the encouraging voices soon fade into the background. The encouraging thought, however, is that even in those overwhelming days, there could be other people watching our every move to take some inspiration to run their own race too. There ought to be hope in our own past days to find some comfort in.

Our assignment is too important to allow the crowds standing on the sides of our lives to cause us to lose our focus on running our race the best we know how. What become the overwhelming steps we manage to take in spite of the many voices that say otherwise, may very well become the footprints someone else will have to follow one day. Even when we occasionally sway from side to side, with the winds of life's pressure blowing on us, let the hope for a brighter day give us the energy to keep trudging along.

The Loudest Wind There

1. The voices say it's gray by the sun when I awake
So a drowsy mind imagines running north.
The heat and dirt
From the distance scare me still
5. To endure the nerve
And emptiness of vacuum
When the little voices drown the zest in my steps.
Now I live in my hand with wrinkles of joy
And the lies
10. And the doubts are loud in vain
In a desperate search for cheering faces
And a God in a man to lead me on.
I hold on dusting off yesterday's dirt
And wipe away the sweat from my neck
15. For it's gray again from there to here
Even in the loudest wind.
If my future is a line,
It is near
The thin white line is not a hanging rope
20. Though I reminisce over the trails of noisy words
That the morning field is not as green
That where I kneel to pray
For what I feel is hollow for cover
Though the day is long with no applause
25. I'll let the wind be as loud as rumble and in vain.
The voices are empty as vacuum
When a heart is strong and woken here
The cracking heels are my true story
The trail of songs is bleeding toes with all the odds.

30 The loudest winds make me chuckle
  The gray in the sun is the life in the desert days
  Where we find meaning to blurry stars
  And escape the mess of a stranger's sting.
  The grace to endure with mercy to forgive
35 The tiniest curiosity runs its course
  When breath is spaced
  Words are bitter, and stranger's blind
  So I'm here to the ending turn
  North of my deepest fears
40 And farther still from my biggest foes
  Grateful for the dirt and sweat,
  For the voices and empty noises
  For bringing me here
  Just where I prayed to be.

BACK TO BEING LITTLE

Never forget the magic of childhood. There were once those thrilling moments when we could dream all day without the limitations, and laugh aloud at the simplest occurrences.

Once in all of our lives, there was that moment when pain and shame didn't mean anything, when we felt so strong and nothing could break our will, and disappointments were no more than breeze passing by. The poem "Back to Being Little" is about finding the moment to begin again, to trust like we did as the innocent and clueless child with no sense of limits, impossibilities, or humiliation.

Innocence sees beauty even in gloomy days because the reference point for their joy is not tied to the fear of the moment but rather the pleasant memories of the past. One of the most compelling moments to live through for all of us is when we are forced to doubt ourselves, and question the same supposedly uplifting and inspiring words we share with others around us.

In other words, when the shoe was on the other foot, on someone else's foot, it didn't take much for us to encourage them. We were conveniently removed from the frontlines of those challenges, so our ideas were rock solid. It is when the same shoe ends up on our foot, that we find out how heavy the soles indeed are, and how uncomfortable it really is to walk in them.

It is a particularly awkward feeling to be so down on ourselves, frustrated at the events of our lives, when the faith we once professed loses its meaning by the minute. The difference or danger here is that we know the encouraging ideas; in fact we have spent our lives preaching them to others, and now make it even harder to subscribe to those same words when we need to the most. It was in one of such low road moments when I remembered how easy life was as a child, oblivious to the real world full of tough breaks and sad songs that I wrote "Back to Being Little."

My mother had a worn-out unoriginal saying, "If necessity is the mother of invention, adversity is the father of success." I never found the author of the quote, but as far back as I can recall, my mother had convinced my siblings and me that she had coined the adage herself. She would refer to it for almost every situation, and by the time I was ten years old I would repeat it to my friends without having any idea what the adage really meant.

It took several years to grasp the meaning of *necessity being the mother of invention,* but it is the courage to invent when our once peaceful world turns into chaos that makes all the difference. Like most people, I wondered over and again if ever I did come to the difficult points, sandwiched by unsure turns and doubtful options, would I have the guts to rewrite the rules to live completely? Can I have the energy to see past the obvious road signs and follow my inner impulse to redraw the limiting boundaries? Can I come "Back to Being Little?"

I spent some of my formative years as a boy growing up in Accra, the capital city of Ghana. We had a homemade and unsophisticated version of baseball that kids my age spent our afternoon hours playing. It was especially fun during the cool *harmattan* season when the sun would set early, but the breeze and clear skies would allow us to play long into the night. Sometimes however, the fog would be very dense, making it almost impossible to find your way around the open field.

The idea of the game was simple. We would throw a tennis ball, or any round object into a tiny bucket and the person or people who were first to score would earn the right to hit. All that the lucky few had to do was to prevent everyone else from scoring by throwing their ball into the same bucket. The technique had more to do with luck than skill, but it could be a very exhausting event for some of us who never mastered pitching the ball.

As a sport, it was similar in concept to baseball. The problem is, the game turned into a not-much-fun activity if you happened to be the unlucky player whose ball falls outside the tiny bucket. The first person was allowed by rule to hit every other ball with any object of his choice, in any direction and as far as he chose. It meant that the probability of another person scoring next was almost zero.

The odds decreased even further when a second person, by some miracle made a good throw and the hitter missed. Beyond that, it was often a long day for the rest of the kids trying relentlessly to score and also earning the right to hit.

I vividly recall some of the *why me* thoughts running through my mind when it was impossible to catch a break. More than once, I recall some of my friends' frustration after running around all afternoon chasing balls, while other kids enjoyed the privilege of hitting them at their expense. Surprisingly, as kids, we didn't give up so easily. Regardless of how frustrating the game turned out to be, we never forgot the bliss of the moments before.

An interesting observation was how the same words of cheer we would tell the other kids didn't make any sense to us when it was our turn to run through the dense fog looking for balls. Ordinarily, some of their suggestions made perfect sense, but in the midst of the crisis, the more a caring friend would assure us that we would soon score, the quicker we would lose our cool.

In retrospect, it is fair to suggest that whenever we find ourselves living in the cauldron of our most overwhelming challenges, it helps to cling to the same words, the thoughts and hopes we profess. If only we do not magnify our anticipation and the likelihood of pain ahead, we can use the memories of our past joys to thrust us into a new season, and with new opportunities to live again.

One afternoon, as we played our ball game, the youngest kid in our group of friends who were usually part of the unlucky bunch, thought of a clever idea. He had the nerve to suggest that there had to be some limits that would regulate the *hitters* and keep them from abusing the *pitchers*. It was his first time playing the game, but it didn't take much for him to think that there had to be a risk factor and a price to pay for a missed effort. If the game was to have any meaning at all, our hard work ought to have a promise of some reward, a prize to look forward to. The little boy had no concept of a baseball game, but was forced through the endless punishing runs to think outside the box, in our case, outside the bucket.

A kid's simple idea made a world of a difference to the rest of us, nudging us to rethink the rules of our game. Interestingly, the rules we devised were not too different from those of baseball as was played in other parts of the world. If only we knew that something of the sort existed, we could have saved ourselves the frustration in the foggy *harmattan* evenings. The flipside is true however; I believe also that if we had known something about baseball, nothing would have forced us beyond our childish limits to invent our own.

Are the challenges we live through a necessary evil for our own development? It is certainly nice to agree that the punishing trials, in and of themselves, have some invaluable lessons, but often quite a different story when we are the ones holding on to dear life.

"Back to Being Little" for me, was to never lose sight of the miracles and magic moments of life. The courage to live, to believe in our God-given abilities, and to trust in our own convictions is indispensable to our daily survival, and my hope is that all of us can envision the new season, and a new day when our unique adversity has made us invent new opportunities for life.

Life works in quite the same manner as we seek to find ways of affecting our own future. I think many people whose successes we admire today all had blindsided moments when they had to choose between living within the same limits that were working to their disadvantage, or reinvent theirs if necessary.

As we journey through life, we ought to find new ways in our own circumstances to develop the resilience and mental fortitude that come out of candidly rethinking our options and ourselves into the driver's seat for our own lives. I am convinced that this mindset holds true also in our personal maturity, interpersonal relationships, just as much as it is true for living a fulfilling life.

There will be many moments in our lives where unless we find it necessary to reinvent our passions even from the same powerful truths we know, it would be difficult to expect a miracle at the end of it all.

In college, I read about the McDonald's franchise and a certain man named Ray Kroc. During the First World War, Ray had trained to become an ambulance driver, but had ventured into other career paths including a paper-cup salesman, a pianist, and eventually a multi-mixing milkshake machine salesman. I have no idea of how many of his endeavors were successful or how well he did selling paper cups, but somehow he had managed to reinvent himself into new roles and used the same stories of his failures to jumpstart his success.

In California, he met the two brothers Richard and Maurice McDonald who had opened the first McDonald's restaurant in 1940. Ray Kroc, together with Harry Sonneborn who is known by many to be the financial wizard behind McDonald's, came up with another idea. There is an almost general misconception about the success of McDonald's, in that most of us had assumed that the defining innovation of their empire had to do with franchising.

As we found out, that is probably true to some extent, but franchising what? I contend that there ought to be some driving force in all of us that can trigger a hope to act, and see green lights where everyone around us is staring at red lights and stop signs.

Harry Sonneborn did not care as much about hamburgers and fries. Instead, he chose to redefine the scope of McDonalds' business and convinced his partners that the real business they were in was real estate, not hamburgers. That probably was one of the least talked about risky business propositions of the time, but the courage to live beyond immediate understanding is what makes genius out of the simplest ideas, and a fulfilling life out of mundane day to day living. In the McDonald's story, the idea for franchising came out of this concept, but it first started with a careful redefinition of the parameters.

Contrary to what I had thought was true as a little boy, redrawing the rules of the game is not throwing caution to the wind. Rather it is the art of staying afloat by engineering our own experiences. When we are flustered on all sides and seemingly walking on thin ice, we should be careful not to let our own doubts force us to question our own resolve. As I thought about this story, the principle could not be much simpler: *widen your playing field and give yourself more room to play.*

Chapter 20: Back to Being Little

The Sonneborn and Kroc idea to *flip* a simple concept changed the course of a company's history. As I write this, I am drinking a chocolate milkshake from McDonald's, thanks to Ray Kroc. In our society, we refer to such people with that uncanny knack as visionaries, but when you deem it necessary to grow, you manage to ride through challenges instead of succumbing to them. All of us are visionaries of our own lives, only if we can find the strength to hang in, even when it seems like we are hanging alone.

Like the McDonald's entrepreneurs, many children on the streets of Accra where I grew up playing ball games every afternoon threw out the rules that made their life hell. Running through the dense fog in search of game balls, we kept our hope alive with the powerful idea that the same fog could be to our advantage if we could throw a little harder without the hitters knowing from which direction the ball would come.

What these children will never know is that they did more than just write new rules for a game; they set the stage for their own lives. That is what getting "Back to Being Little" does. Another interesting observation was how the kids who lose their turns, stay on the field running all day until the night falls, or they get their opportunity to win. For them, the sun only goes down in our lives when we lose sight of how much control we have in our own futures. Soon, the clouds and fog will give way to the sunny days of a new season.

As I wrote in the poem "Back to Being Little," it is not a matter of *if*, but *when;* because *magic moments* certainly will come sometime. For instance, I honestly am not bewildered by the truth that I will die someday but rather inspired by that reality to live my best life today. Someday when our lives' twists and turns come to a close, how much of life we would have lived may be defined by those seemingly insecure moments.

How much we may have done for ourselves may very well be defined by whether we shrank at our roadblocks, or used them as road signs to redraw our life's paths. It is in this realization that I encouraged myself to find the strength to live through the dreary days, and even the painful moments.

Hard as it may be, I have had to learn that every one of those turbulent times is another one of our life's many learning chapters, however colorful. Those experiences teach us to be slow in assuming the worst in others, but also to acknowledge that we all have enough energy to keep our heads up even when the bottom is falling out around us. Ultimately, like a little kid whose short-term memory overrides any past regret, a series of introspective dialogues helps us to relive the moments. I pray that we can all manage to stand tall no matter where we are, and to never lose our sense of wonder.

From simple habits to the weirdest inclinations, as difficult as they have been, I have had to train myself to develop mental images that reinforce healthy choices. In my private moments when I felt especially downtrodden, I had to tell myself the same uplifting stories over and again. Sooner or later the stories sank in. The power of those inspirational ideas doesn't lessen because we are the ones going through the crisis. Often I ask myself this: if a person's character is who he is when there is no one watching, who really am I?

That is a question I bluntly ask myself over and again, because it is true that the people who are able to redefine their own limitations learned to confront the rules of the game honestly. They are the people who evaluate why things work the way they do, not why things happen to only them, who imagine how much more they can do in spite of the blinding fog, and who live their lives in *cranked-up* mode.

I have mentioned before that these inspired individuals have their fair share of low points too, but they adjust their sails when the sun is no longer on their side, and are ready to jump at the first sign of sunshine in the next moment. Most importantly, they *get real* with themselves, in anticipation of a brighter future beyond the current state.

Chapter 20: Back to Being Little

Many years ago, I heeded a friend's advice to ride the Dungeon Drop in Astroworld theme park. The Dungeon Drop is a two hundred and fifty feet tall scream machine that lifts at about sixteen feet per second and drops at about sixty two miles per hour. For the moment you see the entire city below. It literally feels like sitting on top of the world, except that may very well qualify as the single scariest moment in an amusement park.

Strapped into one of the seats, you are lifted over twenty five floors high, your feet dangling in the skies and with your friends on the ground no bigger than little ants. As we were hoisted up into the sky, I started wondering why on earth I had agreed to this meaningless adventure in the first place. The surprise however was in the fact that, many years before, I would cry and beg my parents to let me on anything that looked as exciting as the Dungeon Drop. How crazy must I have been to be coaxed into this thrill? I was scared to the bone.

A little girl next to me assured me that I wouldn't die, so I faked a calm posture. In what must have been the longest 45-second ride of my life, I imagined all that could possibly go wrong. How many people have died in the past on such rides? What if the seat comes apart, the hinges come loose or the control switch malfunctions?

It was in that same moment when it dawned on me that all the operators and the control units below were a couple of teenage kids, and that I had trusted my life to amateurs who might not know what they were doing. The little girl could read through my grin, and told me that I should have *courage*.

Really? That simple?

The upside of being a child is that sense of calm under the most unthinkable predicaments. If she had been where I had as an adult, and seen some of the horrible things I had in my life, courage would be the farthest thing in her mind. "Back to Being Little" is about the innocence and the apparent ignorance on the little girl's thought process which enabled her to be confident in her seat and enjoy the ride, while the rest of us were gripping tightly to anything, holding on for dear life.

Luckily, we landed on the ground without a hitch, but only after a few screams and a wild adrenaline rush. I had lived through it, I did not die and we did not crash. The more I thought about my chat with the little girl in the air, it made sense that sometimes being naïve eliminates mental limitations and gives us the strength to hang tough. I never sat on the Dungeon Drop again, but I dared to be a little naïve in the face of the many seemingly daunting challenges when I didn't know where to turn.

I believe also that each of us will get the opportunity to live beyond the mental blocks and carve new paths into a rewarding future. No matter how high in the sky we find ourselves and with our legs dangling several hundred feet into the sky, we can still redraw new lines of hope, and have the courage to push beyond the roadblocks to our rewarding lives.

From my own first-hand encounter with some of the lowest points of life and the feelings of dejection, I am living testimony that finding just a little courage to heed our own words even when everything else is falling apart, is not an impractical expectation.

Until we can stare at ourselves in the mirror, look ourselves in the eye and honestly say that we are giving life our best effort, you and I still have a little more work to do. My proposition is that in those days when we feel like questioning our faith and doubting the reassuring truths that we have come to know, it will take a little nerve sometimes, but we have all it takes to make through the long days and the doubtful nights also. That is getting "Back to Being Little."

Back to Being Little

1. I think I am strong enough
   If I could,
   I won't stand on concrete bars to feel so tall.
   I smile when no one's smiling
5. And the frail in my heart is in brightest circles.
   I'm too scared to be strong alone
   The day will be gone in a moment
   And the murals of my painted life will peel in pieces
   Up high and hoisted into the heavens
10. A little heart waits for the sun.
    I'm searching for something closer to courage
    Like the sun shines on a road signs
    Like a man's soul glaring without fear
    A genius is scratching scalps before the nightfall
15. Losing touch with his soul with his doubt
    Another chance in sight to seize the moment
    A fine-spun sculpture but still unsure.
    Bliss is once in a while
    A promise of cure to crippled hopes
20. To buy my fate a nickel at a time
    And save a scream worth all there is to life.
    The music has no words to be heard
    It's a carol, or so I wish
    A magical tune but without the tremble
25. Fill my ears and make me go
    Where horseshoe shaped hopes abound
    And I'll be strong enough to stand again.
    The sun goes down to shine again
    The lane will turn, the morning will come

30 The stains will pale, the bruises will heal
Fig trees will wither, lonely leaves will live
The tips of stars will not be sharp to hurt
Make me believe in the brightest colors
And take me far away into the wonder moment.

THREADS OF LIFE'S TAPESTRY

In the winter of 1996, I rented a small North London apartment in Stoke Newington, England with a roommate, Calvin. It took a while for me to acknowledge that he had a somewhat different set of guiding principles to his life, of which integrity was not a part. It probably may have in fact been the farthest thought from his moral curve; he stopped at nothing to lie about anything and to anyone.

Two months into our rental agreement, I learned that his application information was false, he had sold some appliances from the apartment, and even swindled the old landlord. Calvin must have carefully planned his mischievous adventures and set out to accomplish every bit of them, and one would imagine that people go through life with at least a good sense of what is right and wrong.

Every one of us has a core set of beliefs upon which we operate. How we have acquired them may be just as important as how they affect us, inspire us, and challenge us. They are the threads from which the intricate fabrics of our lives are woven together.

I recall in my own life as a child when I would do something that my parents did not approve of. My mother especially will stare into my eyes, as if to pluck my brains out of my head and her interrogation often ended with this stern rebuke, "Don't lie to me." I won't assume that everyone heard such a speech as a young kid.

Over the years I took that to be my parents' way to make certain that deception, dishonesty and shame did not become a part of my early childhood makeup. In many ways, we get the opportunity to exercise integrity as we grow up and it is by far one of the most important attributes of a person's character.

Throughout my formative years in different countries, I met more than my fair share of deceit. A chunk of my frustration was born out of individuals I had trusted or cared for, but who would repay me with dishonest actions. Like any other attitude, regardless of how firmly it is inscribed in you, integrity does not automatically become a part of our habit. The next step is steady practice and application to our everyday lives.

"Threads of Life's Tapestry" is one of the few poems that I wrote at a decisive juncture and a desperate point in my young life. Living in Europe, away from the family and friends I had grown accustomed to, I learned that real life was swift, and opportunities often appeared and disappeared before we could think through them. Good-hearted people did not stop with signs along the way to help you, even if you desperately needed help.

I had made a bold decision to follow my dreams and along the way pursue a law degree in London. When I first realized that I was many thousands of pounds sterling short of my first day on a college campus, my heart dropped. To this day, I still cannot recall what my

Chapter 21: Threads of Life's Tapestry

exact plan of action was, but none of the schools which I applied to responded.

In the following years, I worked long hours throughout Central London and stayed up all night scheming my next move. It was during these same years that I also had my first lessons in the importance of knowing my specific motives before seeking advice from others. Even the most well-intentioned person could unknowingly manipulate your circumstances from their own perspective, and before long, you would be farther off track than you were before.

My inability to enroll in college was to become the easiest part of my troubles. For the next several months, I had to struggle working menial jobs throughout London just to have enough money for food and even basic shelter. The only safe haven and refuge I had was my afternoon walks in Dalston Mall, where I would sit for hours writing random ideas and reflections in my little notebook.

Little by little, the pieces began to fall apart. My life had drifted farther away from the beautiful dreams that I had as a boy, and it seemed to be getting worse with every day. I was out of work, and two weeks away from homelessness. All I had was the person I had become, the resilience I was developing, and the desire to continue dreaming.

Amidst all the chaos, I signed up for one more foolishly charitable task. I gave my entire life savings, which were not much up to that point, to my roommate Calvin, who was in direr need than I was. His close relative had been admitted to the Intensive Care Unit of a local hospital and he desperately needed money to help with some of the expenses. He promised to repay me in full in just a few days.

Two days later, Calvin left England for good. I found out later, that apparently I was just one out of eight people he had swindled with his bogus sad story. We all learned a fairly remarkable lesson that morning. Most of us gave Calvin our money because we had assumed that he would be honest, at least with us who we thought were his friends. We had all reasoned that although he lied and deceived almost everyone he came in contact with, certainly he would not do that to his closest friends.

Core beliefs and true character are nurtured by repeated actions and reactions to daily events. We do not exhibit any trait overnight, but it requires a conscious effort for a person to become the image they seek to project, whether admirable or otherwise. Not much of a relief to me, but several people had lent our friend Calvin portions of their retirement savings, and they were on the brink of a nervous breakdown.

How did we all miss the same obvious warnings? I was still a teenager with meager financial experience, but how come these older men did not think for a minute that their good friend could be out to swindle them? Many years later, I have come to understand that this life abounds with many people who would sell their souls for a penny if they could. Such people may not subscribe to the same moral tenets that you and I do.

Regarding Calvin's story, we all missed a fairly simple truth that most people often easily ignore. The common misconception is this: the fact that you and I are honest is no guarantee that the next person will be the same in return. As a value we place on our own lives, integrity has nothing to do with reciprocity.

I contend also that personal integrity, for example, is an individual choice. For those who truly have it and cherish it, it becomes an outstanding character trait. There may very well be as many poor people as there are rich ones who door do not have it, because value systems have nothing to do with status in life, wealth, or position.

Ultimately, our own philosophy on life becomes a framework upon which we live and function. Both consciously and subconsciously, these deeply-rooted and often ingrained basic values become the dominant influencers of our daily life's actions.

Chapter 21: Threads of Life's Tapestry

Aside from my roommate Calvin's story, I am often surprised to learn how many people are indeed dishonest at one thing or another, and that may very well be because our human nature stops at nothing to satisfy its selfish desires if we are not mindful of our thought processes. I did have to learn this the hard way, because I trusted over and again, often naively.

Not every person will make sense of Dennis Kimbro's quote, "Your ideal is what you wish you were, your reputation is what people say you are, and integrity is what you are." Not everyone cares about who or what they become; but even then, a character is being developed with one act after another, one thought after another.

In writing "Threads of Life's Tapestry," I sought to retrace my steps without reliving my frustration. I did not plan to understand why other people's attitudes would be different or even what I considered moral flaws in judgment. I instead replayed the encounters that had created the *bitter sketches and portrait of my life*. Throughout life, all of us have different benchmarks and grading rubrics for our every action. Human nature may be fallible by its inherent need for gratification, but our conscience serves to guide us should we deviate.

I learned to be careful of presumptuous assertions, because the degree of tolerance in each of us varies according to how much each of us can endure. The truth is, several aspects of our lives and our stories may be alike, but in some distinct way, all of us come from different places with very different sensibilities. As we age, without any conscious redirections, we become mature versions of who we have always been. Our sense to uphold any value will largely be a reflection of who we truly are when no one is watching.

I once told a group of young children at a local YMCA about how important it was to understand that every human being, regardless of age, faces some genuine kind of adversity. Even the most inconsequential occurrences affect our makeup in the long run.

Although that supposed difficulty might seem trivial to the gray-haired ninety-year-old fellow who may argue that he has lived long enough to see every kind of problem in life, it does not necessarily make it any less pertinent. The only difference, I believe, is that the older person has lived longer, experienced more of life and thus probably developed a more constructive response to hardship and difficulties.

A little boy, Tristan, pulled me aside after the session, his eyes filled with tears and he could barely force the words out. He told me of his ordeal on the internet where other kids in the chat room did not say particularly nice things about him. I thought to myself, "You can't possibly be serious with this trivial issue."

Many years ago when I first learned about chatting online, I also learned about developing a thick skin. You quickly realize that sitting behind a computer and engaging in conversations with people halfway across the world can unleash some brutal interpersonal communication. People do not care about ignoring you, nor do they have any remorse about intentionally hurting your feelings.

"What about switching chat rooms, Tristan," I asked. That was the most logical answer I could come up with in all of my infinite wisdom. Ever since I could remember, I have always tried to evaluate the value of any challenge, in my attempt to avoid assigning the same value to all of them. That had been my way of dealing with challenges, but my mistake was in thinking that my technique was how everyone one else should deal with their set of challenges.

The little boy stared into my eyes, partly surprised at my almost insensitive response and said, "It's not that simple for me." What was so difficult here?

Many years earlier in my London apartment, an old lady had an answer while the rest of us lamented how naïve we had been. She sat next to me and said, *"You may be a lot of things son, but God isn't one of them."* In her own way, she warned us to never think we know so much that we can think for other people.

The ten-year-old Tristan reminded me of something I had effortlessly overlooked, that life for him was not as simple as flipping a switch. His best friend was among the kids online saying awful things about him, and that was why it hurt his young heart. At least he thought they were his friends, and that for him meant and did hurt more than an insignificant online conversation.

Immediately, I played back my own life stories in my head, about how other people brutally ignored my painful experiences as trivial happenings. I recalled a lot of premature advice from friends and people who often meant well, but had failed to understand that I was a unique person with a uniquely different set of emotions.

It's not too difficult to understand why people often reflect on their own circumstances when offering counsel and eventually confuse the act of drawing from their own experiences to empathize, with judging your experience from theirs, to downplay your feelings. Now it made sense and it clicked for me. I could have been *a lot of things* but God certainly wasn't one of them.

A sequence of supposedly trivial disappointments and honest associations had once made me bitter, had turned me into a *pale pilgrim*. Yet somehow I forgot that other people, like the little boy, dealt with their own hurts too. If I could offer one powerful idea to him, it would be that someday he would use these tough days as building blocks to construct his own character.

Little Tristan still spoke highly of his friends and was disappointed that they did not return the favor. It was no different from my bitter memories of my roommate Calvin bolting with my cash. Tristan learned something else about integrity in his young life, and was now exposed to the harsh fact that there is no such thing as automatic reciprocity.

A good action in life is not inevitably rewarded by a good response. We have all heard stories of good people often suffering from their honesty when other people take advantage of it as a sign of weakness. My *"life is not fair, get over it"* speech was not going to work here. I had learned to address my emotional responses and now will have to use the opportunity to teach a young boy the same lesson.

While I wrote the poem "Threads of Life's Tapestry," I coincidentally read a psychology journal about how we cultivate responses to emotional letdowns. There is something experts call "the three states of being." It suggests that some of these mental states are learned from our environment and others are instinctive—we operate in them often without knowing it.

For instance, there is the *victim mode*. This is often the easiest to identify by people around us, mostly because we talk about it ,or it is evidenced in our daily lifestyles. There are other justifiable synonyms for it, but the common one that I know of is the *pity-party*. It is the obvious dwelling on the negative circumstances that may have happened to us and perpetuating unconstructive and usually unhelpful thoughts.

It is also the *why me* syndrome that potentially turns into the *"it's only me"* thought process. Inasmuch as we would love for it to be just, life is far from fair, and we cannot afford to let that drag us into doldrums. If all we see is a *mirage of happy days* and *dark loads tumbling in*, we do no more than set ourselves up for misery and depression.

There is also the *symmetry mode*, where you are neither going up nor going down. Perhaps this could be a transition phase, but the *Calvin stories* and the *Tristan frustrations* were challenges for me to keep pushing higher, and not get stagnant in a supposed mental equilibrium. I oppose this notion from a psychological outlook because I am of the firm belief that there is no period of absolute equilibrium in life. The fact is that at any point in time, we are either going up or going down.

I further contend that just in case you are not sure which direction you are going, you probably are going down. My rationale for this point of view is not difficult to decipher. People on an upward movement know it, because it requires effort, a mental assertion and actual work to undertake that task. People who are on a mission in life do not live in a figment of their imagination; instead they work at every stride to achieve their goals.

Finally, the three states of being have a *cranked-up mode*. The fact is that once we understand that life is somewhat like a twisting cyclone, or whatever imagery we assign to it, we can give ourselves the opportunity to actively engage in the business of life. Perhaps in the same vein, the disappointments wouldn't so easily throw us off course.

With every new day, we have a new opportunity to repaint the portrait of our lives; however we can imagine it, not just *bitter sketches*. *A victim mindset* only sees the roadblocks, the setbacks, the broken dreams and the *mirage of happy days*, not the chance to change their moment, and move on with their lives.

I have often shared how at every point in our lives we are faced with a variety of choices. Most often the immediate repercussions are unclear and unpredictable, but our instinctive responses reflect our core attitudes towards life itself. The heart of the poem "Threads of Life's Tapestry" was my responses to the challenge to my core attitudes.

Once I was discussing this idea with a group of friends over lunch. Dr. Cinturon shared this thought, that a person's "Choosing not to do anything at all is also a choice." The rest of us sitting at the table smiled in agreement, and went on to spend the rest of the afternoon sharing personal stories and events in our lives when we had to force ourselves to rise above solitude and the disappointments of life.

The effect of some of these choices on me was the regret which in turn became the chassis of my apparent emotional loneliness. I did ask a lot of the *why me* questions, but the more I asked, the louder I heard the insensitive response *join the club*.

The circumstances we all face are different, but surprisingly, there is nothing novel about them. Many times, I felt the desolation that distance from my family and childhood memories had created for me. I had been immersed into a society where genuine friends had become a seasonal happenstance and I was constantly on the lookout for emotional and mental wellbeing. There were many baffling, challenging and rough, rugged rocky moments when I almost felt I could not carry on any longer.

Surprisingly however, similar events had in fact happened to many more people than I thought. The longer I reflected on my version of the "Threads of Life's Tapestry," the more I realized how much of other people's stories it was. It is crucial to be aware of how our internal dialogue eventually becomes the mirror image of our observable actions, and affects our attitudes.

The fact that life is not always fair should not make us abort our inner roadmaps, simply because no one else appreciates them. Truth is, wherever in life we choose to stop, we can always find a hundred legitimate reasons to give up. It is for reasons such as those, that I talked earlier in this chapter about my care to avoid presumptions and generalizations about how any of us ought to live our lives.

My humble suggestion is that life is always worth living and sooner or later it will amaze you how you may not be the only one *sitting in limbo*.

I am certain that if life were designed to be easy, you would not need my experience to learn from. If it were intended to be difficult, however, life would perhaps have an operating manual. The closest thing to an instruction manual is not sitting on a bookshelf, but rather it is the unpublished work called personal integrity. Doing the right thing may not seem convenient, but not doing the right thing could cause you and others a lot more inconvenience in the long run.

I think of the year 1991, when rapper M.C. Hammer released a successful record and called it "Too Legit to Quit." All of us, through our own experiences, are too legit to quit on doing the right thing, when we could be living our fulfilling lives in a cranked-up mode.

Many years ago, I had a colleague who was notorious for pointless trivia. In a group discussion, I was making a point about happiness when I quoted Abraham Lincoln as once saying, "People can be just about as happy as they make up their minds to be." His sarcastic rebuttal was, "If Lincoln knew this secret, how come he resorted to antidepressants for his misery?"

That is a reasonable question to ask, but perhaps Abraham Lincoln would be the best person to respond to it. The answer to my classmate's question was, *I do not know.* What I know however, is that Lincoln was right about one thing; if we plan to be either happy or miserable, we can very well execute that plan to perfection.

Maybe it is impossible to acquire an objective stance on life if we do not go through the molding process, that character transformation cycle. In spite of the impact of disloyal and dishonest friends, or the disappointing setbacks we all live with, I believe wholeheartedly that the most intimate part of the world as we live it begins with our thought process and then is followed by our actions. Becoming conscious of the way we construct and utilize our ideas is the crucial element to any attitude we build up in life.

I like to think that the poem "Threads of Life's Tapestry" reflects on the different ups and downs throughout my teenage years and into adulthood. This introspection, as self-motivating as it had been for me, did also teach me valuable lessons about not wallowing in self-pity. I chose to not *hide behind the moon* for fear of what hides behind it.

The most important lesson is that relational integrity translates into our personal quest for progress in whatever activity we engage in. I am confident that through our own experiences, we can be encouraged to form an affirmative and encouraging perspective to the choices we make and not quit on our sense of honesty because of how unfair others have been to us.

The reference to *strangers along the way* is the symbolism of the associations I formed, and the many friends that through their relationships, brought some significance to my life. The *faded picture in distorted lenses* was the metaphoric depiction of the lowest points on my emotional curve through the pain, the frustration, and surprisingly the self-disdain. At the end of the day, the integrity of our own hearts will always be the guiding light towards the fulfillment of the distinction we strive for.

Over the years, I listened to psychotherapists, religious leaders and different schools of thought in dogmas and credos as they related to individual senses of honor. There is no magic formula. There is however a universal principle. Our value of decency does define our exercise for candor in every aspect of our lives.

How we see life ultimately defines our approach and our actions. The reward may not come readily as I did learn, but I believe still that it is by this principle that we define our limitations or curb our own potential, not by some unseen force pulling strings from the clouds.

For the young man that swindled eight of us, I can only hope that he is still not in that business of defrauding strangers and friends. I however thank him for the lesson and the many more that are presented to us in our different circumstances. All we can do is to live our lives irrespective of which station of opportunity we find ourselves in. The truth is, when we lose the desire to live, we start dying.

When we trade in our heart's integrity, we walk away with a blank check that is drawn on a fictitious account. Sooner or later, it is returned to us, but perhaps with a dose of embarrassment and humiliation attached. It is imperative that we see beyond the temporary setbacks of life and keep on keeping on.

There are enough of our own examples to attest to the fact that life is not fair, but we have every asset and advantage to win at it.

Threads of Life's Tapestry

1 Climbing the moon,
In all that is left in a life to feel alone
In the midst of the unknowns
Life tainted my days
5 Changed my name
And changed even the sun I have known.
Early days distorted by hazy memory
From people to dreams,
And from faith to destiny
10 My escapes and fictional decoys
Tweak the solitude and worry of uncertainty.
The slang that didn't change me
I lived life, loved this life and lived a lie
Until days like this when I can't hang on
15 And the darker loads are tumbling in.
I am the only soul sitting in limbo
And dying for the weakest little hand.
I saved my smiles and my father's songs
So I won't faint
20 And forget where I am
In denial of who I have become
Come too far to middle of nowhere.
A thorny life made me a pale pilgrim
And the strangers I meet along the way
25 Turn their backs and walk on by
An alien from a terra incognita.
All I see is a mirage of happy days
Bitter sketches itching for meaning
And a portrait of my life

30 And a faded picture in distorted lenses.
     No one knows my doubts and hanging cloud
     A glowing space is mine to trek.
     Somehow I'll live through tomorrow
     Not because I loved to live
35 But only for lingering fear
     The fear of what hides behind the moon
     That I won't make it to the grave
     Just to see I wasn't alone,
     Not alone after all.

22

WHEN DECEMBER COMES

One of my father's favorite stories is that of a man driving down a dirt road. Unexpectedly he sees a chicken running alongside his car. As the man speeds up, the chicken runs even faster. The amazing thing about this chicken is that it has three legs. Soon the chicken runs past the man's car at full speed into a small side street. The man was perplexed to see a chicken with three legs, so he followed it with much curiosity. Soon the chicken run to a barn and the man saw a farmer standing outside.

"Did you see that?"

The farmer smiled back, "You mean the three-legged chicken? We raise them here."

The man stood there speechless.

The farmer continued, "Because I like a drumstick, my wife likes a drumstick, and my daughter also likes a drumstick, so this way we all got one." Still in shock, the man inquired, "that is interesting, but how does a three legged-chicken taste?"

The farmer shrugged his shoulders, "I can't tell you my friend, I have never been able to catch one."

Sure, the story may be too farfetched and fanciful to be true. I am yet to see a three-legged chicken in real life. However, the farmer in the story wanted to take a stab at an impossible feat, in the hope of a fulfilling reward down the road. Maybe one day he will be able to catch one of the three-legged chickens and fulfill his fancy.

In the meantime, unlike the strangers who followed the chicken to his barn with puzzled looks, the farmer's plan was to surprise himself. He had a real desire and a hunger for drumsticks, which happened to create an unusual episode for others.

We do not need to raise three-legged chickens to earn the attention of other people, but in our own small way, while we pursue the ambitions of our hearts, we will undoubtedly earn spectators. Many people will be curious to know how we thought about what we are doing and what drove us to forge ahead. How often have we worried about and lost sleep over our challenges and adversities, so much so that one day when we are set free to follow our hearts' desires, we do not even know where to begin?

"When December Comes" is a tribute to the restoration beyond the uphill climb and the dark days when we thought relief was nowhere in sight. How much would our character have been remolded through fear and despair, and crippled our resolve to pursue our heart's ambitions?

Unlike raising three-legged chickens, my friend Chris walked in with a puzzle. He had thought it was very simple, but for some odd reason it seemed much more complicated. This would be my first encounter with the nine dots that formed a square box. At first glance, it certainly did not seem like there was much to it. The challenge is to connect all the dots by drawing four straight and continuous lines.

Chapter 22: When December Comes

Both Chris and I stared at the puzzle for several minutes, determined not to give up that easily. Just before we dismissed the puzzle as one of those with no answers, a man who had obviously seen it several times before asked if he could attempt a solution. In less than ten seconds, he had connected all the dots and as he walked away, he looked back. *"Don't worry"* he said. *"When you look at it long enough, you stop seeing the solution, even when it is glaring right at you."*

The trick to drawing the four continuous lines is that there is absolutely no way to solve the nine dot puzzle without extending the lines beyond the *imaginary* box, outside the square area imaginatively defined by the dots. The man went on to explain how the simple puzzle becomes unusually complicated because in drawing the lines we had imagined in our own minds a boundary around the edge of the dot array.

No one put any such boundary next to the puzzle, *we imagined it,* and proceeded to work within its confines. The cliché, "Think outside the box" was born out of this puzzle.

For us to apply this to our normal everyday lives, the individual ought to first to identify the *box,* whether real or imagined. The problem is that often, when we have lived in the proverbial box for so long, and had every opportunity we once dreamed of vanishing into thin air, we become more equipped for confronting the adversity, and less to celebrate the victory beyond the battle.

"When December Comes" is about our recharged attitude at the launching pad from which our long awaited victory lap takes off. My prayer is that all of us wouldn't be too bent out of shape to celebrate our victory.

A long time ago, I met a professor at the University of Houston's Bauer School of Business. He recommended that I read a book called *Blue Ocean Strategy.* I had always been fascinated with novel business ideas, and this book did not fail on its promise. This innovative business idea is the catchphrase for corporations seeking to gain an advantage over their competitors ahead of the long-established methods.

In the crowded industries of business, traditional head-to-head competition results in a jam-packed and a *bloody red ocean,* with many people fighting over the same pie. In such an environment, there are no new ideas, just a struggle for a bigger portion of the same target market.

For corporations who intend to adopt a proactive strategy for increased profitability, they instead redefine themselves to compete in areas they had not previously thought of. They dive into the *blue oceans* and think outside of their present conditions. Instead of competing with the rivals, they *make them irrelevant.* New habits make the old defeatist and negative tendencies irrelevant. The new thinking eliminates the fluff and put us in a position to see our world from a slightly different view.

Reprogramming our minds, our attitude and our habits, however, is the defining element and the most crucial after we have managed to stand tall to see the brighter days. None of us can afford to take the same defeatist, banged-up and baggage-laden mindsets into new moments of expectancy and step into our fulfilling season.

As is the case with the *Blue Ocean strategy,* in the course of their operations, pioneering enterprises retrain themselves with new processes that are helpful, and employ them. In the same manner, they find the processes that are wasteful or do not yield the desired rewards and eliminate them. The professor's argument was that if this attitude is true for any successful enterprise, why not the same for a successful life?

The fact is, the same attitudes and perspectives that have helped us endure the lonely nights, as useful as they may have been, could very well become the attitudes which stifle any future potential we may have. Author Marshall Goldsmith said it best with the title of one of his most impactful books, *What Got You Here, Won't Take You There*.

If I were writing a self-help book, this is the point where I will require you to take a pen and paper and list ten things you can do differently to *think outside the box*. Then I will ask you, "Does any of the actions look like a three-legged chicken or swimming in a blue ocean?" If you answer no at any point, I will ask you to go back and rethink your answers. We will do this exercise several times until you force yourself to *rethink* the options which do not readily come to mind.

I could tell from my colleague Kristi's voice that something was wrong as she spoke. She kept her composure throughout the conversation, but I reasoned that she would soon break down into tears at any moment. Just two days earlier, she had lost her life savings and investment capital during a sudden economic downswing.

There had been other people in similar situations who had given up on everything they built for their lives; many more were on the verge of a nervous breakdown. Kristi did neither of those, and in fact was determined to not *cash in* her life.

Just before she hung up the phone, she was still hopeful, saying *"No one gets out of this alive. If I could do it before, I certainly can do it again."* She did.

Those were the words of a heartbroken woman who will be first to admit that we cannot afford to live by how we feel. Our human architecture is fueled by our emotions; many times when we feel down and out, that low point could become the start of an unlikely turnaround. How is that possible?

In those adverse moments, when all the pieces have fallen apart around us, it is *what we know*, owing to the little steps that have brought us to our present moments which give us just a little breather to keep living.

It is those recollections and notes of our own lives that *stir our fading hopes,* knowing that each day is a precious gift and so are its experiences. They are the *transcripts of our victory,* no matter how small, that have the capacity to help us rebuild our faith, and to prepare us for the days ahead.

I am witness to the fact that there will always be lackluster days when we have to learn to pull ourselves up, not by what we feel but by, surprisingly, reverting to the trivial triumphs from our own past. Those invaluable memories and unsuspecting keepsakes are the unique and compelling *beige transcripts* of our own life's diary.

In September 1989, I had my first dose of separation from the familiar friends and family I had. After elementary school, I was enrolled in a Presbyterian boarding school where I would spend the next seven years of my life with strangers from all walks of life. Barely a teenager and unsure of the world around me, I had been plugged into a strange playground. In the first few days alone, my confidante was a little notebook which I filled with a world of possibilities.

I wrote about all the things I wanted to be, all my lavish ambitions and how much more interesting life would be once I became those things. I had just turned eleven years old, and the most captivating ambition I had was to be *older*. As I flipped through the pages of my own diary many years later, the only thought which jumped out at me was the sense of optimism, and the amazing fortitude which clothed all my wishful imaginings. Empty as some of those ideas were, it would be those same ones I would turn to for insight.

Twenty years later, it was amazing how much of my life's circumstances had beaten down my enthusiasm, burned my hopes and twisted my fortitude into a life filled with doubts and uncertainty. Surprisingly, those untainted and naïve hopes of the eleven year old boy would become the potent reminder of my ambitions which were still within reach. The big difference was that I wanted more out of

Chapter 22: When December Comes

life than just growing older, but it would take my own *transcripts*, dusty and old with time, to reassure my faith.

The answers we seek in life are often clouded by a host of ups and downs, but all of us need to be on the lookout for the insignificant happenings that redefine the things we had hoped for. Someday, indeed, *December* will come. We are reminded that none of us are victims of any circumstance and cannot spend the rest of our lives blaming the rest of the world for our missed opportunities.

If any of us were paid a penny every time we heard that *life was not fair,* we would all be millionaires by now. Just like you, I have to learn to accept the fact that nothing promises to be any fair anytime soon. In the meantime, there are many people diligently planning their lives and preparing for an opportunity that will launch their aspirations into a new level, and so can you and me.

"When December Comes" encourages us to develop fresh stimulating mental images of ourselves to help us to control our own reactions to the problems we encounter. To a large extent, if we could break our own lives into component parts, and into groups of likeness, we would quickly arrive at one conclusion—that none of our troubles are new.

Have you ever felt like every moment in your day was filled with one rough patch after another? My guess would be that you and I are not the only two people in life who have had the privilege of living through a dreadful minute, day, month or year. Those particularly long days when a minute felt like a day, and a day felt so much like eternity. There have been many moments that we can all recall when the discomfort and crushing situations made life unbearable, and we would pay almost anything to get back the life we once had.

As I wrote *When December Comes,* I recall the words of many people I have met who stories began from an innermost desperation, some helplessness in a moment where everything they tried had failed.

If in fact there is any power in our past accomplishments, and any such thing like *When December Comes,* the memories of yesterday for some people seemingly add much more to the pain than they relieve. What then is there to do? What I know is that we ought to be careful not to carry over the attitudes and introspective dialogue we have had by ourselves, and limit the opportunities ahead of each of us. I wish I had some half-baked and microwaveable answers to give you to quickly soothe your pain, but the truth is that no one does.

A few years ago, I heard about the twenty-one day rule. According to whoever discovered the revolutionary idea, if a person committed him or herself to an activity for twenty-one days, that action became a habit. Perhaps another twenty-one days and it becomes a lifestyle. I cannot say for a fact that I know this rule first hand, and that is because for some odd reason, I never make it past the tenth day.

If only I can make it to day 21, I imagine to myself. Maybe there is a magic feeling that envelopes a person at the end of the trail, but I will argue that no matter what mental overhaul a person accomplishes in twenty-one days, the winning formula is you, not the number of days.

Let's take the idea a step further. Assuming you stick to the hope trail for 21 days to acquire a habit. What happens on day 22? That's anyone's guess. Inasmuch as I have faith in this time-tested thought process, I mention this idea because I have also met people who have convinced themselves that they can never acquire a habit or attitude, simply because they never seem to make it to the magic day twenty-one.

What I know is that we can find the energy to rebuild our hopes one moment at a time and truly appreciate our seemingly insignificant accomplishments one after another; we can still achieve the miracle of twenty-one days, no matter what.

A friend who had lived with a personal nightmare for thirteen years talked about the thoughts that haunted her the most and the

Chapter 22: When December Comes

ache she can't seem to shake off, no matter how hard she had tried. In her world, she had done all she could, and a feeling of deep betrayal by people she trusted the most consumed her every waking moment. Whenever she attempted to talk about it, the pain would be so heavy that you could feel the hurt piercing through her veins. She told me, "I have nowhere else to turn to, and the fact is I have no idea which direction I'm heading."

In her own words, the challenge was not whether or not to trust in the possibilities ahead of her, or whether to forgive the people by whom she felt bitterly betrayed, but a bona fide process to shake off the doubts that prevented her from reinventing her joyous moments. It was the starting point to live again that eluded her. How could she find peace when all she had known was turmoil and emotional chaos?

Where could she find hope when there was nothing but a myriad of disappointments to point to? What was the color of optimism when a person is blinded by the nightmare of their own past and without the energy to stave off the haunting and daunting heaviness?

Many self-help books and good people she knew had given her endless lectures on forgiving oneself and moving on with life. If only it were that simple. If in fact the process of reversing the depressing thoughts was that uncomplicated, I bet there won't be one depressed person roaming the streets.

My guess is that it requires a different shade of perseverance and an almost blinded stubbornness to pull yourself from that dungeon of thought, and that is precisely what my friend's challenge was. People in desperate moments want real answers, not fancy theories.

In listening to my friend's story, I learned also that the best answer she had heard thus far was mine. I had been candid, just as I would have been with myself. It would be impossible to retrace my steps in her shoes because I have never lived her life and never felt her pain. All anyone can give her would be a bunch of fancy theories, but it will be up to her to make some practical sense of it, and take hold of what has some value to her. No one in this world knows her story like she did, and I told her my notion of the "rewind" button.

I liken our desperate moments when we wonder how we got to such a low point to staring at a film unsure of how you missed a meaning in a scene. It is amazing how a simple act of watching a film or television became a life-changing lesson for me years ago. Just as in life, distractions happen every day.

Technology affords us all an excellent opportunity to hit one button, the all familiar *pause* button, when our minds have lost their tracks and we no longer make sense of the same thing which was once a fun event. Next, we hit *rewind*, and that slowly leads us back into familiar territory until we get to the moment we vividly remember. That is where we find a place to start again.

The beauty of *rewind* is that it gives us the much-needed advantage to travel as fast or slowly as we choose. It is impossible to underestimate the value of going back to the moment where the images and the story once made perfect sense to us.

I did not tell my friend anything I didn't know of, or suggested a prescription on how to overcome her setbacks. What I know is that to 'rewind' is not the same as replaying the horrifying events that unfolded in our past or to relive our misery. It is instead the chance to go backwards, a step at a time, and make sense of how we got to where we got to, but starting from the place right where we stand.

Nothing happens overnight, and certainly this process will not be possible in a split second, but the calming power rests in the fact that if we can pause for a moment, we can find that blinding stubbornness within ourselves to relive again.

It bears mentioning again, that no other message and signal is more powerful than the one we give to ourselves, and that is irrespective of how close to the edge life has pushed us to. Hard as it may be to imagine, nowhere in this book will you find a list of suggestions and power tips for successful living. I have none. I am a firm believer in the notion that it doesn't matter what list you and I follow to accomplish our life's ambitions, but rather that the most important process in the adventure is the *self*.

It is up to you and I to introspectively find what works for us, and what doesn't. That is obviously the idea of *self* in the *self-help*, not a tailor-made instruction manual for victorious living.

In "When December Comes," the powerful truth is that the ultimate motivator is the little victories we have had before, the almost insignificant ones that we easily forget, and the ones we relished in for a moment before everything around us plunged into chaos and disarray.

To a large extent, most of our circumstances of the present are altered and redrafted versions of those of yesterday. The locations and the individuals involved may have changed, but the pieces are essentially the same. Often we confess our deep-seated beliefs regarding our own lives without paying attention to how we formed them in the first place. It is those images that we have imbibed and allowed to dwell in our minds over time that generate either motivating viewpoints or the self-defeating kind.

I have learned how our own confessions and words have the power to negate our aspirations and talk us out of our own dreams. To this end, a priest cautioned his flock, when you are done praying to God, shut up. Instead of talking ourselves out of our providence, it helps to recreate the angle from which we look at life and allow our new mindset to change what we want to see change for us.

I have said over and again, almost ad nauseam, that one of the least advertised secrets in life is the fact that no other person has the answer to our problems. Even the best suggestions from the most insightful psychologists and renowned thinkers are exactly that, *suggestions*. All of us will have to be mindful to not drag our baggage into our new season, our *December*.

Our life paths and unique journeys in themselves have the answers to our unique ambitions simply because we ourselves were the authors of them. The individual core values remain the guiding force towards their accomplishment.

The surprisingly simple and innocent notes in my journal triggered positive thoughts to confront the setbacks I lived with in my adult life. In the end, however, I had to let go of the self-inhibiting confines, and dream again. I contend that most of us can find the comforting thoughts which in turn can become a compass to guide us into rewarding directions which we never thought of.

When our burst of enthusiasm suddenly evaporates through our emotional downswings, lossesand disappointments, or kills our precious momentum, as difficult as it may be, we cannot afford to give up and *cash in* impulsively.

I read a story about Stephen King's novel *Carrie*. King had been working on his book for years, and after several rejections from publishers he was convinced that his manuscripts were a failure. Frustrated and disappointed in himself, he crumpled up the work and pitched it into a wastebasket.

A while later, his wife Tabitha pulled the pages out of the trash and secretly read them. Stephen King's wife saw more than crumpled thoughts and scribbled words. She urged him to believe in the simple notes, with the remarkable ideas which he doubted would be any good. Good it was, and the book *Carrie* went on to launch Stephen King's captivating writing career. Today, he will tell you how careful he is not to let his fears thwart his creativity.

All of our past, like transcripts, are filled with concepts and ideas which could reorient our present circumstances in one way or another. Even when it looks like the bottom of our plans has fallen out, surely if we managed to dream sometime in our past, we can dream again in our future. If there is any such thing as a technique, it would be for us to step back and to carefully reexamine how we pull ourselves out of the low points of the emotional spectrum.

Chapter 22: When December Comes

Our memories *worn with time and frail sepia,* and the *scribbled wish from long ago,* have a way of serving the once unimportant details, as the wonderful guideposts we need for the next step of our journey. *December* will come, what matters most is that we would be well prepared to celebrate the season of restoration.

If you and I cannot see any bright stars on the horizon, we ought to stop looking into that direction and start looking at our own lives for the inspirational mementos. It takes a conscious effort to create the life we want and just as it is important to be mindful of the ideas we preach to ourselves, it is important also to be mindful of the notes we make through our simplest behaviors. Most importantly, the simple memories could be building blocks to our own fulfilling lives, and it is imperative that we pay particular attention to how we construct those memories.

When I graduated from the University of Houston, I walked away with one powerful note. It was during a business lecture when Dr. Sherrill said, *if life is a game, you better be sure you are making the rules.* It doesn't matter where we get our inspiration from, but as long as someone else has the pleasure of setting the rules for our everyday activities, we do not stand much of a winning chance. It is our own responsibility to take an inventory of our prior inspirations which could be the springboard that launches us into new areas of fulfillment when we least expect it.

When my friend Kristi talked of losing her savings and hard-earned money, what kept her sane was her being able to savor the simple moments of her past. She felt the weight and anxiety just like everyone else would have. Somehow the same simple memories helped her to cultivate the right attitude to relive the precious moments ahead of her.

She did not *cash in* her life, but would learn to find her inspiration in the most awkward of places. For her, she found the opportunity to constructively reconsider those things which had blinded her amidst the rush of daily living. The interesting part of her story is that she did not only make up for lost time with her mindset, but became even more successful and happier than she was before.

Time is always passing us by, all of us will have the same twenty-four hours in a day and how well we use them is dependent on what we seek out of every fleeting moment. I used this analogy on several occasions: by virtue of our being alive, we are all at a party. What we do next is our own prerogative, but our doing nothing and breezing through life is no more a waste of time than it is to dress in the finest attire for a lavish party, only to hide in a corner and under a table when we get there. We might as well have stayed home.

Conversely, there is also a scary roadblock that arises from our revisit of the very same dreams and ambitions from our past. The minute our past memories become a damper and negative souvenir, they becomes counterproductive, and kill our zeal and drive. Defeats and failure can potentially affect our present circumstances; we have to quickly learn to avoid the reminders that pull us away from what we aspire to.

Self-awareness and self-control lie in our ability to connect with healthy and uplifting moments of our own past. The critical effect of a failure is that it could derail our hopes by our replaying it in our minds. It could be toxic, just like an undetected yet dangerous carbonmonoxide. The mementos ought to serve us in an upward movement, not be a drag and momentum killer.

Professional sports especially employ this process in their regular routines. After every game, there are other people who are paid to keep track of all the athlete's successes, and unfortunately their failures too. There are also professional statisticians who take notes on every action during the game and reinterpret them to mean either a slump or potential.

Professional athletes are trained to not focus their energy on the statistics. Those grim reminders are very capable of drowning their momentum for the next game, just as much as the excellent statistics have the power to slide the successful players into steady complacency.

The interesting observation, however, is how quickly the athletes resort to a defining moment from their past when they face similar challenges. It is no coincidence that the athletes learn to find those same outcomes which were supposed to be downers, and use them to hang tough. Sure, if they had done it before, what stops them from doing it again? December certainly will come, fresh moments will be refreshing, and the pain of yesterday's misery will be long gone.

The saying *no one gets out of this alive* is a blatant restatement of the charge to use our own internal locus of control. It is that understanding that we control our own lives and do not surrender our fate to another person, downbeat forces or pessimistic sentiments. *The sky above not so blue* and the *flaming moments changed the color of day*, but if I could do it before, I certainly can do it again. No matter where we find ourselves, one thing is sure, that many people are busy celebrating their new moments and determined not to fall victim to their past.

I wrote "When December Comes" one New Year's Eve. This is often the day for honest reflections and lavish resolutions. Most of us think of our most aggressive and daunting ambitions on New Year's Eve, but by some coincidence we repeat this exercise every year. Is it possible that nothing changed in our lives because we didn't purposely plan for anything to change? Furthermore, the lavish resolutions will need to have some practical relevance in order to make a difference in a new season, beyond *December*.

All of us have very different desires for life; most of us however enjoy living, although we can admit to not living it to our utmost potential. It may be the time to revive our hopes, remember how we endured the pain of yesterday, and dig our heels in for the new day. The interesting twist is that we know what needs to be done in most cases; we just fail to do it. The farmer knew that the only way to satisfy his family's love for drumsticks with his scanty resources was to raise a three-legged chicken. What's the value of raising three-legged chickens if you can't catch any of them?

The point of the story had less to do with the number of legs the chicken had, than it had to do with the state of mind of the farmer. As it turned out, the farmer and his family in the story were all blind. He reasoned that they couldn't catch any chicken at all, even if it had only one leg. Instead of getting stuck in their handicap, they thought to stretch their luck. They thought to believe for the impossible, and expect that one sudden miracle where we can look back and truly see the long days and nights as a distant history.

Many times in our own lives, we are stuck in a rut, unprepared to change our comfortable routines. On that New Year's Eve, I was home watching a basketball game and I noticed an interesting string of events. As a rule, anytime a ball goes out of the playing area, a player throws the ball to his colleague who has a few seconds to dribble the ball into his opponents half of the court.

Often, the ball is in-bounded to a point guard who without looking up at the clock is very aware of the amount of time it takes for him to get across the center line. In spite of the opponent's defensive positions, the player with the ball assertively dribbles to center court without any formidable opposition.

On one such sequence, an opponent anticipated the steps in the routine and intercepted the pass, which eventually became the turning point of the basketball game. After the game, a journalist approached the player who intercepted the ball for the winning team and asked what prompted him to chase after the ball. His response: "You don't repeat the same thing over at this level and expect to win." The losing team had done the same thing throughout the game and it was only a matter of time before their opponents pounced on them.

It is no more difficult guessing the outcome of a repeated basketball sequence than it is for a life with repeated actions and the same play-it-safe attitude. Leaving our psychological comfort zones requires the same agility and mental toughness as businesses do to swim in *blue oceans*.

In a simple basketball game, you then understand why coaches run along the sidelines with hand signals every minute. They change their plans accordingly and make sure they are not repeating the same process over and again.

There were many other players on the opposing team, all comfortably sitting on the bench, but it would take that one person willing to challenge the *conventional wisdom* with *alternative wisdom* to deliver the winning formula. "When December Comes" expresses an encouraging idea to exploit our own *alternative wisdom* and not just live life with the same prescription we have with our past.

Most journals credit Edward de Bono, a Maltese psychologist and physician with the idea of *lateral thinking*. Just as in 'thinking outside the box', lateral thinking focuses on the kind of reasoning which may not be immediately obvious, and its logic unclear. Traditional step-by-step logic does not work in this area of thought, as a person seeks to intentionally deviate from entrenched business-as-usual thinking.

Years ago when I was in my final year in high school, my mother began a conversation about what I had to do next. In her own maternal concern, she had a map carefully designed for me to follow, with a high probability of success. It was the same script everyone had followed and it only made sense that I signed onto it also. Deep down the inside however, I disagreed with my mother's plan and I had to graciously differ.

A deliberate thought process outside the norm requires one powerful factor, a bird's eye view of our circumstance. Lateral thinkers acknowledge that just as it is important to understand the parameters and rules for life, all of us need to be able to step back from our normal thought processes and account for our innate assumptions and ignored alternatives.

Our life is our own, and taking full advantage of it is our own responsibility. There are many avenues of distraction and our most important asset will be our ability not to dwell on unimportant happenings, or the ever-fleeting temporary emotions. I am a firm believer in the notion that in many events of our lives, the *means* and the *end* are equally important, but too often we handicap our own reasoning to assume that an *end* is only justified by the *means*.

In the basketball story, the winning team won by two points which was the direct result of that one interception of the ball. Not to my surprise, the coach's reaction to the game's turning point was, "We knew it would take a slightly different approach at some point to win the game." Some of these simple stories happen around us every day. We hear of people who are living beyond their accepted perspectives, their internal status quo and pressing forward to create a victorious future for themselves. Why not you and me?

All of us have our own versions of winning formulas but we unfortunately make a choice not to use them. Often we see them on television or read about them in magazines, but seldom do the reality and the truth of the message jump out at us. I believe that all of us can afford to swim in *blue oceans* and make our limitations and competition *irrelevant* to our potential.

We may not care to raise three-legged chickens or ever play basketball, but the barriers we put on our own ideas impede any progress we could even imagine making. My guess is that the natural predispositions of our brain functions may have a role to play in our *thinking outside the box*. Most of us have learned to use the left side of our brain, which is responsible for such activities as computing numbers, sequence and logic. The right side of our brain, where we get to use our imagination and creativity, is often the least employed.

It is particularly intriguing how children, in their innocence and mental freedom, think through ideas. For any one question, the child will come up with a range of answers, most of which are probably unrelated in any way. Most of us adults call that the undeveloped mind, but that freedom of the mind is not restricted to entrenched thought and boundaries. Once in a while all of us are baffled by a child's imagination; we stand back and wonder why *I never thought of it in this way.*

When it comes to the use of our minds in avoiding the nine dots trap, there are no boundaries curbing our enthusiasm and desire to strive for a fulfilling future. If there is any disadvantage to being stuck in our cycle of inactions and mental blocks, it is that we pay full price for things that should be free of charge. It is also when we forget the value of our new seasons, beyond all the pain and desperation, because we haven't unlearned what have become our stifling attitudes.

As we look to "When December Comes," reinventing ourselves may require having to make some quantum leaps, but it is worth every second of our lives. If blind farmers can raise three-legged chickens, surely all of us have the ability to pursue our ambitions with purposeful speed, but it starts with a paradigm shift and a willingness to expect the fulfilling days we have yearned for.

When December Comes

1 I am my wind
A breezy daze in cottage miles away
Green leaves blow to prairie land
And I am gone into the distance.
5 Vanished without a trace of tear
Alone in the wide lanes
On bare feet, I only walk so far
A word or two on colored pages
Worn with time and frail sepia
10 The sound stirs my fading hopes
I was once young with cheerful heart
Now the drips take its toll
The sky above not so blue
And flaming moments
15 Change the color of day.
I lived in the candor of an innocent past
The gloomy air was my choice made
To bask in simple joys to distant end
Along dusty streets and cloudy trees.
20 The color beige is trail of years gone by
The years when God went away.
The years when only the shade lived across the fields
What my son's will write of me
A feeble hope is alive and well
25 And the color of old is bright again.
No sense of strain in sight
The panic of obscure loads are far away
And the pride in heavy winds lead astray
Dreaming day in a flash and a line

30 My wind and moment wear me down.
     Along dusty streets and cloudy trees
     The color beige is trail of years gone by
     Gone until December
     The years when God went away
35 And one more mile from providence.
     The chain of trouble is setting sun
     Swallow my wanting for blustery push
     Living in curves at my world's end
     I escape the limits of my own skin
40 A dreaming mind shatters doubt
     And truth unknown in silent spaces
     December will soon be here
     But I am my wind in my moment,
     If only in my daze.

HALFWAY HOME

A boat is wrecked at a sea's shore. The beams of its stern are falling apart, and the wood of the hull is cracked on every side. The mast, the mainsail and the jib are all shredded by the storm. The boat's rudders are hinged on just as they have always been, and it's not certain the boat can hang on for another sail. The waters have been raging on its way to shore, but its journey is only half over. There will be many knots to travel, every one with a discomfort of its own. The boat at the edge of the shore will have to find the courage to get back into an ocean filled with everything it fears and manage to sail home.

It was past midnight into the New Year when my plane landed at JFK Airport in New York City. In the hallways I saw the faces of what seemed to be friends and families as they clasped onto their relatives, many of whom had traveled from afar for a warm embrace of their loved ones. An elderly lady at the arrival booth inspected my travel documents and reached over for a pen.

"Your first time here, I see," she said in a raspy voice. I nodded. She pulled out a map, marked the spot where we stood and patiently showed me how to navigate one of the busiest airports in the world. I needed all the help I could get walking past the many enthusiastic faces and their different stories, for someone to welcome me, *home*.

"Have a happy life, young man" she said, as she handed over my personal belongings. A *happy life* was exactly what I had planned on. It was that sense of peace which I had searched for all this while, and in that moment, it felt as if I was almost *there*. I remembered all the strangers I had bumped into in the different countries who had wished me well, but never took the time to wonder why many years later, I was still searching for this perfect destination.

"Of all the places you could be, *why here?*" the lady asked out of the blue. She wondered why I chose New York City. I wasn't sure either. I had traveled a chunk of my adolescent life in search of somewhere far and different, which would be a symbol of my pursuit of what I believed to be my happiness. Europe didn't do it, and Africa, not so much. Asia, I wasn't too sure, but perhaps here in the winding maze in America, I would find the complete joy I imagined.

As it is for most people, a part of us always yearns for that fresh starting point, where we can recreate and relive our individual hopes in a renewed promise. Just as a newborn baby lies with innocence in the safety of a mother's lap, all of us occasionally rewind our thoughts to the neutral moments in our lives when our vision of a happy life had a clean slate.

That imagination of harmony is filled with the hope that our enduring hard work can bear fruit in all we aspire to. Some of us spend the rest of our lives in pursuit of this harmony, and I had become one such person. I would rather take my chances and *live*

Chapter 23: Halfway Home

anew than accept my present state as my fate. However long the journey, I reasoned that the decision to climb higher is half the ascent.

"Halfway Home" follows a hunt for happiness, which as it is for many people, is the never-ending quest for fulfillment. At every juncture, I did believe that working towards inner satisfaction is not just an elusive state of mind. We can in fact achieve anything, if we believe long enough, and are determined to work hard enough.

It was not the New York that I was heading to which would make the difference; rather it was the symbolism of a fresh start that I was looking forward to. It was the opportunity to wake up in a day not locked in limitations. Sometimes we may not get to a physical place to start over, and that is why finding that place in our heart—no matter what station in life—becomes the most important first step. There is a freeing and incredible sense of appreciation that comes from recognizing that where you have been and where you are now have not been a sad mistake. It may perhaps be just as difficult to embrace that as the moment that consumes our every wish and every enthusiasm.

One thing we discover is the fact that we could walk through eternity looking for people and places to make us happy, but ultimately that feeling of fulfillment begins with each of us. It is more of an internal battle than an external pursuit.

Eureka is claimed to be what the famous Greek mathematician and astronomer Archimedes yelled out when he suddenly uncovered a method of detecting the amount of alloy mixed with the gold in King Hieron of Syracuse's crown. The story is about how the king, after having felt deceived by a goldsmith, solicited Archimedes' help to prove his suspicion.

The King had given his goldsmith pure gold to be used for a golden votive crown. He suspected, however, that he had been cheated, by the goldsmith removing gold and adding the same weight of silver. Archimedes' discovery became the much sought-after explanation to the King's problem. In the years around 270 BC, there was no sophisticated technology, no calculators and certainly no computers to assess the purity of the extraordinary crown.

Some story tellers believe that equipment for weighing objects already existed in that era, but because Archimedes could also measure an object's volume, the ratio would ultimately give the object's density, a central indicator of purity. Archimedes is said to have been so eager to share his realization that he leapt out of his bathtub and ran through the streets of Syracuse naked. No one knows what happened afterwards, but no one can argue the authentic gusto and unreserved joy of a man who found the moment he searched for.

Eureka has come to mean an expression of triumph upon finding or discovering something. In the United States, *Eureka's* symbolic reference was attached to the state of California, with a reference to the discovery of gold near Sutter's Mill in 1848.

As momentous as the discovery was, the people wanted to be sure they never forgot the unabashed joy of the moment, and never lost the meaning of their long journey. A simple word became the state's symbol, the state motto and was stamped everywhere on the state's seal.

Eureka moments, for me, are almost impossible to explain, just as they are difficult to replicate. I share the opinion that such liberation is a uniquely individual experience, and exhilaration comes from knowing where we once were and how much pain we endured. We remember the nights of disappointments and dejection, and how quickly our dreams unraveled. We remember also, how much closer we will be to our fulfilling lives if we manage to hang on for one more day.

The challenge is to find a reason to go back to that definitive moment in our lives when we had that unquestionable calmness and gratification of a new day. Academic researchers have pointed out the different mindsets required for achievement and maintenance. There is nothing more glaringly true than the fact that the same attitudes that have guided us to this moment may not be the same which can guide us to reach even higher in our dreams. Fundamentally however, the basic elements of achieving true peace and happiness remain the same. We can all learn to come back to the *Eureka* moment.

Over the years, I would meet many people of all ages, races and from very different economic backgrounds. For every one person whose happiness was tied to their status, there were a hundred more miserable people with that same status. Somehow the individual's happiness was not dependent on their specific position, rather on an active engagement, and finding meaning to their lives was defined only by their own mental backdrops.

Life does not provide any us with opportunities for a *do-over* and sometimes, what may seem to be a makeover or second chance at life could come with a hefty price tag. At any point in our lives, the most we can do is to take a careful stock of our own progress, reevaluate our priorities and create our home right where we stand. Evaluation is not an opportunity to beat ourselves over the head about decisions that did not turn out quite the way we thought they should. Rather, the exercise gives us a chance to step back and be able to give ourselves an honest appraisal.

All of us are architects of our fortunes, just as much as we are of our misfortunes. If you have managed to live up till this point, no matter how disappointing some of it has been, it is a step nonetheless. Assuming it is a journey on your life's fulfilling trajectory, you may very well be halfway there.

Sure, the raging sea will have done its best to leave us in a state of shock and allowed despondency to become a familiar emotion. It is, however, incredibly important that we look up to that little ray of sunshine bursting through the cloud as an anchor, and get back into the ocean. Sure, every now and then there will be a huge wave that will remind us of the danger ahead, the uncertainty that looms and what our life could become, but we have enough wind in our sails to press on, and all we need to do is to keep moving. We did not create the waters, so we do not control them; we built our sails, and all we can do is to trust they will get us there, the other half of the way.

The most definitive time for all of us will be when we seize the moment, not as a proverbial ghost in the middle of nowhere, unsure of which direction to go. Instead, to carefully reconsider the obstacles, and determine to make this exact moment in our adventure count, even as we look for the advantages in the direst of circumstances.

No two people will travel the same path. I mentioned previously that we travel unique roads towards our unique hopes and unique happiness, but our lessons could inspire each other to keep pushing harder and walking farther. The symbolism of "Halfway Home" is about my pursuit of a happy life, hoping that I would be home whenever I found whatever it was I was looking for. Could it be that after all the toil and sweat, we are just a shade away from where we set out to be?

Inspired by some of these historical references, *eureka* is that moment of genuine exhale as we find the much-needed insight and relief. My hope and prayer is that someday all of us can find that powerful moment of peace and calm, and appreciate the breath of opportunities that life has afforded us even right where we are.

The problem however, is that like most people, I was not sure of what I was searching for. There were also many moments in my life when I thought to call it quits. If only I knew I could probably have been *halfway home,* I would have lived those moments full of joy and in the anticipation of how much more life could offer. It was through some of this emotional variance that I found that what I thought was excitement, elation and fulfillment to one person, did not necessarily give the same inner rewards to the next person.

Home in our hearts is an individual decision, and whatever it is that brings us that peace and contentment should be defined by our own consciousness. *Home* is not a *place,* but those internal stimuli which give us the happiness, in spite of what is happening around us. One thing I also know is that it is almost impossible to keep our internal bliss, when the rest of our lives are falling apart around us. It is usually those moments when we find ourselves discounting our own accomplishments, and doubt our own resolve.

Just before I completed high school, I was convinced that I should spend the next stage of my life in Australia. I had never been there, but I had this curious fascination with what I called the *far away land.* Why Australia? No good reason per se, except that a person determined to find that "perfect peace" will dare to find solace anywhere.

When I was a little boy, one of my toys was a huge atlas with images of all the countries in the world. I would often lay the book flat on a table, stare at all the continents, and Australia sat in the corner all by itself, serene and quiet. The thought of a country so far away from all pandemonium, in my young mind, was just as intriguing as it was inviting.

I never made it to Australia, but the search for emotional calm and the peaceful alternative to life's stress would drive the rest of my life until I heard the raspy-voiced lady that afternoon in JFK Airport. I also remember the many people I have known looking both far and near to find some place they would call *home.*

Years ago, I wondered if it was possible that all of us are unhappy by default. We spend our days amassing wealth, reputations or tangible prosperity to satisfy our need for that perfect place in our lives. Is it that none of us could perhaps be completely happy no matter how hard we tried?

For most of us, we define our ultimate sense of wellbeing by an artificial criterion built in our own mind. I had to learn that if our happiness hinges on external forces, and situations beyond our control, it is impossible to develop a happy outlook on life. The answer to the question is that indeed we can be completely happy.

The happiest people I had met all lived with their unique sets of problems. They had not taken the path of least resistance; neither did they have access to a magic pill to guarantee a rewarding life. I contend that if our journey has indeed brought us to a halfway mark, *home* will start with a self-motivated declaration to live a fulfilling life in spite of what each day brings. We will have no effect on the sequence of life events but how we interpret experiences will be the critical factor that triggers the emotions we produce for ourselves.

"Halfway Home" also reflects on my one defining element, a faith in God. I chose to live my life in the assurance that my belief in God is not a fluke. I have always intentionally avoided the pointless logic of faith critics who question the basis of anyone's belief. The answers and instinct in that regard are my personal choices, and the unflinching trust in a Godly direction for my life has given me the hope to hang on, when there was absolutely nothing else to clasp onto.

Over the course of thirty years, my life unfolded in a series of bizarre circumstances and several uncanny events. Through it all, my faith became a personal guidepost, stronger than any idea justified by scientific computation or theory. I lived life, however, conscious of the fact that not everyone may believe as I do, but the good news is that none of us are required to explain what drives each of us. When I needed a hope to cling to, it was this conviction which carried me for one more day. Long after my encounter in New York City, it was this faith that would reassure me of happiness right where I stood.

Life is a forward impulse and our inclination toward a positive outlook rests on thinking forward into a future, often with the conviction and hope that our best days are ahead of us. *Home* could very well be the moment we aspire to, but we can endeavor to live our happiness in the present. It is amazing how faith gives us the extra impetus when all the facts around us are inconsistent with what we strive for.

Chapter 23: Halfway Home

I have come to fully understand that our past is gone and irrespective how exhilarating or pleasant it had been, we cannot go back to it or live in it. In spite of how draining or exciting it had been for us, our futures begin from this point forward, and perhaps we should remind ourselves that by virtue of being alive, we are probably *almost there*. The dialogue is entirely up to us.

"Halfway Home" is a recollection of a belief in my *guiding light*, especially in the moments when the pieces of my struggle did not add up. Those moments when I was tempted to dwell on my doubts and nothing made sense about what I was steadily chasing. I joked about how we may not possibly fathom all there is to comprehend about how a black cow will eat green grass and eventually turn it into white milk and yellow butter but it never stopped anyone of us from enjoying it.

Understanding this dynamic of life has made me a much happier person. It could very well be an unwritten code of life or a universal principle that the moment we decide to be happy or enjoy our lives, all the opportunities we seek are those that reiterate that decision.

I also believe that a fulfilling life will be measured by our own ability to look in the mirror, see the man or woman we have become and be able to live with that image. The fact is, our life is never over, the battle is never lost, nor our dreams ever useless, unless we give them permission to be. If there is any consolation in a thought, it would be that the best person to sabotage us is ourselves. Despite the *broken cages of restless joy,* the *bruised palms once warm,* and the long list of *poignant tingles,* the *color of joy* is still ours to paint, and that we can do right where this moment finds us.

Long before the elderly lady wished me well at the airport, I was willing to risk everything I had in anticipation of a bigger opportunity every step along the way. I was busy combing through all four corners of the world for something that probably was already placed in my heart.

Years ago, I had thought that my exciting journeys had turned me into a wandering soul across the planet, but it was all those journeys that would give meaning to the complete whole. I look back and smile at my own transitions over the years, how I ended up where I am, and with the enthusiasm to live the best I know how. I was sure to take my chances and push just a little harder. The extra degree is all that it takes for hot water at 211 degrees to boil at 212. If we have managed to come this far, wherever we are, it is amazing where an extra push could land us.

In different cities and places, there were people who easily believed that they would achieve anything they hoped for, and other places where people rarely imagined a life beyond their present. There were countries where people did not have any worries, and other towns where everyone spent every second dreading tomorrow.

It was in all these places, that I found pieces of who I am, and the realization that our trials and experiences have not been for naught.

My identity had never been tied to a country or a place. There was no event waiting in the wings to suddenly reveal who I had been destined to be. The picture we paint for ourselves through our habits and expectations has an incredible ability to hide the nuggets of hope that fill our every day in plain sight. We could be standing next to miracles on sunny days but because our minds have gone ahead in search of something else out in the world, we miss the opportunity at our feet.

Only when we realize this can we truly leave behind *the fading skies* and the *vague fears that chain our steps*.

As I write "Halfway Home," I do not know your individual problems, neither do I assume to have all the answers, but I will not doubt your resolve just as I never doubted mine. I have no intimate knowledge of what makes your world go round, but one thing I know for certain is that there is still so much life to live.

There is absolutely no reason for us to allow *gravity* and life's drama to send us into even a split second desperate moment when we entertain the thought of driving ourselves over the ledge to end it all. I urge you to not give up on the hope and faith which has guided our determined hearts this far. We are one extra mile away from our utmost potential if we can hang on long enough.

The boat rests on the shore, with its tattered sails on its side, yet it will need one more journey in pursuit of its ambition. But it is cracked on every side. It feels wrecked. It is worn. Logic and human reason scream to stay on the coast and rest there. A faith in a tomorrow encourages it to get back into the ocean for one more ride. Where will the courage come from to persevere? In the distance is a little ray of sunlight bursting through the dark clouds. Will that be enough to rekindle a passion and revive a fading zeal? The only consolation becomes that it is not too late to stretch faith and believe again.

Just when the boat gathers what is left of its sails to try again, regardless of which way the winds blow, it will take courage beyond what we thought we could find in ourselves to trust it will sail safely through a threatening storm to the other side.

The longing for home is a search for fulfillment where our extraordinary experiences—especially when they had been dim and gloomy—will find a rest. We will find the calm to breathe again and believe again. No place is endowed with abundant cheerfulness for everyone passing by, and in fact no matter where in the ends of the world we go, life can be a difficult adventure. Wave after wave, we will find our hearts in a place where we look ahead with assurance, and are grateful that the turbulent days became the internal compasses which gave us the strengths and the wherewithal to pursue the rest of our lives. Often it is in these not so rosy times when we have learned the most.

Just as in our individual journeys, the struggle may be far from over, but the extraordinary peace of heart resides in the fact that we are *halfway home.*

Halfway Home

1 Unfailing heart in wild summer days
Warm with smile, free of aching sweat
I'm home where life takes me
Unlocking daunting tunnels of all I see.
5 The thorn in shrubs
And the coldest breeze all day long
In my heart is still somewhere safe.
When fright of space is now my judge
All I dread in time wanes away.
10 The wealthy love of a father's hand
Is enough to keep me sane.
The bruised palm once felt warm
Broken cages of restless joy
Is forced my walking far from home.
15 The golden mines in Pretoria
Is vain with a happy pledge
The color of joy is mine to paint
On my way somewhere,
Anywhere but home.
20 The waters spilled across the room
For I slip and fall on either way home
The trek alone to a distant earth
Faith is shrunk for a happy guest
The remnant of vague fears chain my steps
25 But here, still strong
And in suede gloves to calm a finger's tip.
No more sting and poignant tingles
For even the brave live in feeble clout
Now that the green in the grass is all withered

30 I know why Mama prayed in sacred song
     Lean on time and chance
     Her son, far away in blissful ride
     Leaving behind the fallen skies
     Halfway home,
35 And down into the sunset.

"For I know the plans I have for you," says the LORD.
"They are plans for good and not for evil,
to give you a future and a hope."

Jeremiah 29:11

AFTERWORD

Many years ago, I bought a small journal at the W.H. Smith bookstore in Victoria Station, London. The plan was to make notes about any idea I came up with. I had no way of knowing what I would use the information for, but I recall my first thought being that I wanted to be someone important in the world. I was not particularly concerned about how to accomplish that, neither did I have the faintest idea of how complicated my life would be in the next decade.

Whatever laws of nature contributed to my existence, it seemed as though at every turn, the burdens increased, and the weight became heavier. The most important task ahead of me would not be to stand like the next person, or chase a dream like everyone else I would have met. My work would be to do what God gave me life to accomplish. Once I have done so, and to the best of my ability, I will have lived every moment without the nagging thoughts of what could have been, or what should have been. When a sudden realization brings you to appreciate the fact that the assignment for your life is too important to let the breeze in a day sway your emotions, you find the courage to see through the darkest fog and to stand again.

Writing *A Poke In My Eye* was the process that unknowingly outlined in me a relatively optimistic approach to life. I had lived most of it without cautiously analyzing the different constituents of it. My perceptions eventually made me evolve into a pragmatic and careful observer of thoughts that inspired the lives of the millions of people around the world, including mine.

The problems we live and deal with are just as alike as they are unique, and perhaps I have not lived long enough to know all the answers even if any do in fact exist. However, these dissimilarities enable us to appreciate the diversity and variety of every one of life's events and learn from them.

One afternoon, I had a long conversation with a counselor at a university. It had been several months since I submitted my application for a scholarship and presented a compelling case to be awarded a grant. In her sincerity, she admitted to having seen my application during the selection process, but ranked me fourth, concerning who should be awarded the scholarship.

Here I was, full of admiration for this counselor, only to find out she could probably be the reason why I was overlooked for a well-deserved scholarship opportunity. The only thing I could think of at that moment was getting up and expressing my dislike for her inconsiderate supposed expert opinion. As if the counselor had purposely prepared an answer for what I was thinking, there was a huge poster hanging on her wall, of a man sitting on top of a hill, and another man climbing the same hill in obvious distress. The caption beneath the poster read, "Life is not fair, get over it."

Next to that same poster was a very popular quote by Al Franken: "Appreciate the mistakes of your life because you learn precious life lessons from them, and sometimes that is the only way to learn them. Even if the mistake is fatal, at least other people can learn from it." The clear message in the words was that whether we acknowledge it or not, every action in our life is a natural contribution to the learning curve, either to ourselves or at our expense.

I suggest that as you read this book, you allow your own life's story to come alive for you also, whether in your personal life, relationships with family and friends, or business endeavors, apply the simple thoughts and expect powerful results. Finally, it is my genuine hope that the distinguishing trait of this book from the millions of inspirational books will be the fact that I can only tell my story, not yours.

My personal journey in life has been a series of turns and twists, none of which I still believe I would have been able to accomplish alone. For this reason, I have attempted to draw from our similarities and even our differences.

In reading this, I invite you to delve into my sincere thoughts about one person's approach to different aspects of life, and perhaps be encouraged by it. In several ways, this project has been a collaborative venture and encouraging adventure for me. The words and the diction are mine, but the encouragement and the emotions, with the expressive underpinnings, come from many people whom I acknowledge and sincerely thank.

There is no intent to either oversimplify any trusted academic and psychological research, nor question the validity or limitation thereof. There is only one aspect of life I am an expert in and without question the one piece I can unequivocally share glaring insights about—my own journey. Often I admit lightheartedly that, "Maybe I am crazy, but that is because I have a lot of living to do."

If I learned anything from my childhood friend K.M. Eyeson, it would be that the most cherished part of the world we live in begins with our thought process and then is followed by our actions. Becoming conscious of the way we utilize and construct our ideas is crucial to any outlook and attitude we develop in life. Through the harsh conditions and a series of misfortunes, we all have the tendency to develop conditioned responses and self-inhibiting reactions to certain scenarios.

From my personal observations and the reflections of the many people I took the time to talk to over the years, adversity potentially breeds a view often more negative than positive. This is where our interpretation of life can either lift us up beyond our difficult times or fast-forward the trip down to the doldrums.

For me, it will take *A Poke In My Eye* to learn about life.

END NOTES

Babauta, Leo (2009). The Power of Less. *The Fine Art of Limiting Yourself to the Essentials.*

Brown, Les (1997). It's Not Over Until You Win. *How to Become the Person You Always Wanted to Be No Matter What the Obstacle.*

Buffet, Warren & Schroeder, Alice (2009). The Snowball. *Warren Buffet and the Business of Life.*

Cosby, Bill and Poussaint, Alvin F. (2007). Come On People. *On the Path from Victims to Victors.*

Dewey, John (1997). How We Think.

Gladwell, Malcolm (2000). The Tipping Point. *How Little Things Can Make a Big Difference.*

Goldsmith, Marshall (2007). What Got You Here Won't Get You There.

Ireland, Kathy and Morton Laura (2002). Powerful Inspirations. *Eight Lessons That Will Change Your Life.*

Kersey, Cynthia (1998). Unstoppable. *45 Powerful Stories of Perseverance and Triumph from People Just Like You.*

Kimbro, Dennis (1998). What makes the Great Great. *Strategies for Extra Ordinary Achievement.*

Kula, Irvin and Lowenthal, Linda (2006). Yearnings. *Embracing the Sacred Messiness of Life.*

Mandela, Nelson (1995). Long Walk to Freedom. *The Autobiography of Nelson Mandela.*

Mauborgne, Renee and Chan, Kim W. (2005). The Blue Ocean Strategy. *How to Create Uncontested Market Space and Make the Competition Irrelevant.*

Maxwell, John C. (2007). Talent is Never Enough. *Discover the Choices That Will Take You Beyond Your Talent.*

McGraw, Philip C. (2001). Self Matters. *Creating Your Life From the Inside Out.*

Meyer, Joyce (2007). The Power of Simple Prayer. *How to Talk to God About Everything.*

Obama, Barack (2007). Dreams from My Father. *A Story of Race and Inheritance.*

Orman, Suzie (2003). The Laws of Money, The Lessons of Life. *Keep What You Have and Create What You Deserve.*

Russell-McCloud, Patricia (1999). A is for Attitude.

Schragis, Steven and Frishman, Rick (2006). 10 Clowns Don't Make a Circus . . . . *and 249 Other Critical Management Success Strategies.*

Shakur, Tupac (1999). The Rose That Grew From Concrete.

Stanley, Charles (2000). Success God's Way. *Achieving True Contentment and Purpose.*

INDEX

A
Abraham Lincoln 259
adawroma 103
aha moment 22
Albert Einstein 64
Alex Corretja 163
Al Franken 304
alternative wisdom 281
antidepressants 58, 259
April showers 209
Archimedes 289, 290
Ashanti 93, 95
Astroworld 245
Attic 161
avant-garde 214

B
Barack Obama 113, 115, 116, 117, 120, 121
Bill Gates 72
biopsychosocial 46, 51
Blue Ocean 268, 281
bobo 171, 172
Brownsville 129
Buddhism 61
butterfly moment 34, 35, 38, 40

C
catecholamine 45
Charles Spurgeon 175, 176
checkered fly 41
chlorofluorocarbon 23
Chongchon River 39
core personality 150
course correction 193, 194, 197, 200

cowboy mentality 129
cranked-up mode 244, 257, 259

D
Dalston 251
David Pollay 222
David Ricardo 108, 109
Deborah Goolsby xx, 100
deja-vu 29
Dennis Kimbro 253
Devale Simmons 33
dissociative 141
Dr. A. B. Meldrum 31
Dungeon Drop 245, 246

E
Edward de Bono 281
Eli Manning 37, 38
elixir 144
equilibrium 256
Essex 176
eureka 292
Eureka 289, 290, 291
Evening Standard 24
expectancy effect 154
extrasensory perception 32

F
fight or flight 46
filmstrip 135, 139, 142
flashbulb moments 121
flipping coins 3
Frank Lloyd Wright 50

G
Galatea 154
General Oliver Smith 39
gravity 2, 6, 7, 8, 9, 11, 296
Gravity 4, 5, 8, 13

H
Hackensack 69
harmattan 239, 240
Harry Sonneborn 242

J
Jane Austen 179
Jane Tewson 60
je ne sais quoi 122
Joel Osteen 228

K
Kaiser 97
karma 57, 62
Khalil Gabran 135, 138
King's Cross 24
Korean War 39

L
Lakewood 228
Larry Walters 92, 93, 94, 96, 101
lateral thinking 281
law of garbage truck 222, 225
lupus erythemathosus 57

M
Mark Twain 169, 174, 176, 177
Marshall Goldsmith 268
McDonalds 242
M.C. Hammer 259
mirage 146, 256, 257, 262
Mount Everest 182, 184
Muhammad Ali 225, 230
Murphy's Law 119

N
National Association for the Advancement of Colored People 92
Nelson Mandela 187, 188
neuroscientific 110
New England Patriots 36
New York Giants 36, 38
nyankonton 96
Nyankonton 95, 103

O
Oprah Winfrey 162
Ottoman Empire 136

P
pale pilgrim 255, 262
paradigm shift xiii, xv, 26, 56, 283
paranoid personality disorder 70
Pay It Forward 60
Pete Sampras 163
Philomela 161
polite persistence 17, 20
polystyrene 69
preproduction model 119
program objective 119
Pygmalion 154

R
Randy Polk 118
Ray Kroc 241, 243
re-constructive thinking 177
red ocean 268
relative exposure 131
Richard Roeper 221
Robben Island 187
Rocky Marciano 225
Roger Ebert 221
Roy Plunkett 23

S

Saint John 89
sanguinity 118, 158, 213
selective ownership 24
self-concept 129, 141
self-enhancing bias 27
self-inhibiting 276, 305
self-limiting beliefs 44
self-loathing xiii, 8
self-protecting bias 27
self-serving biases 27
self-therapy 72
Sorbibor 229
Sorbonne 219
stargazer 41
Stoke Newington 249
Sutter's Mill 290
symmetry mode 256
Syracuse 289, 290

T

Taliesin studio 50
Teflon 23
Tereus 161
terra incognita 262
tête-à-tête 89
Theodore Roosevelt 219
Thomas Edison 164
Thomas Malthus 108, 109
Timebank 60
Tom Brady 36

W

Walter Cannon 45
W.H. Smith 303

www.ingramcontent.com/pod-product-compliance
Lightning Source LLC
Chambersburg PA
CBHW020608300426
44113CB00007B/551